PSYCHOPATHOLOGY
AND *Family Dynamics*

MICHAEL
BOYLE

Cover image © Shutterstock, Inc. Used under license.

Kendall Hunt
publishing company

www.kendallhunt.com
Send all inquiries to:
4050 Westmark Drive
Dubuque, IA 52004-1840

Copyright © 2016 by Michael Boyle

ISBN 978-1-4652-9209-4

Printed in the United States of America

Contents

Chapter 1
Research as It Applies to the Family

Bildagentur Zoonar GmbH / Shutterstock.com

The study of research methods in psychopathology and family dynamics in this text considers research as it applies to the family. There is a need to understand things more clearly and a need to add to the knowledge we already have. The purpose for research should be to help people understand why behaviors are the way they are and why people act as they do. One important reason for research is the need to get it right. There are many theories and, over time, incorrect as well as correct information is discovered. The goal must be to avoid harming people and not realize later that more harm than good was the result. There's a fellow who came up with a new therapy method. He engaged in tickle therapy to get the patient to open up by overcoming fears, etc. To his surprise, he was sued several times for assault and battery. Researchers must avoid incorrect assumptions to ultimately not harm the individual. The goal of research should be to add to the field of knowledge.

It is important to ask questions and then to look for answers, which requires creative and critical thinking. It takes creative thinking to come up with ways of asking questions and then researching them in a way that's meaningful. Why do people allow themselves to be physically or verbally abused, and what causes the criminal to be a criminal? This is the first step of research. I will complete this chapter for the first edition.

Chapter 2
Family Traits that Engender Psychopathology

Steve Allen / Shutterstock.com

This chapter will consider those traits or problems within families that can bring about pathology or plant the seeds of mental disorders. To begin this topic, an important point to consider is systems theory (VonBertalanbby, 1968). This theory states that every member of a family is part of the family system. Also, one can view the family as a dynamic system, and the purpose of the system, besides raising offspring and sending them out into the world, is to maintain balance in the family so it can in some way function. To illustrate this theory, consider the Kaibab forest, which is in the four corners area of the United States—Arizona, New Mexico, Utah, and Colorado—near the Grand Canyon, and is isolated. In the 1950s, it was discovered that these very old trees were dying. It was finally determined that the trees were dying because the farmers and ranchers around that area had completely annihilated the coyote population. This may cause one to ask why this would cause trees to die. With the coyotes gone, the ecosystem that had developed and was maintained for thousands of years was now imbalanced. There were no natural predators to keep the deer, mice, and rabbit population in check. With the coyotes gone the deer, mice, and rabbits all proliferated and the populations increased. They all needed to eat and, because of the overpopulation, they wiped out the range grass and seeds, and when that was gone they started eating the bark off of the trees. These trees had existed for hundreds of years and were dying because stripping the bark off the trees is like taking the skin off a human being, and because of this they were open to disease and were dying off. The coyotes had to be brought back to reestablish and maintain the balance that was disrupted by their removal.

In light of this, consider the family. Each family is a system, and each member in the family typically fills a certain role, but in most cases, these roles change as the family system increases, decreases, or modifies itself due to circumstances that may leave the family in flux. When considering a healthy family, they will adjust to the changes that come their way. As an example, when a young couple gets married, they typically start out blissfully, enjoying each other and enjoying their time together. They usually don't have many responsibilities, except for work and maintaining the household. They do have to adjust to each other even though they think they know each other fairly well because of the engagement. Living together as a married couple allows each to see the other person's little quirks, such as one being fanatic about putting things away while the other may not. While this may potentially cause problems, most couples learn to work these types of problems through.

The next significant adjustment comes when the wife becomes pregnant. The expectant parents are excited. They get to buy new baby furniture, baby clothes and so on, and this is a positive experience in their lives. But as soon as the baby is born, the system changes abruptly, even though the couple had time to prepare for the baby. They likely did not know what was coming or what they were getting into. The baby is born, the parents come home, and their entire life is altered significantly. They can no longer go to dinner when they want to because they have the baby to take care of. They can no longer go out to the movies or take off with friends, and so on because they have a child to care for. This may be difficult for some individuals, or couples, but a healthy couple will make adjustments. They give-and-take. They take care of each other, as well as the baby, and they adjust and move on.

When the second child comes along, the first child has to make some adjustments, and the parents have to make changes, but they accept it and enjoy the addition to the family. When the third child comes along and again comes an imbalance in the family system, and one difficulty is there are three children and only two parents. This means that in some cases one of the older children must be ignored, or left alone, because of the needs of another child. Other adjustments may include changing rooms, the place at the table, and so on. When the children get older, they go to school which is an adjustment. When the children mature they have outside activities such as sports, music, dance lessons, and so on. The family is always busy, and it seems as though the children are the main focus. Then the children, one by one, get into high school and do not come home for dinner because they have athletics, plays, or band practice. Ultimately the child graduates from high school and leaves home for college, the military, or work. Which brings about another major adjustment.

Just like when the child came into the family a big adjustment took place, when he/she leaves home, the family again makes adjustments. When the last child leaves home, mom and dad are by themselves and they are empty-nesters. Many couples think of this as a great time in life because they are free of many responsibilities. They are back where they were in the beginning of the marriage, able to do things without having to worry about children and pressing responsibilities.

A healthy family will work things through and adjust. An unhealthy family, on the other hand, does not make adjustments, or when they do make them they do not do it very well. An unhealthy family may be enmeshed (Kivisto, Welch, Darling, & Culpepper, 2015) or tightly intertwined with each other emotionally. If one person steps outside of his or her role, the rest the family will put great pressure on that individual to come back and conform. An example might be a family member deciding he wants to change political views. The rest the family will put pressure on that individual to come back and be what he was to begin with.

This enmeshment is often seen in family therapy where one family member starts to get better. The others may have pathology or problems such as depression or anxiety. As the one person gets help and begins to improve, the unhealthy family members will try and sabotage that person's progress with the intention of keeping him or her from getting better and thereby stop the disruption of the family system, as unhealthy as it may be. Or one family member may decide to live independently and get a lot of pressure from the other family members not to move. In cases where this works, the family will never change and all family members stay in the unhealthy rut, and that can be one place where pathology will begin. The remainder of this chapter will consider other traits that may engender psychopathology.

Lack of Direction

Lack of direction is a common problem. One area of concern that constitutes a lack of direction is not understanding the needs of children. If parents don't understand the needs of children, they will not know how to teach, and establish consistency, as well as meaningful limits, which is one of the greatest needs of children, because they thrive on routine. Students of psychology learn early in their career about circadian rhythms (Ferreira, Miguel, DeMartino, & Menna-Barreto, 2013). These rhythms cause one to become tired at a certain time every day, to eat at given times and to awaken at the same time each morning. Not only do these rhythms give the child a sense of structure and security, but so do other constants in his or her life. If, on the other hand, a child is raised in a family where there is no consistent bed or meal time, the child will likely feel frustrated and confused.

A number of families are not consistent in giving clear direction to their children. In this case, it can leave the child feeling unsure about his or her place in the family. In instances when expectations are unclear, not knowing what the other person is think-ing or feeling it leaves many children with no recourse but to begin to push the limits to find out where the person really stands. Older children might compensate for this discomfort by spending a lot of time at a friend's home, or with another family and possibly become a part of that family where things are predictable and peaceful. Those feeling that they have no direction often feel at loose ends and confused. This in turn can lead to a lot of bickering and fighting, whether it is the husband and wife or with the children. Others may withdraw and, by so doing, contribute to the deterioration of the family.

Another need children have is limits. Imagine living on a busy street and allowing a 3-year-old child to play in a front yard that is not fenced in. No parent would allow a child to play in the yard alone. The parent would supervise the child and make sure the child knows the boundaries of the yard. He will eventually learn to obey before being allowed to play in the yard without supervision. But why do parents do this? It is for the child's safety and well-being. In an example such as this most parents have no difficulty being consistent. If the child tests the limits and tries to go beyond the boundaries of the yard, he will likely learn quickly that no means no every time, which gives the child a sense of security.

On the other hand, if the limits are inconsistent, the child will have no recourse but to push to find out what the rules or limits are. On any given day, mother may say no and mean it. On another day mom may say no, but after much pleading, begging, and arguing she might give in. If this is the case, it will leave the child confused. Another day mother may say no again and try to mean it, but because the child has experienced inconsistency in the past he will likely press the issue hoping to get his way. This inconsistency is confusing to the child and the resulting behavior is frustrating to the parent. If mother gives in sometime later, even though she set the limit earlier, this will also confuse the child, and the child will have no recourse but to continue to push and test to find out if what she means today is the same as before, or will this time be different? Children will think that they can get what they want if they continue to get their way by pushing limits. This will give children a sense of insecurity and a lack of direction, which is the result of the parents not understanding the needs of children.

Another problem with lack of direction is an adult not verbalizing what he means, or needs. This often leads to couples arguing and fighting with each other, which is often the result of one person not verbalizing his or her thoughts or ideas. Imagine being with someone who never tells you what he, or she, is thinking. Most individuals in such circumstances are left to guess what the other person is thinking, which is typically negative. The person starts thinking what's wrong with me, don't you like me? The result is taking the other person's silence, or withdrawn behavior, personally. This will likely lead to upset feelings, and the person will get mad and start questioning or probing to get information or direction. The quiet person may then shut down and retreat further into his world, which oftentimes will lead to such emotional and mental problems as depression or anxiety for both individuals.

Some individuals are not able to establish themselves as a person. Imagine being with someone who is always agreeable and never says what he or she wants and never clarifies being unhappy with something. This can cause a lot of problems in families because, by not establishing one's self, it leaves other people guessing. Not verbalizing can result in a lack of direction, which can cause confusion by not knowing what to expect. The result of this is the person either becoming aggressive and/or angry and upset.

Emotionality

Another problem that causes difficulty in the family is emotionality, which means that people act on their emotions or impulses rather than following their common sense. Often when people are emotional they are actually frightened, insecure, or will use this tendency to manipulate others to get their way. As with lack of direction, acting on emotion leaves the other person, or people, confused about the emotional behavior. Most often family members become anxious and, to calm their anxiety, they will try to calm the persons down, which is actually reinforcing the poor behavior. An adult child lived with his parents because he was unemployed. Since childhood he would become upset and emotional and would continue until his mother or father would attempt to calm him by giving him what he wanted. The parents argued with each other because of their son's behavior and the result was the son never learning to control his emotions. He was unable to hold a job and no woman would date him for more than about 2 months. One woman told him his personality was too stressful, that she could never relax when with him for fear of him getting upset. Many people say that to be with such a person is like walking through a mine field; they never know when an explosion will occur.

No Clear Expression of Thoughts

The next trait that contributes to family dysfunction is the lack of clear expression of thoughts. In many families one or several members are not very clear in expressing their thinking. There are several ways this happens. One is talking in tones that distract from the intended message. There might be a parent or child who speaks very softly and almost childlike, which can be very distracting from what the person really wants to say. This is usually because of feeling unsure, or timid, and thus act on fears of rejection, so the person talks in soft, childish tones. A middle-aged mother talked childish, and the entire family had to work hard to figure out what she wanted. All of the children were anxious and fearful of not pleasing others, all because of mother acting in this manner.

Another example is the person talking too fast or loud, which can distract from the intended message. The anxious person might say "I'm hungry" in a loud voice, which might come across as being angry rather than anxious. The loud voice can be extremely intimidating to family members. If one talks in loud tones and intimidates everybody, the family may either ignore the person, or interact with him out of fear, not respect. A father who was raised in a large and loud family acted this way all through his adolescence until he had a friend tell him to stop being angry about everything. The young man said he was not angry. His friend said it always felt that way, and he needed to stop, which he did except at home.

The tone of voice can be very sarcastic. One could say "I love you" in a sarcastic tone even though unintended and cause hurt feelings. The youngest son in a family learned to be sarcastic from a friend he idolized. After talking this way for the better part of a day his father became upset and told the boy to leave his presence. The father later reported that he felt the boy was acting condescending and not respectful which hurt the father. The boy soon returned and asked the dad why he was angry and the father told him how his sarcasm hurt his feelings. The boy apologized and never talked that way again. Such a problem can cause a lot of upset in the family, especially in a marriage because of unintended messages. Parents sometimes talk very abruptly to their children, which can cause intimidation.

Another problem is a lack of clear expression of thoughts or not saying what one means. A person might say "it's kind of hot today, I would like cool off," when the person actually wants to say "I would like some ice cream." This sort of problem typically stems from one's fear of being rejected, so instead of saying what needs to be said different messages are sent to protect the individual from this anticipated rejection. The person may want to say "I would like to go to the movie," but will act on fear by not actually saying what he means or what he wants, so not to displease everybody. He might then act upset because he did not get what he wanted, which can cause confusion because no one knew what he wanted. One might say in an indirect way she wants out of the house by saying "I want to go the movies" thinking that is what the other person wants. Since the individual never clarified what she really wanted, she may feel disappointed or upset that the other person did not care enough about her desires to do what she really wanted. An elderly couple was returning from a church activity and the husband stopped to purchase gas. When he was getting out to put gas in the car, his wife asked him if he was thirsty, to which he said no and pumped the gas. He got back into the car and as he was driving his wife started crying. He asked her what the problem was and she said he was a tight wad and stingy. He asked what brought that on and she said she wanted a soda from the gas station and he did not get her one. He defensively replied that she never told him she wanted one, and he would have gladly bought her one if she had asked. She said she did by asking him if he was thirsty. Another problem with not expressing one's thoughts or desires is the person is expecting others to read her mind. This is typically the result of the person fearing rejection and taking what he thinks is a safe route by hoping the person will know what he wants rather than expressing his desires.

The Fearful Person

The next subject is the fearful individual. People acting on fear can create significant problems in the family, which can lead to pathology. Why? Because fearful individuals will often act in unpredictable ways, which once more can leave others guessing what is going on. One fear people have is doing something wrong and getting in trouble. Many individuals with this fear will always be agreeable on the surface and sacrifice what they need at the moment. An example is a father who was determined to raise his children the military way. As a result the oldest son never told his father what he needed. One time while visiting relatives he became ill and acted in way that came across as being defiant and was reprimanded by his uncle. Soon after that he vomited, which caused is uncle to feel guilty for scolding the child. The child later said that he was afraid of getting in trouble for feeling sick. His father was a verbally and physically abusive man that left the child feeling fearful of letting anybody know he had a problem.

Another fear may be being ignored. This is usually the result of feeling inadequate, or the fear of disapproval, which can be very strong. If an individual is raised in a family where disapproval, ridicule, or being ignored is common, this fear of disapproval is likely to be developed within the child. If the individual develops a pattern of acting on fear by holding back and withdrawing from people, that puts the person in a bad position by reinforcing the fear of disapproval. This is because the fear of disapproval is strong, and immediate relief from the fear is experienced when the person avoids the situation by not speaking up. The person never lets people know what he or she wants, thus leading to further doubts or feelings of being rejected which can then be the beginning of doubt and possibly develop into depression or a social phobia.

There are those people who are afraid of being hurt emotionally or physically. They fear being hurt emotionally by taking a risk, such as saying to mother "I love you mom" and mother ignoring the child, or responding with something like "leave me alone," or "what do you really want?" One particular patient stated that as a child he was afraid of telling his parents he was failing a class because they would get mad. He would keep it to himself and continue struggling and ultimately getting a poor grade and was then punished for not doing better and was told that was not very smart. Many other examples can be given of people acting on their fears which usually lead to harming the family. This trait then can help plant the seeds of psychopathology for family members and cultivate them within the individual.

Manipulation

Another problem seen in families is when one person manipulates other family members. When a child is born he or she has no way to express his/her needs except to cry, or act upset. When this occurs mom or dad attempt to satisfy the child's needs. As the child gets older he learns how to verbalize these needs, but will still have the same tendency to want to get something by acting upset. If the parent says to a 3-year-old "you cannot have a cookie, it is too close to dinner," the child will likely get mad and have a temper tantrum. If the child learns to get his way with pitching a fit to get the cookie, he will likely try that behavior again. What then may occur is this behavior being brought into adult life. As an example, a father has learned that through temper tantrums and outbursts he gets his way with his wife and the children. Another example is a newly married husband who wants to play softball with his friends, go to a concert with his buddies, or go fishing and his wife says "dear, I really need you home." If he learned as a child that a temper outburst got him what he wanted he will likely get mad and pitch a fit hoping to get his way and go with his friends, but his behavior will utterly destroy the relationship. One couple had this problem. They had a newborn son, and the wife told her husband she needed him to help her clean the house. He got mad at her and started yelling and saying "I do everything around here, you're lazy. You don't care about me." Actually, he did very little around the house and did not help with the baby. "You just think about yourself." The one time she needed some help he reacted in a strong and negative way and she was devastated, cried, took the son, and left him alone to watch TV.

Another form of manipulation is pouting. A certain family's father would pout if something did not go his way, if someone would disagree with him, or they did something wrong. He would not get outwardly mad, but would withdraw and say something like "I guess I'm just a bad person and am not very good." This would put a guilt trip on the other person and the entire family would rally around dad and try to make him "feel better." This was reported when he was 70 years old and was still using this rather childish behavior to get his way. This behavior leaves people guessing about what's going on with the person, and the behavior makes others anxious, which causes them to try harder to please the manipulator so no one will feel uncomfortable.

Some other types of manipulation include arguing or withdrawing. If, by arguing long enough, the person can wear the other individual down the manipulator is very likely to get his or her way. The person being manipulated may fear that by disagreeing the manipulator will not like the person, which may be difficult to accept. So by not arguing the person thinks he will not have any conflict. The problem is that the conflict still continues because he is not being honest with himself and the manipulator and will likely see other problems arise because of cowering. Others will try to argue by looking for loopholes in what the person is saying, and as the other person tries to defend her position the manipulator continues to counter by seeking the loopholes, which again leads to wearing the person down. Withdrawing or shutting down and pulling away is a strong tool for manipulation. "If I don't talk and shut you out long enough, you're going to give me what I want." At times one has to shut the other person out for healthy reasons, but to withdraw to continually manipulate is not healthy. One patient would spend weeks withdrawing from his wife to get his way, which was to allow him to come and go as he pleased without being questioned. Another method of arguing is accusing the person of the faults the manipulator has so the person is sidetracked by trying to convince the manipulator that he is innocent, which takes the focus off of the manipulator.

Manipulation destroys the family and the people being manipulated often end up with negative thoughts and feelings about themselves because in their mind they are being treated this way because there is something wrong with them. "You argue with me because you don't like me, or you think that I'm wrong." The guilt caused by withdrawing, the pouting, the arguing, temper outbursts, and all other manipulation tactics leave the person thinking "if I could just be perfect you would not do these things to me." These individuals being manipulated fail to understand that no matter how perfect they are the other person will continue acting in this way because the manipulated person will continually try to be better and that this behavior is actually reinforcing the manipulator's behavior. He does not have to change because this behavior will most likely get him his way.

Communication

Another problem in the family is poor communication, which is a two-way street. Often couples will come to counseling and, when asked what the problem is, they often say "we just don't communicate," or "we have communication problems." It is well understood that if a couple has problems communicating they will not be able to work through any difficulties they may be facing. It can also leave one vulnerable to manipulation because of doubts and fears that "I'm saying the wrong thing" and so forth. Again, communication is a two-way street. One reason people have a hard time with communication is not being able to be a good listener. Imagine coming home from work at night and the spouse is upset because of something not working or because she had a bad day with the children or work. If the other spouse is feeling unsure about what to do he may attempt to fix it, so the stress will be eliminated. If a person acts on his or her feelings problems usually ensue. For example, one may not want to listen because of the fear of being trouble. When an individual has a hard time listening, he or she will cut the other person off. When this occurs the cutoff may take different forms. Some do this by making fun of the person or by changing the subject. Others may do it by ignoring what is said or even by belittling the person.

One of the most common ways of stopping the communication is by giving advice. The person is typically thinking "I want to come to you. I want you to be a good listener." Almost everyone has experienced this. The person needing to talk might have a problem or want to share something important and wants the other person to listen. In many cases as one is actively listened to, that person likely will end up figuring out the problem or answering her own question. One patient had a difficult time listening to her husband because of the fear of him doing what he would talk about, such as buying something that was expensive. She would become so anxious she would lock herself in the bedroom for several days waiting for him to forget about what he wanted.

The other side of the problem is cutting off by not opening up and talking about concerns, or even positive things in one's life. When one doesn't talk and let people in his world he leaves people guessing where they stand, and when left to guess, the person will likely come to the wrong conclusions, which are typically negative. One reason for not opening up is fear. One patient's husband was an accountant. He would leave the house about five in the morning before anybody else was awake so he could avoid talking to anyone. He would come home late at night after the family had eaten and put his dinner in the microwave. He would then go into study and figure out sports statistics such as batting averages. His wife divorced him because she did not feel like he loved or cared about her. Another husband started communicating when his wife filed for divorce. He started opening up and found that it was a very positive experience and the marriage was salvaged.

The Double Bind

The next trait to be considered that causes problems in the family is a phenomenon called the double bind. A double bind is a message that has two parts, or expectations, and one contradicts the other, leaving the individual confused and conflicted (Bateson, Jackson, Haley, & Weakland, 1956). It was originally thought that the double-bind caused schizophrenia. Schizophrenics were found in families where poor communication existed, which included the double bind. The mother might say "Johnny get me a glass of water," and he may think "Oh boy if I get a glass of water for mom she will be happy with me." Johnny runs to the kitchen and gets her a glass of water and brings it to her and she gets mad at him because she did not want it in a plastic glass. This confuses Johnny and leaves him in the double bind by thinking "no matter what I do it is wrong. I can't ever get it right." One may get in trouble for not cooking something correctly such as the food being too salty, or not salty enough one time and the opposite the next time, or it being too hot, or not hot enough. This can be confusing for anyone raised in this type of environment. It has been discovered through many years of practice that a double bind is typically manifested in a different way that does not bring about schizophrenia, but engenders severe problems such as depression, anxiety, and even may lead to bipolar disorder.

One such family situation where the child is put in a no-win situation is the example of a parent using a young child as a confidant. It may be that mother becomes very close to her daughter and confides in her about mother and father's marital or financial problems. Mother is upset so she starts talking to her daughter who is about 10 or 12 years old. She tells the child about her problems, but because the child cannot understand what mother is talking about this becomes destructive because the daughter wants to help, and because of naiveté she feels she has to "fix" the problem. She starts doing things she feels will help, but eventually finds out nothing changes, no matter what she does. This is detrimental because a child this age is not able understand what mother is talking about, let alone what she needs to do to help. Parents should never go to their children with their problems.

Other Problems that May Contribute to Psychopathology

Other problems that can contribute to pathology are lower socioeconomic circumstances, family illness, substance abuse, abuse of any type, neglect, divorce, and blended families, as well as mental illness of one or both parents, only to name a few. Any of these problems can lead to pathology such as depression and other mood disorders, anxiety, chemical dependence, health difficulties, personality problems, and even thought disorders. Can people change? Yes, if they get the proper help and are motivated to change. The purpose of the text is to help the reader better understand how problems are acquired so effective treatment can be provided. Without understanding how a problem is acquired, or developed, one cannot have a clear picture of the paths needed to take to help the person.

One case was a couple who came in for couple's therapy. They had recently celebrated their 50th anniversary and the wife announced that she wanted a divorce. The husband said he did not want the divorce and was willing to do anything necessary to save his marriage. He was extremely insecure and always fearful that others would think poorly of him because he was not as good as other people. As a result, he was manipulative and always wanted his way. This caused him to feel like everything had to be perfect, which was very frustrating to his wife and three daughters and they could not tolerate being around him. It had been that way through the entire marriage. He was prone to depression due to his doubts and fears because everything had to be perfect. One example was the Fourth of July Parade that passed by their house every other year. For about two weeks prior to the parade he was impossible to live with. He was on everybody's case to make sure the house was perfectly clean and the yard was perfect. This type of behavior resulted in a depressed wife and 3 anxious daughters, and they all did not want to have anything to do with their father. He revealed that he was raised in a poor family and had hand-me-down clothes. Because of this and other circumstances related to their poverty he promised himself that he would never be in a position of ridicule again. Because of this he was controlling and always upset, fearing that somebody would look down on him. He soon realized that this was destroying the family when his wife filed for divorce. At the age of 73 he decided to change by not giving into his fears, and to act lovingly and kindly to his family. Many would say that this change would be impossible because of his age, but he did change and it was permanent. He said he was still anxious, but found a better way to act.

Instability in the home for whatever reason can affect the family negatively, which can bring about depression, anxiety, or other problems. People who were raised in such a family circumstance typically watch and are vigilant trying to keep on top of things so problems can be avoided, or so they think. In such situations family members could develop chronic illnesses such as headaches, digestive disorders, or even immune disorders, heart problems, and other chronic illnesses that can become very serious.

Chapter 2—Worksheet

1. Which family trait appears to be most interesting to you?

2. How would you view the double bind as a problem in the family?

Chapter 3

The Role of Learning and Psychopathology

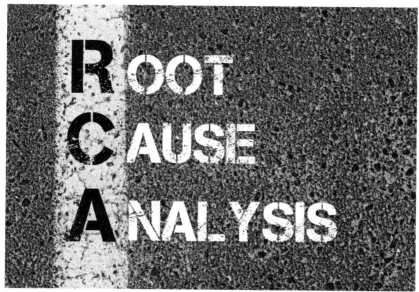

Constaintin Stanciu / Shutterstock.com

When considering psychopathology it is important to look for the root of the problem—where it started, and what is causing it. The perspective of this text is that behavior and most psychological disorders are learned. If the behavior, or disorder, is learned it has to be taught, and if the individual can learn, and wants to, the person can change. A clarification needs to be made that everybody can learn even if there are certain limitations. A person may have cognitive limitations, physical disabilities that are considered limitations, or limited mental capacity, so it may take longer for some individuals to learn certain concepts. Again, people can learn. When does learning begin? Of course, when the child is born one could say that is when this process begins. Actually research has shown that learning begins in the womb (Kisilevsky, Haines, Jacquet, Grainer-Deferre, & Lecanuet, 2004). Children are able to learn such things in the womb as to differentiate sounds (DeCasper, & Spence, 1986), the mother's position, the difference in intensity of light and possibly the mother's mood. Another indicator is the movement the baby makes when mother lies on her back, which causes the baby to lie across mother's spinal column; this is rather uncomfortable. The baby will start kicking and moving to get away from that discomforting position. One couple enjoyed attending their college basketball games. The wife was pregnant and she noticed at about the last trimester of the pregnancy that every time the team made a basket the pep band would go through a little drum roll which would cause the baby to jump. They thought this was quite unique and realized the baby could hear while in the womb.

If behavior is taught, who teaches? It is the parents or significant caretakers of the child. With this in mind, consider parenting styles and patterns. Through her research, Diana Baumrind (1971) identified four different parenting styles. The first is the authoritative parent who is said to be high in acceptance and high in control. This parent loves the child and relates to the child on an emotional level, but is also one who is willing to set the limits for the child. The parent will lovingly say "no, you do not talk back" or "do not hit people", and so on, but will also teach a child through love that he or she is an important person, and the parent is a safe individual. On the other hand, the authoritarian parent is high on control, but low on acceptance. These are parents that are controlling and have little, if any, emotional connection with the child. Earlier this parent was labeled the iron-fisted parent. This parent is the one who says, "my way or the highway," or expects the child to learn what the parent tells him the first time and not ask questions or make mistakes. In other words, "when I say jump, you ask how high on the way up." The next pattern that Baumrind identified is the permissive parent. This parent is high acceptance and emotional closeness with the child, but low in control. This parent will allow the child to do whatever he or she wants. "I love you so much. I'm not putting restrictions on you." Ultimately the parent will cave in to the child's demands and limit testing. Next is the neglectful parent. This parent is low in control and low in acceptance. This parent is emotionally and often physically absent from the child. This is common with parents who have mental or emotional problems, are consumed in their own world, and don't have enough well-being left over to attend to the child. As a result, the child is pretty-well neglected, or left alone. Another group of people, negligent parents, are those who were chemically dependent, those addicted to drugs or alcohol. These parents are again so consumed in their own world they don't know how to interact with other family members including their children.

One can learn about the different personality types and the traits that these parenting styles bring about. The authoritative parent typically raises children who are self-assured, motivated, and get along well with people. They also tend to have a good self-concept. Authoritarian parents, on the other hand, usually raise children who can be very controlling, but also in many cases, children who become passive as adults, afraid of authority, and keep to themselves. Permissive parents, on the other hand most often raise children who are aggressive and test limits in order to get their way and have very little empathy for other people. The neglected child is the one who stays to himself or herself. This person doesn't trust people. He will typically become a loner and have no use for people because he never learned how to interact with others. If they do interact with others the individual will typically feel awkward and oftentimes act rudely.

With this in mind, it is important to consider how behaviors are taught. As mentioned, behavior is learned, and if it is learned it has to be taught, and the teacher is usually the significant caregiver for the child. It could be a parent, a foster parent, grandparent, or someone in a facility. Whoever has the primary responsibility for nurturing and caring for the child is the one who becomes the teacher. In most societies it is typically the mother. She is the nurturer, the protector, and the reinforcer. She is also the person to make the child feel better and the encourager. In many cases, the mother is the one who does not want the children to get hurt so she may keep the child home where he or she is protected from anything that would potentially cause harm.

One mother was extremely protective of her two younger boys; the oldest lived independently. The two younger boys were in the early adolescent stage and spent all their time in the home and only came out on rare occasion. One day the older boy, who was about 14, was riding his bicycle and wore all the protective gear including a helmet, elbow, hand, and kneepads. He was riding his bike up and down the driveway, and that was as far as he was allowed to go. He and his younger brother were homeschooled and sheltered and protected by their mother to the point where they began to talk like some twins and developed their own particular language with each other with their own peculiar accent.

The home is where teaching and learning typically starts, but from there learning continues. In all cases, though, it is the responsibility of the parent to be sure the child is taught. Children learn at school both academics as well as how to interact with other children their own age. If the child learns at home to get away with certain behaviors, the child will likely try it out in public with his/her friends, or even adults. This will also carry over to other places such as church, day care, sports, and other activities and organizations. Again, the behavior patterns seen in public are most often started, or allowed to continue, because of what takes place or is taught in the home. If the child has learned through experience at home that he or she can argue with the parents to get her way, this will continue outside the home such as with the school, the music teacher, the coach, the teammates, etc. However, it is ultimately up to the parent to make sure the child learns well. These learned behavioral patterns acquired in the home are the beginning of either mental health or psychopathology. With this in mind, consider the methods of teaching, and the methods are simple.

There are two methods used in teaching. The first method, which is the most familiar to many adults, is example. This is done by acting a certain way and then the hope is that the child will follow what he saw the parent do. One example might be teaching a child how to set a table for dinner. Mother or father would set the plates, water glasses, and silverware in the proper places and hope the child would follow the example. In other instances one may teach manners, proper use of language, and so on by example. Consider, though, attempting to teach a child how to read by example alone. In this case the parent would have books in the house, he would read to the child, and even possibly get excited about reading, but that would be the extent of the teaching. Many parents report that they are continually attempting to teach by setting a good example, but cannot understand why the child will not follow. Of the two methods of teaching, example is the weakest, although it is necessary. The teacher will set the proper example of how to do a certain task, such as how to set the table, but if that is where the teaching stops then little is learned.

The other method of teaching is by precept. In reality this is the method that actually brings about the learning. First of all, one must understand the definition of precept. It is defined as a law, rule, or a command (*Merriam-Webster Dictionary*, 2016). Using setting the table as an example, once the parent has set the example, he then invites the child to follow the example while holding the child accountable to the standard just given. If the child makes a mistake father immediately corrects the child and holds him accountable to the standard. This occurs as often as necessary until the child has learned the process and can do it independently and consistently without having to be corrected. Once this has been achieved, the learning has taken place and the teaching by precept can stop.

Imagine again attempting to teach a child how to read. This is done by both example and by precept, but like many other instances this takes place one step, or precept, at a time. The teacher will establish the precept by setting the example and then invite the child to practice following that rule and holding the child accountable to the precept. The first step in teaching a child to read is to teach the alphabet. The child has no clue what she is doing or why she is saying the alphabet. She simply repeats what the person says. This is typically done by singing the ABC song. If the child makes a mistake, the parent corrects the child and has her repeat it again and practice it repeatedly until the child can do it correctly and consistently. It may take hundreds of tries before the child is able to say the alphabet consistently and without mistake. The next precept in reading, then, is what letters look like and how they sound. The same method is applied again. In each case the child is given the example and then invited to practice it while being held accountable to the standard initially established. If one is learning to play the piano, it is mostly by precept. The person must learn the scales by practicing them over and over until he has mastered the task.

Consider teaching by precept and example and see how it applies to teaching behavior. We use the same methods in teaching behavior that we use in teaching academics. We teach by example by acting the way we are supposed to ourselves, but we also teach by precept. One example is teaching the child how to act with the living room couch. The rule in most families is to sit nicely and to not jump on it; it is not a trampoline. Unfortunately, most children will attempt jumping on the couch because it looks fun, or they have likely seen someone else do it. When the parent sees this, he or she will tell the child to stop. Here they are establishing a rule, but unfortunately in many cases, the behavior does not stop because the parent does not follow through by enforcing the rule, or precept, and they fail to teach. In other instances the parent may put a stop to the jumping but fail to teach how to act on the couch, which is to sit nicely. Next is holding the child accountable to the precept by reminding him each time he sits on the couch to not put his feet on it, not wrestle, jump, etc. After a while he will automatically act appropriately on the couch. If the child makes a mistake, we correct them and stay with the precept until he is able to behave the right way.

With this in mind, the question often posed by parents is why do children misbehave? When this question is asked back to the parent, the most common answer is for attention, or sometimes they will say children misbehave because they want to get even with the parent. Others will admit that they think it is because they are not good parents. Other times, people will say children misbehave out of curiosity, or they simply want to try something out, which is often the case. One young boy who was about a year and a half old, was put to bed to take a nap. After a few minutes he was heard saying water is nasty. Mother walked into the room to find he was trying to drink a bottle of hydrogen peroxide. It didn't taste good and he was foaming the mouth. He most likely drank this out of curiosity or possibly thought that it was a bottle of soda. If the theory were correct that a child misbehaves for attention one would expect the behavior to stop once the attention is given. If the parent gives the child attention while he or she is misbehaving the misbehavior may stop for a moment because he or she is getting the attention wanted. In reality, though, the parent is actually reinforcing the misbehavior by giving the child attention. If on the other hand the parent thinks the child is misbehaving to get even with the parent, that mother or father will most likely retaliate in a harsh manner.

The reason children misbehave is to find out what the parents really mean, where the parent actually stands, what the rules are, or if what they are doing is okay. In other words, children are seeking clarification to understand what mom and dad are actually saying; "do you really mean what you are saying, or do you mean something else?" Going back to the example of jumping on the couch; "mom and dad, you said don't jump on the couch, but if I jump on it and ignore what you're saying will you leave me alone to do I want?: Additional examples are the 10-year-old daughter being told to go and wash the dishes, or the 12-year-old son asked to vacuum the living room rug, and the child ignores the parent or pitches a fit. The child is hoping the parent will say "never mind I'll do myself," or get someone else to do it. If the child learns through experience that the rules are not consistent—sometimes they mean it and sometimes they don't, or if I push long enough, the odds are in my favor for getting my way—the child will learn it is okay to function in that manner. On the other hand, if the child is taught that such behavior will not get him what he wants, that he has to do what is expected, the limit testing will cease, and when such behavior is consistently stopped over time the child will learn how to control himself and not misbehave. Now the mature parent can set the limits very kindly, firmly, and meaningfully. The permissive parent will not set the limits or make a feeble attempt at setting them. The neglectful parent will ignore the child, which leaves the child without a sense of direction. So why do children misbehave? It is to get his or her way or to find out what the rules are.

The next question that needs to be addressed is why do parents have difficulty teaching children? Is it because they are not educated, or is it because they do not have the right to tell the child what to do, or because the child is mentally challenged and can't be taught? Actually it is not any of those reasons. Parents have a hard time teaching children because they allow their emotions and feelings to get in the way of common sense. To illustrate, one's feelings and emotions are the result of the way the person thinks about the child, which is the attributions the parent has toward the child (Heider, 1958). For example, if the parent grew up feeling very safe being by himself because he was always ridiculed by his parents, this will likely leave him feeling extremely inadequate. If one day one of the children says "I hate you, I don't want you to be my dad anymore, and you're not fair" the parent will be devastated and this feeling would interfere with healthy parenting and teaching.

Now consider how these old feelings that one learned as a child can very easily come to play in adulthood. It is often easy for parents to feel sorry for the child if the parent feels bad about himself or herself because of something that happened as a child. If this is the case the parent will likely be afraid of making the child feel bad so father or mother will typically not set the limits for the child for fear of making the child hurt. The authoritarian or iron-fisted parent may think about children and parenting in a completely different way. If this is the case, the parent will act on negative emotions, such as anger, and exercise harsh control. This is likely with a parent who was raised in a strict and harsh family. If this is the way the parent thinks a child should be raised, those thoughts and feelings then would likely cause the parent to act controlling and emotionally distant and possibly unloving. Regardless of the family circumstances, adults act on their emotions in many ways that can be destructive. If, on the other hand, the parent has learned in childhood that rules are there for a purpose and it was expected that the person abide by them as a child, and was taught in a loving way, the person will likely bring this tendency to act in a kind, loving way into his or her adult life. Then, as an adult she can teach children how to act in a healthy and mature manner.

Typically these thoughts and behaviors are carried over from childhood experiences, but this might also be because of what is going on at the moment. If a young wife is to stay home and care for the children while the husband is always gone playing sports, the building resentment may cause her to treat children differently than if everything was well with her and the husband. Consider a divorce. That situation can cause one to think about children in a different way. A large number of divorced parents feel sorry for the child, and as a result are very permissive. Any one of these instances can interfere with a parent's ability to teach a child by precept as well as by example.

A single mother felt sorry for her two boys because their father had passed away, and as a result she was permissive because she did not want to hurt them because of not having their father. Another parent might feel guilty because he can't give his children what they want, such as new tennis shoes like everybody else is wearing. They can't have the latest video games because the parents don't have the money, or they can't have music lessons or go to sports camp. One may feel guilty because she feels she needs to be a better parent than she is. These sort of thoughts and feelings can get in the way of helping the child. Some parents are fearful of doing something wrong. These are parents who are afraid of hurting the child's feelings so they give the child what he wants. Some parents are afraid of the child getting hurt, so they protect him, such as the shy child being uncomfortable, and so the parent backs off from insisting that the child socialize.

There is a new term that is being used in the field of mental health the last several years, which is **attributions** (Heider, 1958). Attributions are what we attribute the behavior to. Attributions are either internal or external, stable or unstable, and global or specific. For example, if one attributes the child's behavior to being hardheaded, this will first of all be viewed as internal as well as stable and global. It is internal because of this part of the child's personality. Furthermore, it is stable because it is a part of the child's personality, and global because the child acts this way all the time. Another parent may say his daughter is acting out of sorts because she doesn't feel well. This will then be viewed as external, unstable, and specific to the moment. The way a parent attributes his or her child's behavior will determine then how the parent will interact with that child. If the parent sees unacceptable behaviors as being internal, stable, and global, the perception will likely keep the parent from expecting anything different than what he or she is seeing. That is going to interfere with being able hold the child accountable.

One parent introduced his son, Robert, as hardheaded, and as a result he treated the boy as such and was unable to teach his son how to behave. This resulted in Robert getting away with all sorts of unacceptable behaviors both at home and in public because it was never expected that he act correctly.

Susie had a hard life. She was born with a physical disability and, as a result, she could not play like the other children her age, or so her parents thought. As a result this attribution was viewed as internal and stable, as well as global. They felt sorry for her and became permissive. This resulted in the girl thinking she could have whatever she wanted if she only asked, or begged. If a parent views a child as capable internally, globally, and stable, it will be easy for the parent to expect the child to accomplish tasks assigned to him or her. Again, the way a parent thinks about the child will ultimately affect the way they feel about the child and the way the parent will go about teaching.

The problem with acting on one's emotions, is inconsistent teaching, and when teaching is inconsistent the child has no recourse but to keep pushing to find out what the parent means, which causes most of the problems seen in children. This is also the cause of problems between parent and child. As mentioned earlier in this chapter, parents lose sight of common sense when they act on their emotions. Also, it is important to remember that one's emotions are the result of his or her thoughts. All parents have common sense, or they intuitively know if something is right or wrong. Is it right or wrong to let a child up way past bedtime three or four times during the week when the child's about 10 years old? It is wrong because the child needs a consistent bedtime. Another example, is it right or wrong for a child to eat her vegetables or fruit? Of course, it's right to expect that. Even if she doesn't want to, she can learn how to the same as other children. Is it right or wrong to allow fighting? Some parents say they let their children fight to work out the problem, but when asked if that is acceptable most will admit it is not. They typically admit to something along the lines of hearing other parents saying it is okay so that's what they do for fear of maybe being wrong for stopping it.

So what happens then if parents act on their emotions and against their intuition? They fail to teach correct behavior. In most every case when working with parents who have problems with their children, and this is pointed out to them, they will say something like they are afraid to do something wrong. One mother said that her 5-year-old son's shoelace broke so she told him they would go to the store and buy a new pair of shoelaces. He was excited about it and when they arrived there he saw two different kinds of shoelaces. One kind had ABC written on them, and the other shoelaces were plain. He was asked which laces he wanted. The mother said she had learned earlier to not give her son choices because it would take forever for him to decide what he wanted. After much indecision mother decided to play a game by hiding them behind her back and said "you choose which hand," and he chose the plain white laces. Then he said that he wanted the others and started fussing. At that time a lady in the store came to the mother and said she should give him what he wanted. She went on to say that she knew when children are bad, and she could see that this young boy was good and mother was being mean to him by not giving him what he wanted. The mother did not know how to respond so stood there quietly. The woman gave the boy a dollar and told him to buy the laces he wanted. Mother went to the cash register and bought both shoelaces. When she got to the car she told her son firmly that he would not get the shoelaces with ABC printed on them because of the way he acted in store. She knew not to give him the idea that if he tested limits he could get what he wanted. Shoelaces were not the problem; the behavior was and had to be dealt with.

The next question posed by parents is how should they punish their children when they misbehave? First of all punishing is not effective in teaching correct behavior. Most parents think that if they can make the child hurt enough he will conform. Research has shown that the subject, in this case the child, will likely behave correctly in the presence of the punisher, but away from the punisher the child will resort to the unacceptable behavior patterns (Chance, 2008). A child might say a bad word and get soap put in his mouth, or may be scolded or given some other type of punishment. Punishment means paying for something the child did wrong. The concern should not be paying a price because many children believe that once the punishment is finished and the price is paid they can go back to what they were doing and not change the behavior. Another problem with punishing, or lowering the boom on them, is it can actually bring about feelings of fear of getting in trouble even when the fears are unwarranted, and even cause a low self-esteem in the child.

A patient was jailed for a brief time for breaking the law. During his probation he was not allowed to use any mood-altering chemicals, and he admitted to craving marijuana. Because of probation he did not smoke it for over 2 years. He said on many occasions that when he got off of probation he was going to buy the biggest bag of marijuana he could find and smoke to his heart's content. He didn't see this as a chance to change behavior, but only paying the price. It is not surprising then that so many individuals who have been incarcerated go back and reoffend.

The point to be made is that individuals such as those mentioned are out of control. What does the concept of being in control mean? It doesn't mean that the person doesn't have any feelings or emotions. It means the person is going to manage how he or she will act, regardless of how the individual feels. Adults have a desire for things, but will they let their emotions or impulses dictate their behavior? Will an adult who is in control steel or buy something on credit when he cannot afford it? If he can afford to pay for it he will act on his desire, if it is within reason. All adults have a sex drive and they are in control if they act on it appropriately and at appropriate times. So it is with teaching the child to control his or her impulses. What child wants to be told what to do or not to do, such as not jump on the bed, go and do the dishes, or pick up the toys in the family room? If the child gives in to the impulse to not do what she is supposed to do, she is out of control. The problem is not that she has the feeling, it is that she is acting on it when it is not appropriate to do so. When individuals act on their impulses and are out of control they, the family, and society are negatively affected. Under such circumstances someone must step in and either help the person gain control or take control for the individual until either he is able or willing to.

With this in mind comes the question of how parents should discipline? A term often used by the author is the bench. It doesn't mean that the parent needs to go out and buy a bench at the store. It is a term used in sports. When the athlete isn't doing well he is put on the bench until he is ready to go back into the game and function as he needs to. This is nothing more than timeout. Timeout, or the bench, is giving the child opportunity to go somewhere and sit down and come to terms with what he or she was doing, and decide what he or she needs to do to fix the problem, or change. In essence the parent is saying, "Suzy you're out of control, go sit down and when you've decided you're going to be in control come back and tell me what you are going to do to be in control." As a parent, or preceptor, she is establishing a precept she wants the child to obey. As an example mother tells Suzy to pick up her toys after playing with them and put them away, but Suzy goes in the family room and continues playing with the toys until it is time for dinner. Mother tells her again to put them away and she still doesn't do it. She's out of control so mother puts her in timeout. How long should she be in timeout? It is actually up to her. She can come out of timeout when she has decided to be in control. It is up to her to convince mother she is ready to manage herself and do what she has been told to do, or to be in control.

There are several rules to consider when using the bench. First, it is not a punishment. As such the parent does not place a time limit on how long the child is to stay in timeout. This then becomes a punishment rather than a teaching tool. If a time is placed on the timeout, the child will likely be concerned about how long she has to sit there rather than decide that she is in control or act as she is supposed to. When she commits to managing her behavior as expected, the parent is to then invite the child to show that she means it by acting accordingly. Then the parent is to hold the child accountable to her expected behavior. This is teaching by precept. The second rule to follow, especially with the younger children, is to not put the child in his or her room. this is because in the room there are too many things to play with and many distractions. This keeps the child from working through the problem and deciding what she is going to do to fix it. Furthermore, mom and dad must put the child in timeout immediately. This is no different than teaching the alphabet. The parent says the alphabet and invites the child to repeat it. If the child makes a mistake he is corrected immediately and is invited again to practice it until he can recite it correctly and consistently. The parent is telling the child to stay on the bench, or in timeout, until he has decided to be in control. It is up to the child then to come back and tell the parent how he is going to act. It is not enough for the child to come back and simply say, "Okay, I'll be good." The child must be sincere and willing to work on the problem. There are two other mistakes that parents often make. One is wanting an apology. What the parent needs to hear is how the child will remedy the problem and act. It is easy to say one is sorry and still not change. The other mistake parents often make is asking the child to tell them what he did that was wrong. The typical response is "I don't know" which often leaves the parent frustrated by thinking that if the child does not know then the parent cannot hold him accountable for being out of control. If the rare occasion arises to explain, the parent can briefly clarify the misbehavior and then send the child to timeout until he is willing to manage himself. In most cases the parent needs to send the child back several times to the bench until he figures out how he will do better. In all cases the parent wants the behavior to change, not a pound of flesh, or a debate about what is or is not acceptable.

An example might be asking a child put the toys away and she ignores the parent and walks away. She should be immediately put in timeout and to stay there until she is willing to be in control. She has to indicate "I will go put away my toys when you tell me," and she is then asked to show the parent she means it by doing what she was immediately told to do. Timeout does not mean just sitting on the bench. A child may be out of control with video games by playing on them too long, or acting moody while playing, or not doing homework because of the games. In this case the parent may take the game away until the child has decided to only play with it when mom or dad says he can, and only for a certain amount of time. The child may be put in timeout because of arguing. She may want to explain something, and that can be okay, but if arguing is a way of testing the limits, or to get the parent to back off, that is not acceptable. Whenever the child is out of control he or she must learn to stop the behavior and get back into control. Another example is a teenager misusing the privilege of driving by not coming home on time or going places she shouldn't. This behavior is telling the parent she is either not able to, or not willing to, manage the privilege. The parents would be wise to take the driving privilege away until they are fully assured that she will be responsible and in control with the car.

Again, the term "out of control" covers a broad spectrum of behavior from hitting and defiance to being shy and withdrawn. There is a myriad of misbehaviors that children engage in. Out of control behavior may manifest as being shy. Why is a shy child out of control? By letting her shy feelings dictate the behavior to the point where she will withdraw from people and not interact. This is harmful to the child because she does not learn to relate to people in a world where interaction with others is essential. People do not invest in those who push them away or avoid them altogether. In all cases it is the responsibility of the parents to teach their children how to manage their emotions, feelings, impulses, and behavior so the children can become healthy and productive adults. On the other hand, one who is continually defying authority by acting impulsively is out of control. Such is the case of the 15-year-old male who refuses to go to school and is out with friends who are shoplifting and committing other crimes. Society does not need people who have to be controlled by others because they choose to not control themselves.

The general principle to be understood here is that as one learns to manage his or her impulses and behavior, the person will experience more freedom. As a child learns to obey mom and dad she will then be allowed to do more with friends as well as have other freedoms within the family. An example would be the 16-year-old daughter having adriver's license. If she has proven to be responsible with time management, chores, obedience to mom and dad, and in control of her impulses, she will most likely be allowed to use the family car when she wants to. If a 6-year-old is able to function without a daily nap then he will likely be allowed to stay up throughout the day. One example is a young 15-year-old boy who was continually arguing with his stepfather. As a result he had very little freedom because he was continually grounded. He was amazed to find that when he managed his behavior and stopped arguing with the stepfather both mother and stepfather relaxed with him. As a result he was able to earn their trust. By managing his behavior he was allowed to do pretty much what he wanted within reason. As a child matures and learns to manage himself later in life, as adulthood is achieved this person will have opportunities and freedoms that others who are not in control will never have. The question often posed to children who are testing boundaries and trying to always get their way is "who do you want to control you?" Children are then given three choices; either himself, his parents, or the law. When children have this question posed to them they typically say they want to control themselves.

The purpose of this chapter has been to illustrate the importance of teaching acceptable behavior. This is where either mental health or psychopathology is developed. As an example, if the child learns through experience that by testing the limits and misbehaving he will get what he wants, he will take this behavior through adolescence and into adulthood. If this is the case, the individual will continually experience conflict within his personal life as well as at work, in social settings, and close relationships. This can bring about depression, anxiety, bipolar disorders, as well as other problems such as personality disorders. On the other hand, if an individual is raised in a home where adequate behavior is taught and the individual learns self-control, he will then be able to live a productive life within his profession, personal life, and social life. To illustrate this point imagine someone attempting to play a musical instrument such as the piano. Many individuals who play the piano try to create their own music. Those who have not had lessons, or adequate training, usually create music that is less than appealing. On the other hand, those who have had formal lessons and learned the rules of music are able to take those rules and apply them in ways that would allow the person to create music that is pleasurable and interesting. In life when a person understands the rules, norms, and folkways, and is able to function within them, he or she can apply those rules as needed and live a productive life.

Chapter 3 — Worksheet

1. Why do children misbehave? children misbehave to find out what the rules/limits are.

2. Why does an anxious parent cause the child to be anxious?

3.   Why is consistency important?

Chapter 4
Parenting and Mental, Emotional, and Behavioral Patterns in Children

Rawpixel.com / Shutterstock.com

This chapter will consider the role of parenting and how it establishes mental health and disorders, as well as emotional and behavioral patterns in children. The previous chapter considered how behaviors are taught. It was established that if behavior is learned it has to be taught. With this in mind the question often arises concerning when learning begins. Over the years research has shown that very rudimentary learning takes place in the womb. The purpose of this chapter is to consider learning that starts in the home, and thus sets the foundation for the learning process. To review briefly why children misbehave, it is simply to find out what the rules are. Do mom and dad, or anybody else, really mean it when they say don't jump on the couch, go do your homework, do the dishes, be nice to your siblings, and so forth? When a child knows what the limits are, and that they are consistent, as mentioned earlier, it gives a child a great sense of security.

Imagine driving across a bridge high above the water and there are no lines painted on the road to give one a sense of where the lanes of traffic belong. Furthermore, there are no signs up to give direction. Then imagine there are no guardrails to keep people from going over the side. Would very many people want to go across the bridge? Most people would say no, it would be too frightening. However when the lines, signs, and guardrails are in place one would have a sense of security. On the other hand, if there are only bits and pieces of the guard rail and lines placed randomly on the bridge, it would still be very frightening. Compare this to a young child going to school for the first day of kindergarten. She is going to a new school and the father intends to give orientation by explaining what is expected, and then leaves. At this point in time most children are typically very fearful and unsure because of not knowing the rules, the teacher, and other children. Once the child settles in and learns the routine and gets to know the teacher and gains friends, school can become a very pleasant experience. Some children will misbehave to find out what the rules are in an attempt to gain a sense of security and, if the teacher is inconsistent, insecurity and continual testing follow.

To continue with the same theme, a brief review of operant conditioning and schedules of reinforcement (Travers, 1982) need to be discussed. There are two types of schedules of reinforcement—ratio and interval. Interval schedule reinforcement is a certain amount of time that lapses between reinforcers. An example is every 5 minutes the subject gets a reinforcer regardless of what the subject does. Ratio, on the other hand, means the subject must perform a specific task or behavior a certain number of times before getting a reinforcer. An example of a fixed ratio of one would be a person getting a candy bar of his choice every time he smiled. Because of the reinforcer, the subject would likely smile quite often. In order to cause the behavior to become more entrenched, in this case smiling, one would begin to thin or stretch out the number of times a person smiles before he gets the reinforcer. An example would be getting a candy bar every third time the person smiles and then possibly every seventh time and maybe even up to 10. Theoretically the subject will keep smiling knowing, or anticipating, he will get another candy bar.

To cause a behavior to become strongly established one would then go to a variable ratio of reinforcement. In this case the person is given a reinforcer on an average of five tries over a series of 100 reinforcers. The subject may get a candy bar after smiling twice and then the next time he might not get one until he has smiled 15 times. The next time maybe 22 times and the next time possibly after 3 tries and so on. One cannot get the subject to behave by immediately using the variable ratio. To get it started the ratio has to be a fixed ratio of one, or every time the person smiles she would get the candy bar. Another prime example is that of gambling. One plays the slot machines, which are set on a variable ratio. It might be that the machine will pay out on an average of every 100 pulls, but this could vary from between 20 to over 1000 tries. It is the anticipation of the reward that keeps people putting more money in the slot machine knowing that eventually there will be a jackpot.

This variable ratio of reinforcement is a pattern that many parents unwittingly engage in when trying to teach their children, which causes inconsistency. One couple had a child who was always getting into trouble and they said over and over "we are really consistent." What they were actually saying was they were consistent in telling him what not to do or what to do. The problem, however, was they were not consistently reinforcing what they were saying because they did not actually mean what they were saying. Even though they would tell him either to do or not do something he would keep doing what he wanted. All they would do was tell him and threaten and coax and plead, and spank once in a while, but they never actually stopped the problem. One example was sneaking food out of the kitchen. They would scold him or put him in timeout for a brief period of time, but they were inconsistent by varying the times they would actually follow through with putting a stop to the misbehavior. On occasion they would give up and not follow through at all. By not meaning what they were saying they were inadvertently establishing a variable ratio schedule of reinforcement. Eventually the father got the message and decided the boy was not going to take any more food without permission. The parents made sure that he was not left alone and that food was not accessible to him because he was not able to manage his impulse regarding the food.

What initially occurred was mother and father saying no to something and thinking they meant it, but would not enforce the expectation. Over time it may take longer and longer to wear them down to get out of the restriction, but it usually worked. If the parents do not mean what they say, the child's pressing the limit will ultimately work. This is often seen with children wanting something like a cookie before dinner. Of course, mother or father would say no if it were 10 minutes before dinner time. Parents know that the cookie will ruin the child's appetite, so they say no. What does the child do? He gets upset and starts whining and crying while mother or father continue saying no again and again. After enough pressure what do they do? End up giving the child a cookie to stop the conflict.

Another example is one family visiting another and the cousins wanting to play miniature golf. The cousins from one family know if they asked, the answer would be no, but the other cousins knew if they asked again and again, after a while their parents would give in to the pestering. So by asking over and over again for about 20 minutes, the mother finally got in the car and all the children were taken to the miniature golf course. Mother reinforced the behavior through the variable ratio. If the child persists long enough and asks enough times, the odds may be in his favor to get his way, and also consider in this case the interval, or the time between starting the limit testing and the child actually getting what he wants. This behavior is reinforced by the child knowing that if he waits long enough, parents will change their mind and give him what he wants. Again this inconsistency causes the behavior to become deeply entrenched.

So how does one stop a behavior? To stop a behavior one simply stops reinforcing it. What happens though when the reinforcement stops? The child's limit testing continues and will even become stronger because he is used to persisting until he gets his way. This is called a response burst. The child may think "I have to try harder and persist longer so can I get what I want" because it worked in the past. If the parents truly decide on a limit they will not change; no matter how hard the child tries the effort will be for naught. Again, the child is convinced that mom and dad are going to change so he will persist. In this case the child may have asked 10 times in the past and the parents would finally cave-in so the child thinks, "well if I ask about 10 times I should get what I want." So he persists by asking over and over again and when 10 times doesn't work he might continue to 15 or 20, but will eventually realize it is not working and he will stop. He may come again later and try, but if the results do not change he will eventually stop the behavior completely. This is when the behavior is extinguished, or becomes extinct. One must remember though that this limit testing can begin again very quickly if the parents give into the testing under other circumstances. It is not fair to the child when the limits are inconsistent. It leaves a child very upset, frightened, insecure, and frustrated. It is these circumstances that leave the child no recourse but to continue pushing to find out what the parents mean. If the child is unclear about the limits, other problems will occur which can become very serious. The problem is that the child is in a state of conflict which leads to pathology that will be discussed in this chapter.

Conflict is typically defined as the result of something that used to work, but no longer does. Another example is trying to choose between several options with no clear understanding of which is the best, or correct. The widely held theory is approach–approach, approach–avoidance, or avoidance-avoidance (Lewin, 1935). In these cases one has to decide between one of two good choices where either are acceptable, or the choices have good and bad aspects to them, or a choice where one has to choose between the lesser of two evils. But conflict with a child exists between the child and parent when the child is testing limits, or misbehaving. This situation causes an adversarial relationship between the child and parent because of the limit testing. So mom and dad say no. The child starts pushing and as the child pushes a feeling of animosity between the child and the parents emerges. The first point to be made is that children are not happy when pushing. The parents become upset, the child is frustrated and possibly mad, and this animosity causes a significant strain on everyone, and in many cases even those not directly involved in the conflict. One example might be going to work and being about 30 minutes late. Typically the closer one gets to work and the later she is, she starts going through some specific feelings that are unsettling, which is conflict. This typically involves at least three different emotions or feelings, the same that children go through when pushing the limits. Number one is anxiety. Because the child is pushing the limits he will become anxious and this is not the anxiousness one feels Christmas Eve. This is a negative anxiety, or feeling unsettled. The next feeling is fear. Fear of what? The fear that if he pushes this too far the entire roof may cave in on him, or the result may be getting into real trouble because of the conflict created by the pushing. There is always that fear of the unknown, or "when have I gone too far?" The third emotion or feeling that comes into play is guilt over the problem that has been created. "I'm in real trouble and I feel terrible because of what I've done." Most children feel guilty after the pushing has stopped and they have gotten their way because the fighting and turmoil was not worth it. After all of the conflict the guilt is so strong that they didn't enjoy what they got away with. For some children guilt comes later. When one packages together anxiety, fear, and guilt one sees a very insecure and upset child. Insecurity is one result from conflict.

The insecurity that the child feels because of this conflict is real, which typically entails the fear of losing the love of the parent, fearing that the parent will not care about the child, or will hate him. Children often say that mom or dad don't love them because of the conflict. Another phenomenon that takes place is fear of never being able to get out of trouble and that they are always in trouble. Also, it affects one's health. When a child is in trouble her stomach may be unsettled and maybe they can't eat or they want to eat continually for comfort. Along with problems regarding appetite many children who are always in trouble can have heart problems. This conflict will likely also affect the immune system and the autonomic nervous system (Weiten, Dunn, & Hammer, 2015), which can leave a child prone to illnesses. Another result of this insecurity can be concentration problems. When a child is in trouble, it is hard to pay attention to what is going on around him because he is consumed with the problems with whom he is in conflict. It's hard to pay attention in school when the child is in trouble. One has a hard time concentrating on anything when that person is worried about something. Furthermore, when a child is in trouble at school, with a friend, or is disobeying the parents, they may not know what the problem is, but can discern the child is in trouble by the way he acts. He will manifest some type of behavior change such as acting moody, upset, or withdrawn and not wanting to be involved in the family, or acting in ways that will keep people away. This is because the child knows he is in trouble and will likely think others know, and that can cause him to act defensively.

The Oppositional Defiant Child

With this foundation several common childhood disorders will be addressed. Many of these disorders begin with behavioral problems that will eventually lead to emotional and mental disorders in childhood as well as later in life. The first of these disorders to be considered is the Oppositional Defiant Disorder. This diagnosis is described in the DSM-5 as Angry/Irritable. This includes frequent loss of temper, being touchy and easily annoyed, or often angry and resentful. Another group of symptoms include argumentative/defiant behavior. Here one would frequently see arguing with other children or adults, often defying or refusing to comply with requests from authority figures, often deliberately annoying others, often blaming others for his or her mistakes or behavior, and also being spiteful and vindictive at least twice in the past 6 months. Mostly what is considered in this case is a child who is defiant of authority. It is important to remember that these are children who argue with parents and others in authority because they know that if they argue or annoy them they will likely get their way. Again these are children who are always testing the limits to find out what the rules are. Remember, though, that all children argue because they want their way, but in this case the arguing and testing is far beyond what is considered the normal functioning of a young child. Also these are children who are selfish, self-centered, and demanding, and this behavior typically starts out early in childhood.

One couple had an infant son about 6 months old. He knew how to get out of staying in church during the worship service. He would sit quietly during the first part of the meeting, but after the opening of the meeting was finished the boy would begin fussing and immediately mother would take him out to the foyer where he was put on the floor and allowed to crawl around and play. He learned at a very early age to get his own way by acting oppositional. This disorder typically starts in early childhood. What parenting style will bring about this type of behavior? Usually it is the inconsistent parent. These are parents who don't consider themselves inconsistent, but feel they hold to the rules. Unfortunately they may verbalize the rules, but as soon as the child begins to mount pressure the rules change and the parents rescind the expectations or rules. With inconsistency the child will ultimately develop this pattern of arguing and testing to get her way. Unfortunately this is a very common pattern seen with children. This is seen in school, at play with peers, and most frequently at home.

Whenever one reflects back on childhood, that person will remember some children who were always pushing to get their way. A young boy about the age of 14 had stolen a blank check from his father's checkbook. Later that evening at a social gathering with friends he asked another boy his age to help fill out the blank check. He told his friend that he needed to buy parts for his motor scooter. His friend later said that he was frightened and he did not want to get in trouble with the law so he refused to help the other boy with the blank check. The boy with the blank check became upset, started crying, and said the other boy said that he was a chicken for not helping out. The boy finally found somebody else to help and, over time, this practice became common. His father never pressed charges so the young man learned that his parents would not enforce any rules or expectations. He also learned to pressure some friends enough that they would also cave in.

Another way a child may be oppositional defiant is by acting sneaky to get his way. This child would be seen as a child arguing and debating, but in a kind and nice way. There was a young lady in the psychiatric unit who was a classic example of oppositional defiant disorder. She always argued with her parents and in most cases would eventually get her way. She was admitted to the psychiatric unit because of the continual turmoil and conflict at home, at school, and with friends. About the second day in treatment while in group therapy she refused to participate by acting silent and refusing to talk, and at about 10:00 a.m. she was put in timeout and was told she could come out when she was ready to participate and act appropriately. She stayed in timeout the entire day and into the evening. She was allowed to have her meals and go the bathroom, but that was all. Her parents attended the parenting group that evening and returned home after the class without talking to her. The next morning her therapist noticed she was out of timeout and asked the nurse what happened. She said that after the therapist left the previous evening the girl got the nurse's attention and tearfully asked when she could get out of timeout. Would she have to stay in the room until the next morning? The nurse said no, she could come out whenever she was ready to comply to the expectations and rules of the unit. She thought about the situation for about 20 minutes and finally said she decided to manage herself. The next day she was a perfectly compliant young lady and this continued throughout her stay. It was noticed, though, that when her parents came to visit she immediately reverted back to her old behavioral patterns of being oppositional and defiant.

Another young girl in the unit learned how to be oppositional defiant from a former boyfriend. She would passively defy the parents by sweetly saying no about her business, going and doing what she wanted. She actually feigned being psychotic. It was apparent that she behaved that way because her parents would give her what she wanted when she acted "psychotic." On one occasion she laid on the ground in a busy intersection in town and stared up at the sky because she thought it was beautiful. This frightened the parents and left them feeling helpless and unable to do anything to correct the behavior for fear that if they did she would do something irrational and get hurt. Finally, they were helped to see through the manipulative behavior and they put a stop to it. They said, "Because you're so out of control and your behavior is so unpredictable, we can't let you out of our sight so you will have to be with someone at all times, even your younger sister if necessary." Mom and dad saw an immediate change in their daughter when they took control for her and she soon decided to manage her behavior because she did not want them to manage her.

Another type of parent that can bring about the Oppositional Defiant Disorder is one who is afraid, fearful, or anxious. These parents will put up with a lot of limit testing and give in because they are afraid of the child developing some kind of mental or emotional problem. When parents get anxious and feel they do not know what to do they become unsure and inconsistent, and the result can be ODD. Parents who are extremely controlling to get their way can also bring about ODD because of the child seeing that this type of behavior gets people what they want. This Oppositional Defiant Disorder is obviously reinforced by getting away with continual limit testing and defying authority. These children are also selfish and are used to getting their way. Furthermore, they do not want to share their things with others, and are typically moody because moodiness gets them their way. They are also moody because of always being in conflict and always being in trouble. They also have a very limited sense of accountability, but feel entitled. "I deserve everything I get even though I have to cause of lot of commotion and hurt to get it." With this comes significant insecure feelings within the child because when a child is pushing as was pointed out earlier, he will always wonder when he has pushed too far and his entire world will cave in on him. This also engenders insecure feelings and poor self-esteem. A child never learns how to develop a healthy self-esteem when she is in constant conflict. Self-esteem comes when one has a sense of value. A child with poor self-esteem will have a hard time losing a game, and will not know how to relate to others in a healthy way because of the continual conflict.

They get upset, mad, and have tantrums, and may even try to change the rules so they can win.

If these behaviors are allowed to continue the child will later be prone to mood disorders including depression and bipolar disorders, or even anxiety. They also have a hard time relating to others on a meaningful level and will likely have difficulty getting along with people. Very often, they don't have a lot of friends. Furthermore, the result of the problems from this disorder is that the child is not very sure of himself because of constant conflict and as a result may be easily manipulated. Also the Oppositional Defiant child will gravitate to those people who will put up with the poor behavior and they are typically children who are troubled themselves. Again, this disorder is the result of inconsistent, or over controlling parents, where limit testing is either allowed or not noticed because it is away from the parents.

The Conduct Disordered Child

In some cases the limit testing may go beyond the oppositional defiant child and become Conduct Disorder. The Conduct Disordered child is often seen as a juvenile delinquent. This child has no regard for the law or for other people's rights (DSM-5). They only think of themselves and this typically starts developing in early childhood. They are often viewed as having no conscience. These are children who have a history of running away, who have problems at school, are often involved in drugs and alcohol, will commit crimes such as breaking and entering, theft, assault, both physical and sexual assault, and other types of illegal and destructive behaviors at a very early age. They are in continual conflict at home as well as in society (DSM-5). Most families lack consistency and do not give clear direction to their children. When expectations are unclear it leaves the child feeling unclear about the rules, and many children see no recourse but to begin to push the limits to find out where the person really stands. Those children feeling that they have no direction often feel at loose ends and confused. This in turn can lead to a lot of bickering and fighting whether it is between husband and wife or with other children. Others may withdraw, and by so doing contribute to the deterioration of the family.

Because of this type of behavior they have a poor self-esteem and typically grow up and become more isolated and have few friends because others cannot trust them. It becomes an ugly picture. These are oftentimes children who are also raised by overcontrolling parents. The controlling parents are the overly demanding parents who always insist that things go their way. One particular child was in a rough neighborhood, and while in Jr. High indicated symptoms of conduct disorder. His father was in and out of jail and on one occasion he bragged about his father's boots having razor blades in the toes for fighting. His father was also one who would not tolerate anyone disobeying him. If anyone such as one of his children did, they paid a heavy price. He also talked about how his older brother was always in jail. He acted the same way and had no sense of responsibility for other people's well-being. He was frequently in juvenile hall for breaking and entering, fighting, shoplifting, stealing, etc.

In other cases, these individuals are raised by parents who are unable to set limits. They might say they set limits, but they rarely follow through with what they say. Oftentimes Conduct Disordered children come from families like previously mentioned where the parents are diagnosed as Antisocial Personality Disorder. Conduct Disorder is a diagnosis for the child until he reaches the age of 18 when he receives the diagnosis of antisocial personality disorder. In some instances they may come from a family with a history of extreme conflict, or even drug abuse. Another young man in a chemical dependency rehabilitation hospital came from a home with a lot of conflict. His mother divorced his father and married another man who was alcoholic and extremely physically abusive with the children.

In many cases there exists a comorbidity of a learning disability. This is often the result of a serious disregard for parental or other adult authority and resulting conflict. These difficulties in school typically result in poor grades because of incomplete assignments, not attending school, and most commonly, conflict with teachers and school authorities. It is also manifested through difficulties relating to peers because of arguing, limit testing, and lack of respect for others' rights. One high school patient stated that he was having difficulty in school with a classmate who was always trying to pick a fight with him. His parents told him to stand up for himself, which he did, and it caused a fight. The young man lost the fight, but when his parents were called in to discuss the matter they were told that the other young man had been a problem for years, and if they would allow their son to be suspended they could expel the other young man from school. The parents gladly agreed and assured their son that he would have a two-day vacation.

Again, these individuals typically have a history of running away, hurting other people, and even sexual assault. Furthermore, they can be guilty of physical assault or assault with a deadly weapon. They also have a hard time dealing with rejection and dealing with people saying no. They commonly take it very personally. Typically, they have few friends and are often seen as loners, and as a result they have a poor self-esteem. The result of these problems is the inability to understand what other people are going through because they have not learned to consider others' situations. This also leads to not developing a conscience. It needs to be noted that the earlier the problems are manifested, the more difficult it will be to treat. This is because the longer it exists the more entrenched it becomes. These disorders have to do with defying authority and not wanting to follow the rules of society, to varying degrees, and if a child learns to act this way while growing up these patterns will be taken into his or her adult life. Unfortunately, many young people with Conduct Disorder are in the prison or legal system.

It is also necessary to remember that both the Oppositional Defiant child and Conduct Disordered child lack a sense of accountability. One such example is the young man who broke into several homes and took money and jewelry from the families. He later stated that it was okay to steal from them because they had plenty of money and they should not have left things out where they could be stolen. An adult who had symptoms of antisocial personality disorder said that when he was about 12 years old, a boy from a neighboring farm had taken a toy from him. When the boy returned the next day to play with this person again, he shot and killed the neighbor boy. He showed no remorse and said the boy deserved it, and he was not convicted of any crime, which left him feeling no responsibility for the matter.

The Mood Disordered Child

A common problem with children lies in mood disorders. Some children experience depression, which can be a single episode and can be mild, moderate, or severe (DSM-5). Some children can also have the diagnosis of dysthymia, which is a long-standing depression for at least 2 years with no significant respite from (DSM-5). When depression is considered in a child, such problems as difficulties with concentration and frequent daydreaming with his or her thoughts somewhere else occur. Also there are other symptoms such as appetite changes, which may be either overeating or lack of appetite. There are also problems with sleeping. Some children don't sleep while others do nothing but sleep. Like adults the root of depression in children is negative thinking, which is very destructive. These thoughts can likely be "I am no good; I'm never going to amount to anything." In many cases the child will think that if he or she can be perfect there would be no problems. When a person thinks that way, the result is the child feeling down, hopeless, as well as helpless, and the child starts feeling unsure of himself. Once this thinking starts the child will feel inadequate, and then she will turn from positive to negative feelings. This will have a profound effect on the child's behavior. The pattern of thinking leads to one's emotional state, poor self-esteem, and poor, inadequate behavior that ultimately reinforces the thinking, and it becomes a vicious cycle.

How does the child act out depression? Adults usually act out depression by isolating. Children will act the same at times as adults, and will act out their depression by shutting down emotionally. They will often get upset and moody, which may be viewed as angry, or give the impression of being irritated and tired. On rare occasions, these symptoms may go so far as to appear to be a psychotic episode, where the child may lose touch with reality or become suicidal. To better understand depression consider the parenting styles that engender such symptoms. Most often this is seen with parents who are very demanding and expect perfection. This leaves the child feeling he is always wrong and never adequate.

An example of a demanding parent is a father who was a pillar of the community. He was a farmer and had to have the best farm in the county. He was also on the City Council, the school board, and liked to have a large number of friends and extravagantly entertain people. His daughter was a senior in high school and was the valedictorian, a starter on the girls' basketball team, and was everything that a parent would ever want, but she was miserable. When she graduated from high school, she went to one of the major universities in California, which is an honor and very difficult to gain admittance to. In the middle of her first semester, she committed suicide. One major contributing factor was most likely being raised by a very demanding father whose expectations she could never meet, at least in her mind. She couldn't because he was never accepting of her accomplishments. She could have always done more or done better. Even when she did excel she had to keep it up and could never relax and enjoy her successes. He was insecure and felt inadequate which caused him to view himself as never being good enough. This affected the way he viewed and treated his daughter and caused her to start thinking of herself in a negative way at a very early age. She was always trying to get mom and dad's approval and felt she never could as she stated often in therapy.

Another type of parenting that can start depression in children is the double bind which was described earlier. This leaves a child feeling troubled no matter what they do. The double bind is a very serious problem because it leaves one feeling helpless and hopeless because she can't get out of the problem. The emotionally distant parent can contribute to this. Parents who don't relate on a feeling level are not adequate teachers, and because of the emotional distance, often leave the child with the same feeling found in the double bind situation. Why is this the case with such parents as the double bind and the emotionally distant parents? Because children need to know where they stand. It gives them a feeling of security and that they are okay and acceptable. A point that needs to be introduced here that was not discussed earlier is egocentric thinking. Santrock (2008) defines egocentric thinking as the "inability to distinguish between one's own perspective and someone else's" (p. 247). Within the context of this text it means that the child thinks that everything is a result of him. An example is a child coming home from school and finding mother in a bad mood. Most likely the child will think it must be his fault, or if he does something right mother would be happy. Children typically think they are not a good person if the other person is not acting in an accepting manner or doesn't give approval. If the person acts in a way that is interpreted by the child as negative, it will leave the child feeling anxious and fearful of getting in trouble. "What I did caused mother to be in a bad mood and I must correct it somehow." This is in essence of egocentric thinking. The double bind then means the child is not able to separate himself from what others are saying or doing and is not able to understand that how the other person acts is not the child's problem.

One example is a young man thinking for most of his life that it was best to stay quiet and not be noticed so he would not cause problems for his parents who were always fighting. He, like others, thought the arguing between his parents may have been his fault. Because of this reasoning he eventually feared most adults including teachers so he would avoid them. Then he would become caught up in the negative thinking and emotions because of his poor performance in school and act on the feelings by isolating, which left him time to dwell on how negative his life was.

In most cases when the child is acting depressed it leaves the parents feeling bewildered and unsure about what to do. As a result, they often leave the child alone hoping he will work the problem out on his own, or grow out of it. Again these are children who typically withdraw and ignore people because they think they are of no worth. This can start at a very early age maybe 6 or 7 years old. Some children become moody and want to be left alone. On the other hand, others will show their depression by being demanding and defiant. They test limits because they feel bad about themselves and want some type of recognition, or they feel that other people are disapproving of them, which causes them to feel defensive. These are children who are continually seeking approval and are oftentimes fearful of losing it. They constantly want people to say they are okay but are scared that they will lose that person's approval. Again, they fear doing something wrong, which gives them the sense of being in trouble and as a result they usually have difficulties in school and socially, causing them to be withdrawn and shutdown, or the opposite. On the other hand, the overachiever may also be a symptom of depression. In this case the depressed child is the one who goes way beyond normal in trying to achieve perfection and be the best at everything, including being a straight A student. Earning top grades is acceptable and encouraged if the child is not doing it to get people's approval, and not because he or she is insecure or fearful of being in trouble. Most often these are children who give up and quit over time because they feel they cannot keep up with the stress. The overachievers are rare and often misdiagnosed because the child is seen as hard-working and successful. The depressed children can, as they get older, continue to develop one of the mood disorders.

The Anxious Child

Another result of negative thinking is anxiety. This negative thinking not only causes the child to feel anxious, but also fearful which again has a do with the negative thinking. These are children who are continually caught up in worry that is, in most cases, irrational (DSM-5). They have a hard time concentrating on things such as school-work, completing chores, and even carrying on a complete conversation because of being distracted by their fearful thinking. They typically don't isolate and are usually busy, trying to keep their world in control, accomplish the things they need to stay out of trouble, or avoid situations of which they are fearful. But at the same time they are busy, they are plagued by their negative and worrisome, fearful thinking. The type of thinking they are consumed by is typically "what-if thinking."

One form of anxious thinking is indicated by children refusing to go to school. They will say they are afraid that mom and dad will get hurt, or even die, and they will be left alone. One example is an anxious child who learned fearful thinking from his mother. At the beginning of the fourth grade he came home from school and told his mother his stomach hurt. He later admitted to being teased at the bus stop for school. This teasing was allegedly no different with him than the other children, but it made his mother anxious and fearful of him being hurt. For the next several weeks she constantly asked him if the other children teased him. After being questioned daily he became so worried that all he could think about was being teased by his friends. After a while because of her repeated asking he would not go to the bus stop unless she were with him. Over time his fears became such that he would not go to school unless mother drove him and picked him up. Finally, he became so fearful that he would refuse to go to school and mother, out of fear of making things worse, would allow him to stay home. She received therapy and worked through her feelings of fear for the boy and was able then to put her foot down and insist that he go to school like he was supposed to.

Often when one sees an anxious or fearful child one will find an anxious parent behind him or her. These parents usually suffer from an anxiety disorder themselves.

They are typically concerned about such matters as money, the weather, keeping a job, that somebody may be angry with them, or a fear of failing, etc. One such case was a young boy who kept thinking there were people out to get him. He wouldn't go on the playground at recess so he stayed in the classroom with the teacher or other people. His behavior was unhealthy and he eventually became a nuisance to the teacher and others. The teachers were very concerned about this and asked the school psychologist to talk to the father and mother about the boy's behavior, but dad was always working late. Finally, one day, the psychologist learned that the father was home so he called and asked him and his wife to come in so they could discuss the boy's problem. The psychologist told the parents that he appreciated them coming and he knew it was difficult to get them to come together because of the father's late working hours. The father looked rather surprised and said that he worked normal hours but was late getting home at night because he feared people were following him and he had to take a different route each night so not to be followed. Immediately it became apparent that the boy had learned this fearful thinking from his father. As the father voiced his fears, they were soon picked up by his son and he began to look at the world through his father's eyes. Almost all children will be anxious at times, but the child who was raised by an anxious parent will hear what the parent is saying or observe the way the parent is acting and assume that is reality. It is also difficult for the parent to teach a child something that he or she is not able to do themselves. To review, the anxious child here is one who is usually worried and as a result will always feel anxious, jittery, fearful of taking risks, and is likely trying to please others.

The Attention Deficit–Hyperactive Child

The child's anxious thoughts and feelings can lead to other problems including Attention Deficit–Hyperactive Disorder (ADHD) which encompasses attention difficulties and impulsive or hyperactive behavior (DSM-5). One young man was a classic case of an inability to pay attention. On one occasion while on a scout trip he was made to wear a dishcloth on his head during the morning hours. When the scoutmaster was asked why he had it on is head, he said it was to remind the boy to pay attention to what he was doing. About a year and half later the boy was dead. He and his friend were riding their bicycles a certain distance to earn a cycling merit badge. They were riding alongside the highway and were thirsty so they stopped at a gas station to get a soda. Because they each purchased a soda, the station owner gave each boy a small balsa wood glider airplane, which he was giving away to customers as part of a sales promotion. Both boys put together their planes and were playing with them in the parking lot of the gas station when a gust of wind blew the impulsive boy's plane across the highway, and without thinking he ran across the highway go get it. He was struck by a car going about 55 miles an hour and was killed instantly. His parents were offered help in parenting the boy on several occasions, but they always refused saying they would take care of the problem.

In most cases ADHD is learned. Some will disagree. They think it is either neurological or neurochemical because many children do better on medication. This may be true in many cases, but too often people forget to consider the cause of the problem which often goes back to family dynamics. One can see very clearly where this is learned. Imagine a child going to school and trying to learn when back home there is continual fighting and disruption. In this case the child's mind is usually preoccupied with the conflicts and trouble at home. The child will go to school and attempt to learn, but it will be very difficult because of the chaos in the family. In other cases there may be such worries as money and not knowing where the next meal will come from, or if the family will be evicted and so forth. It could be that the child has difficulty paying attention in school because he or she is worried about getting in trouble at home or at school. It is also common that inconsistency with rules and expectations can bring about ADHD of any type. No clear direction from a significant adult is likely to lead to conflict with the parent. When this is looked at carefully, one will likely see a large number of families whose children are diagnosed with ADHD. There are other cases where a family will appear to be normal and will have a child who was diagnosed ADHD, but again when considered carefully, inconsistencies are easy to detect. An example here might be a child who is unclear on what is expected, which can leave him feeling anxious as well as unsettled, and as result the child will likely not even attempt simple tasks for fear of being wrong or doing something incorrectly. Children in this circumstance may also be seen as those who daydream on or are disinterested or have their mind elsewhere. In such a case teachers will often say the child is pleasant and causes no problems but just never does anything.

On the other hand the child may be diagnosed as ADHD impulsive type. This is typically seen in the family where there is either open conflict between the parents, between the child and a parent, or both parents. If conflict between the parents exists it will likely leave the child feeling anxious and fearful because of not knowing what to expect and will assume the worst. The feeling that this conflict is his or her fault is also common. Oftentimes such children act impulsively out of fear of somehow being in trouble and as result emotional and mental conflict may be manifested as not being able to pay attention to her surroundings. The child might be seen as one with little self-control. Another problem in the family that would engender impulsive type behavior would be abuse of some sort. In such cases, children are so overwhelmed by the negative feelings of the abuse that they interact with others out of fear and they don't think very clearly. Also inconsistency of rules and limits can bring about impulsive behavior. In this case the child is continually pushing to find out what the rules are like in other examples given. The result of this is internal conflict including anxiety, fear, and guilt, which can cause a child to act on impulse. As mentioned earlier most children think egocentrically and the outcome is misinterpretation of other people's behavior. The result is the thinking that it is her fault for other people's problems. When children are thinking in this way it will likely leave them feeling anxious, fearful, and confused. Such children will try to fix the problem, whatever it may be, with no success and the resulting anxiety this will increase turmoil and may be acted out as impulsive. Other types of family problems to consider are divorce and separation or death of a parent or sibling. To summarize, a number of different family situations can likely bring about anxiety and uncertainty in the child's life which can be manifest as ADHD inattentive, impulsive, or both. Healthy families give children the stability they need and as a result these types of disorders usually do not exist.

The Double Bind

Another family trait that can bring about any one of the above-mentioned disorders in children is the double bind. Because of the double bind children often have this mistaken idea that if they can be perfect and do exactly what the parent is expecting there will be no problems. Unfortunately, they do not understand that the adult's problems are not caused by the child, and there is nothing the child can do to help alleviate or fix the problem. One example that is commonly seen is the parent discussing his or her personal problems with the child, or simply being open about problems in the presence of the child. Because of egocentric thinking, the child will likely assume that it is his responsibility to take care of mother and fix things. It might be that the mother is telling the young daughter that she is upset with father because he does not earn enough money or other problems.

One patient was placed in a serious double bind. As a young girl her father would take her with him to his girlfriend's house and have her babysit the girlfriend's children while he and the girlfriend would go off and do whatever they wanted to. He would then tell his daughter on the way home not to tell mother because if she did she would destroy the marriage. This left the young girl with an overwhelming feeling of guilt and fear because of what she knew about her father and how he was hurting her mother, and she could do nothing about it. The result here was the girl trying to become perfect in school, at home, and socially. She also developed an eating disorder thinking that this is the only area of her life over which she had any control. Her depression and anxiety were worsened by the idea that she was a failure because she could not help her mother or straighten out her father. Her parents remained married, but the family was never very stable and this girl carried her problems into her adult life and as a result struggled with depression for many years.

Another example was an adult who experienced significant anxiety and depression most of his life because of the double bind. This interfered with his personal life as well as with his marriage. He would try to control his wife and children, feeling if things were not right he would be in trouble. He would then feel fearful and guilty because of hurting her feelings. As his problem was explored, he revealed that his parents were in continual conflict and he was placed in the middle of this conflict. He was the youngest of three boys in the family and because of his age he had no way to get away from his parents when they were engaged in arguing. His older brothers found other ways to escape from the family. If he was in the car with his parents and they were fighting his mother might say "tell your father that he is wrong," the father would say "no, you tell your mother that she is wrong." He was stuck in the middle with nowhere to go and no way to fix the problem and get out from under the pressure he was experiencing. As a result, he was so depressed and anxious that he almost destroyed his marriage.

In other cases the double bind may exist with parents who are divorced. And in therapy it is often heard that one or both of the parents will use the child, or the children, as a weapon against the other parent. One parent may say it was the other's fault that they are not together, or "I just never was good enough so nobody likes me." It might be that one of the parents will tell the child "if your mother or father does not cooperate with what I want" that parent will go to jail. The comments in such circumstances place the child in a destructive situation and will leave the person feeling completely helpless.

Summary

Children who are fortunate enough to be raised by mentally healthy and mature parents will likely have a safe and meaningful childhood. On the other hand, children raised in dysfunctional families will probably not have a chance to learn the skills needed to succeed as adults. Since behavior is learned, the child can change if given the proper guidance and teaching in a loving atmosphere.

Chapter 4—Worksheet

1. What type of parenting contributes to childhood depression?

2. How might an anxious child effect the family?

3. How might some of the symptoms of Oppositional Defiance be manifested?

Chapter 5
Parenting with the Adolescent and Young Adult

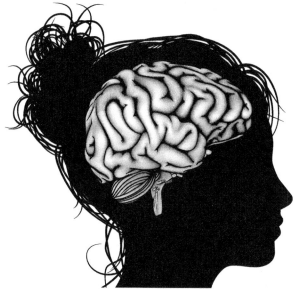

Christos Georghiou / Shutterstock.com

Parenting does not stop in the early years of childhood but continues essentially as long as the child lives in the home and often beyond. Chapter 5 will address the problems of adolescence and early adulthood. On one particular occasion, a group of three girls from the nearby junior high school were walking across the neighboring college campus. They were all dressed as adults with skirts or dresses, dress shoes, were carrying purses, and had makeup on. They were looking grown-up. Immediately after they were observed, a group of three boys jumped out from behind some bushes and started chasing the girls. The girls screamed, threw their purses into the air, and ran off like little schoolgirls, not acting as they were imagined to act because of their appearance. They may have looked like adults, but they were actually still children. Because the young adolescent changes physically and appears to be an adult, it is easy for parents and other adults to think of the child as more mature than she actually is. This can cause problems because of misguided expectations of performance and the immature behavior of the adolescent that might lead to a misinterpretation of defiance, or disrespect.

It is well understood that puberty brings about physical and hormonal changes. These physical and hormonal changes will likely cause disruptions in one's emotions and bring about some degree of emotional instability. One common outcome of these physical changes is the child thinking that because he or she has an adult appearance he or she should automatically be treated as an adult. Unfortunately, the child may become upset or disappointed when not having the privileges that older adolescents and adults have. So what happens during this period of time is the child thinking and making such statements as "I want more freedom; I want to be treated like a grown-up." They often say to their parents "I'm grown-up, look at me. I want to do everything you are doing."

So what is seen here is in essence the same phenomenon that a child goes through when he or she learns to crawl, to walk, to talk, and to do other things independently. Once again the child learns that the horizons are beginning to broaden. When the child is able to crawl she can go places not before attainable, such as to the bookshelf, or the flower pot, or to the kitchen cupboard where the cleaning supplies are stored. The child will begin to get into the things that are dangerous. In such an instance the parents then must teach the child where he can and cannot go. As explained earlier, when the boundaries are set the child will push because she wants to do whatever she wants. With this in mind, consider the behavior patterns of an adolescent. If she has learned throughout her life that mother and father mean what they say and cannot be manipulated she may protest briefly, but will conform to the parents' wishes. If on the other hand the child has learned that he can manipulate and very likely get his way, this behavior will continue into adolescence.

One example may be bedtime. As a child matures physically she may think that she can stay up as late as mom and dad and still function well in school the next day. When the parents tell the child it is time for bed, and it is earlier than the child thinks it should be, she will likely protest and if the parents give in, this behavior is reinforced. Some friends may have cars, and others may be allowed to stay out later at night or go to parties. In these instances the parent is the teacher, and of course is wiser than the child and the parent should set limits that are in the best interest of the child's welfare.

A personal example comes from observing young transplanted trees in an apartment complex. It was at the end of a long drought and storms were coming through. It was noticed that after each storm one or several of these trees would be broken off and down. On one occasion when going to the car, a broken tree was noticed. While approaching the tree it looked as though a beaver had gnawed around the trunk and cut down the tree. The problem was where the tree was broken was too high off the ground for a beaver to do the damage. On further investigation it was discovered that the tree had broken off at the weak point in the trunk. When a young tree is transplanted it is typically supported by several stakes in the ground and rope or something tied around the stake to support it until the root system becomes established. This was done, but the mistake of not loosening the rope about once a month became the tree's demise. Even though a tree grows up, it also goes out and where the rope had not been loosened the tree was growing around it, which became its weak spot. When storms came through and blew, the weak spot broke and the tree was destroyed. Think of this when parenting children and adolescents. Parents want to teach children to be happy and productive and to become prepared for adulthood so they can stand on their own when the time comes. Some parents, though, like the trees that were described, are too restrictive and controlling. When this occurs and the children go out on their own and face opposition they are typically not prepared to handle the situations and as a result the children, figuratively speaking, break off. Parents want to make sure their children do with her supposed to, but too often they become so preoccupied with protecting the child they forget that the children need to do some learning on their own with proper guidance from the parents. On the other hand, if the ties are too loose, support is either too broad or nonexistent in which case the child does not have the support needed while maturing. As such, the children find themselves getting in trouble at a young age and, as young trees without support, figuratively fall and typically have difficulties the rest of their lives.

One young man, 16 years of age, told of an experience he had when he was allowed to spend the night with a friend. His friend's parents were permissive and lax in setting rules, and as a result the friend talked the young man into going out of the house without permission to a party down the street. When they arrived at the party some of the young people in the house were excited about how drunk several others were and that they were passed out in one of the bedrooms. The young man became uneasy with the situation and told his friend he was leaving. The friend became upset thinking the young man was weak and made fun of him. The young man returned to his own home where he found comfort and safety. This person admitted that his parents trusted him, and because of his understanding their standards felt uncomfortable at the party and followed his good common sense to return home. He found out later that his friend got in deep trouble for being at that party and drinking himself. Furthermore, the young man decided to sever the relationship with his friend because of the discomfort knowing he might get in trouble because of what his friend was doing. This example illustrates where one boy's parents were teaching and gave support by allowing him to exercise some freedom and he handled it well. The other young man was raised by permissive parents and as a result had no sense of self-control or self-restraint. When a child has no sense of self-restraint it leaves him weak emotionally and mentally because of the conflicts resulting from the lack of direction.

Typically, there are two general patterns of behavior seen in adolescent's behavior. One is the openly defiant child who blatantly refuses to obey and will challenge any authority. The second behavior pattern is the quiet, withdrawn child. Of these two patterns the quiet, withdrawn child appears to be the most difficult behavior pattern for parents to cope with. The openly defiant child is more likely to be dealt with, even if unsuccessfully, because of the obvious behavior. In either case pathology is likely to be the result because of the internal conflict created by mismanagement of behavior. It is important to remember that conflict is manifested by feeling anxious, fearful of pushing too far, getting in deep trouble, and guilt because of the problems that were created. In all instances the kind parents are those who help the child eliminate this conflict by learning healthy and correct behavioral patterns that eliminate or significantly decrease this conflict.

The Withdrawn Adolescent

To continue with the subject, it is important to consider the two general behavioral patterns seen in adolescents and young adults. Both patterns must be considered as forms of limit testing or unacceptable behavior. Of the two, the shy child, is the most difficult behavior pattern for most people to work with. Most people would not consider timidity and shyness as misbehavior. This is because the shy child is viewed as helpless, not causing any problems, and in most cases is pleasant, but also difficult to get a handle on. There may be a myriad of reasons why shy children act as they do. One is they might be overwhelmed with life and as a result feel frightened. In this case the behavior can be considered unhealthy because the child is either not learning to, or trying to get out of, responsibly working problems through. Now there are cases where children are in an environment where they have no resources to learn how to cope with problems. As a result, people typically leave them alone or excuse the behavior because it is not viewed as an openly defiant behavior. Parents will often say the child has a right to be shy and as a result the behavior is allowed to continue. Again, if this misbehavior is allowed to continue it will lead to difficulties in the child's life.

One young girl was shy in early adolescence. She kept to herself and as a result she had no friends. Ultimately her parents noticed that she was not getting out and making friends. Her parents told her that she would have a party and invite all of her friends from church. She did not want to because she was afraid no one would come. She was told to invite everybody anyway, even the young people who were not popular. Her parents helped her with the organization and carrying out the party. She made all the phone calls, made the arrangements, and everybody showed up at the appointed time and had a great time. Her parents told her she had to interact with everybody, start up games, and so forth. After the party was over her parents insisted that she continue talking with the friends at church, at school, and even on the phone. She soon discovered that she had a new large circle of friends who would often call her and ask what the activities were for the weekend. If her fears would have ignored, which was her desire, she would have continued in a negative behavior which would have made her problem worse.

There are those children who use a similar tactic of being quiet and withdrawn hoping to be left alone and allowed to do what they want. Others want people to do for them, and they will try to get their way by pouting or withdrawing. Others try to get their way by shutting down and doing nothing. One young man, aged 16, was caught smoking. Where he lived the law against young people smoking was enforced. He had to go to Smokers Court and appear before a panel of peer judges his age. They gave him three assignments which included paying a fine, serving a certain number of hours of community service, and write a long essay on the negative aspects and the ills of tobacco. His mother sought to help him because she was worried about her son not getting his requirements completed on time. To help pay off the fine she tried to get him to complete chores around the house and pay him for them. She reported that he would either ignore her or, if he did do the chores, they were done poorly. In actuality he was expecting mom to take care of him by giving him the money without completing the responsibilities. She admitted that for the better part of his life she had done exactly that. When asked why she was so worried she admitted that she felt a significant amount of responsibility for his well-being and feared that she might be in trouble, as well as him, if he did not complete his sentence. She was asked if she made him smoke, or if she bought him cigarettes and so forth. She said absolutely not, that she did not believe in the use of tobacco. She was then asked if this was really his problem or hers, and she was able to admit finally that he was the one who chose to smoke, and it was his problem. Once she decided that, she told the boy it was up to him, and she did not care what happened. As a result he went out and found a job and earned enough money to pay for the fine. He also figured out a way to take care of the community service hours and with only a day or so left finished his report on tobacco.

Other children might phase out because of abuse. In this case phasing out is a form of protection from potential emotional and physical harm. The abused child will be addressed later. Other reasons for children to act out might be family conflicts. In such cases, the child may act out more to be heard or listened to. One young lady was raised by parents who were outwardly and loudly arguing daily in front of the children, and this continued throughout the entire marriage. This young lady stated on one occasion that if people were not mad at her she thought they did not love her. She equated arguing and fighting with love. Such instances as this will likely lead to potential pathology in adolescence as well as in early adulthood.

The Depressed Adolescent

A number of young adults and adolescents present with depression. With adolescents depression is typically manifested as moodiness, not caring about anything, isolation, and so forth. Depression starts in the thinking, and the thinking patterns depressed people entertain are learned. This learning takes place throughout one's life and because of one's experiences. An example is the adolescent, aged 16, whose father was continually critical of the boy. The boy admitted that he always thought that he was stupid and would never amount to anything. Because of this he saw himself in a negative light and would never take a risk with anyone, or anything. He was failing in school because of his fear of trying and many of the faculty at school thought he had a learning disability. As he learned that he was able to comprehend information and could learn the subject matter in school and would not act on his depressed feelings he started succeeding. Another example is a young adult who always thought that he was inadequate and was never told otherwise. His father, like the other young man just mentioned, was severely critical of this person throughout his whole life. On the other hand, his mother felt sorry for him and as a result was permissive. What he learned was that he did not have to risk because mother would always protect him, and there was always a way out responsibilities. His thinking was negative, which then led to his behavior, which ultimately reinforced the idea that he had little worth.

If the person has learned to view life negatively for whatever reason that will then determine the person's mood. A poor self-esteem is always found as a result of depression. If the young person is thinking negatively it is typically about himself or herself, and going back to the 16-year-old boy whose father was critical, he was always in a depressed mood. Because of the way he was thinking, he had poor self-esteem and thought of himself as a "loser." A young girl whose mother was permissive had poor self-esteem because she saw herself in a lesser light than her friends because she was not able to do what others were capable of accomplishing. She was always in a depressed mood and thought of herself again as someone who was inadequate. The mood is often dysphoric, meaning that the person is quiet or sullen and withdrawn.

This thinking that is learned by the child will then be manifest by his or her actions or behavior. When the individual is thinking negatively he or she will not want to be around others, which then brings about isolation. The problem with isolation is that, when alone, there is nothing to occupy the person's thinking except those negative thoughts that got him or her there in the first place. Adolescents seek a place of refuge such as the bedroom or some other part of the house where no one will come to bother them. Some young people will spend days in the room with little or no contact with family or friends. Another place or refuge is being away from home; this could be at the park, in the woods, or some other place away from the family. A 12-year-old boy named Greg and his pet dog would spend all day in the woods behind his house looking at trees, animals, and whatever else would attract their attention. He said that nobody in his family cared about him and that his best friend was his dog because he would never yell at him or get angry with him. Another 15-year-old boy named Stephen spent his time in the treehouse behind his home and had nothing to do with the family except to eat. Eventually the boy became so depressed that he committed suicide.

It is because of this thinking and acting on these thoughts that the other symptoms are not only apparent but reinforced. Because of negative thinking one will not view activities as exciting or fun, and as a result will have little energy or enthusiasm about anything. Along with this, a child's appetite is typically changed; in most cases depressed individuals in this age group lose their appetite although some will increase their eating to cover up the feelings. Furthermore sleep is disrupted because of the negative thinking. In most cases when the child tries to go to sleep, it is difficult because he or she is alone in the bed and there's nothing there to occupy the thinking except the problems he or she is facing. Concentration is also a problem simply because it's difficult to pay attention to something when your thoughts are consumed by problems.

To better understand depression one must understand these and other related symptoms and why they exist. Without understanding the symptoms and the causes, it is difficult to help the person through this and other disorders. In some instances children are misdiagnosed with Attention Deficit Disorder when they are actually depressed and are unable to concentrate on school work and so forth. Other children who isolate may be considered Oppositional Defiant because they don't want to be a part of the family. Some parents become upset thinking the child does not love them or care about the family, which will cause conflict.

Typically when a child is depressed the parents feel overwhelmed and unsure of what to do so they will often leave the child alone. This is because they fear that by intervening they may make the child worse. When the parents do try to interact with the child they are typically ignored or told to leave the child alone. If the child is isolating, the parents will in many cases allow the child to continue isolating. The child may also feel irritated and become argumentative because of the way he feels about himself. Unfortunately most parents give into their fears about making things worse and leave the child alone or will continue to pick at the child, but never resolve anything. This behavior, if allowed to continue, deepens to depression. Again, this like many other behaviors is a form of manipulation with a child wanting to be left alone. If the child is left alone this poor behavior will be reinforced like any other misbehavior. The wise parent will not allow the child to isolate but will insist that he or she come out of the bedroom, and be part of life, society, and the family.

One 15-year-old boy was depressed because of problems at school. He was failing his classes and when asked by his parents how he was doing in school he would become upset and accuse his parents of being nosy and not trusting him and would pout and ignore them. His parents felt rather helpless and as a result left him alone and quickly avoided asking him about school or anything else. When they sought professional help they reported that their son was not going to school and spent most of every day in his room on the computer, playing video games or sleeping. He would come out to get his dinner on a plate and go back to his room without ever saying anything to the family, and this had been going on for about four months. It even got to the point where he was ignoring personal hygiene by bathing only once or twice a week and not even brushing his teeth or changing his close regularly. The parents were helped to understand the negative thinking and how that caused all the other symptoms. Through insight they felt comfortable enough to help him stop acting on his depression by becoming firm enough to set limits and not allow his manipulation. Over time he realized that his parents were not going to leave him alone, which resulted in his doing his schoolwork, interacting with the family, and reestablishing old friendships.

A 17-year-old girl who graduated from high school as valedictorian would become so depressed that she would show signs of psychosis. She would go into a state of psychosis and catatonia about three or four times a year. She finally revealed that she would visit her mother who was divorced from her father since she was about 5-years-old and become so upset over her mother's lifestyle that she would lose touch with reality. Because her mother would not change the girl thought her mother's behavior was her fault and that because she was not persuasive or good enough. She would eventually go into this depressive mood and end up in the psychiatric unit. Her stepmother revealed in therapy that when the girl would go into this state and end up in the hospital, friends, family, and people from church would rally around her and do what they could to make her feel better. After about a week the symptoms would go away and she would return home and go back to school. By revealing this the stepmother was able to see that even though the girl would get frightened and upset she got payoff and support from well-meaning people who tried to make her feel better. Her father and stepmother decided to tell her that if she did this again she would have to pay for the treatment herself because it was a financial drain on the family. It was reported that she never had an episode like that again.

Some individuals can have an anxious mood which will be rather tense because of the negative thoughts and ideas. This is typically manifested by fidgety behavior and often a negative or bad mood that will come across as upset or agitated. This depressive thinking is negative where the individual is thinking that if he or she is not perfect, trouble result. As was the case with the 15-year-old boy who was depressed because he could never live up to his stepfather's expectations. This in turn left him feeling anxious and fearful of getting in trouble when, in most cases, he had no idea what was going to cause the stepfather to be upset.

Adolescents and Bipolar Disorder

Young people may also show symptoms of bipolar disorder, especially the manic phase, by having grandiose ideas, limitless energy, not needing sleep, and the inability to settle down. In such instances this is the result of negative thinking that can trigger the need to be better, or eventually thinking that he has a solution to the problem and then act accordingly. In these cases, again parents will either leave the child alone or become irritated and angry out of frustration by not knowing what to do to get the child to settle down. In either case they are contributing to the child's problems by either ignoring the situation or trying to control the child by arguing, debating, or making threats. The same approach applies to dealing with a person struggling with bipolar disorder that would be used to help a child with depression. If the parents are intimidated, or unsure, they will fail to do the proper teaching. Again this results in poor self-esteem and negative thinking, and it might take some work to find out what the negative thinking is, and what it takes in order to help the parents understand how to help the child work this through. In some cases the adolescent may, along with the parents, need to receive therapy if the adolescent is willing to honestly work on the problem. Many do not want to work the problem through because of feeling nothing will help, or that there may be a payoff for the behavior. A young girl, aged 14, was admitted to a psychiatric unit for children and adolescents with symptoms of bipolar disorder. She exhibited behaviors that were both nonsense as well as dangerous, and the parents were bewildered and afraid for her well-being. The girl was medicated, which helped calm her down and allowed her to talk about her feelings in therapy but nothing ever changed. Her parents were finally able to receive help to understand the daughter's behavior and to see it as a manipulation.

Behavioral Problems with Adolescents

The next disorders to be considered are behavioral, which are typically learned in childhood. A good number of young people continually defy authority and are diagnosed with oppositional defiant disorder. These are children who continually argue with parents and other authority figures and are continually pushing the limits to get their way. At home they typically refuse to cooperate with the family and participate in activities. If asked to do something they do not want to; they will argue their way out of it. They want to do what they want and typically do not consider other people's needs. At school they will argue with teachers as well as administrators, such as the principal or guidance counselor, and in most cases will not do their work. These young people will ignore the rules of home, society, and school. This defiance is typically open and confrontational, although there are times when they will be rather quiet and devious, and attempt to fly under the radar. One young boy tried with success on several occasions to get out of going to a specific class in school by putting a pencil point in the door lock and breaking it off. When confronted he would get mad and upset and tell people that they didn't like him. As a result, they would back away and leave him alone. These are children who learn to manipulate to get their way by being defiant and oppositional in their behavior toward others. This is typically even carried over into friendships where they are constantly manipulating friends to get what they want.

In other instances the Oppositional Defiant child may sneak out at night, not come home when he is supposed to, or go places he's not allowed to. These are children who are raised by inconsistent parents who give in to the limit testing rather than have to put up with the fight and the arguing. In this case a child learns quickly that authority is meaningless and that manipulation, to one degree, or another pays off. The young man who was caught smoking and had to go to smoker's court is another example of Oppositional Defiant behavior. This young man had learned early in life that if he ignored his parents or argued with them enough they would cave in. One teenage girl knew that she did not have to abide by her parents' rules and authority and could get away with everything by ignoring them. The father would only deal with her by teasing, and the mother would always back away when the girl was being defiant. Unfortunately for the girl, she was this way with her friends and as result had only one or two friends who would tolerate her behavior.

In all of these cases the Oppositional Defiant behavior was encouraged and reinforced by parents who did not establish limits and maintain them. As a result the child then does not develop a sense of accountability which leads to continual testing to find out where people really stand. This behavior can be corrected and requires the parents to not act on their emotions and feelings, and establish limits they will stick to under any circumstances. As with all other disorders if the child continues in this behavior the conflict will deepen and can ultimately become part of the personality which then is difficult to change. When parents become consistent and do not change their limits the oppositional defiant behavior will increase because of the child thinking the parents will eventually change like they did in the past. If the parents remain consistent and unmovable, the child will eventually learn that the poor behavior will no longer be reinforced or tolerated and will ultimately conform to the established rules and expectations.

A group of young men between the ages of 14 and 18 were placed in a halfway house after having spent at least one year in state juvenile detention. Part of the reintroduction to society was to attend group therapy with the goal of changing their behavior and not returning to the system. These young men were all incarcerated because of drug-related crimes, which included armed robbery, sexual assault, assault and battery, and breaking and entering. Because of their behavior issue these young men had the diagnosis of conduct disorder, which is significantly more serious than Oppositional Defiant behavior. These adolescents typically defy the rights of others, run away, are truant from school, display physical cruelty to animals or people, use a weapon, fight, and so forth and this diagnosis can only be given up to the age of 18 (DSM- 5). In these cases the sense of accountability appears to be nonexistent. They typically feel that nothing is their fault and if people leave them alone and give them what they want, they would not have to act as they do. In many instances these individuals are raised in homes and families where such behavior is either ignored or encouraged.

A 13-year-old boy named Robert had an older brother who was in and out of jail continually. Robert was following in his brother's footsteps and joined a gang. A friend of his, named Ronnie, was also Conduct Disordered but was not incarcerated as often as Robert. A family member of Ronnie stated that when Ronnie reached adulthood, he still had the same problems. As this was discussed further, the family member said that no one else raised by Ronnie's parents had similar problems, but the parents felt helpless when dealing with Ronnie and eventually gave up trying to teach him how to manage himself. It is not as common to see girls with this diagnosis, although it does exist. One 13-year-old girl was admitted to an adolescent psychiatric unit because of running away. She had no regard for the rules of the family or any other rules. She was failing school and was involved in drugs and sexual promiscuity. She also participated in theft and shoplifting with friends. Another girl was living with her father and step-mother. She was the oldest in the home of the five children. This girl never did abide by the parents' rules and the parents were eventually told by the younger children that when mom and dad were out, and she was alone with them, she would abuse them physically. When confronted, she would fight with the parents and tell them that they were mean to her and did not care about her. She eventually ran away and after about six months was placed in jail for participating in armed robbery and selling drugs.

In these instances, as mentioned earlier, for adolescents raised in homes where such behavior as described in the previous paragraph is allowed, the parents can help stop the problem behavior. If the parents are willing to do what is necessary to help the adolescent, they must become completely resolute in their decision to follow through and not revert back to old patterns. Along with this is the need for accountability. Conduct disordered children have learned that if they defy the limits long enough, then they are left alone, and as a result are given the impression that they do not have to abide by the rules that others do. It is when the parents finally establish the rules and maintain them that the children will either leave home and stay away for long periods of time, or runaway. Some will learn how to make it on their own, but it is typically outside of the law. Unfortunately, if the unacceptable behavior is allowed to continue in the home the influence on other family members can be devastating.

A young boy who was a junior in high school started using drugs and alcohol and would come home at night inebriated. His mother would put him to bed and try to make him feel better. Even the father tried to help him, which gave the young man the impression that there was no accountability. It did not take long for the younger children in the family to begin to act as they wanted and defying the rules with no regard to other family members' welfare. It also caused difficulties in the marriage because the parents started fighting over how to stop the problem. He was also stealing money from his parents, which put them in a very dangerous situation financially. Since the boy was unwilling to change, the father finally told him to leave the home. He did not hear from his son for over one year. The father's family members and people from his church disapproved of his tactic, but after about a year of absence the boy called home and told his father that he was in rehab. He told his father he wanted to come home, that he didn't like living the way he was, and that he would abide by the family rules. Father agreed on the condition that the boy would live appropriately, which he did from that time on.

One problem that needs to be addressed is the runaway. Adolescents running away today is not as common as it was in the 1960s, 70s, 80s, and into the 90s. One reason we see less of it today is because of parents not enforcing rules and giving into fears of negative consequences if they do runaway. On rare occasion children will run away for self-preservation or safety. In most cases though, they run away from home because they are not getting what they want and are hoping that mother and father will be so upset and distraught that when the child decides to come home, she can do it on her own terms. One boy ran away from home at the end of summer vacation because he knew he was in trouble. He was hired by the neighbors to watch their home while they were on a two-week vacation, and he discovered a freezer full of ice cream treats to which he helped himself. The day before the family returned he ran away and was taken in by a friend's family where he stayed for about three-fourths of his senior year in high school. His father initially tried to coax the boy to return home, but the boy said he would if dad bought him a $2000 keyboard. Dad sought the advice of a therapist and was counseled to completely leave the boy alone, which dad did. Over time the boy sought out his parents and said he wanted to come home. He agreed to live by the rules and did. He admitted later he was significantly happier after he took control of his life and lived as he knew he needed to.

The Young Adult

As an adolescent approaches adulthood, becoming independent is a reality. For some young people this is an exciting time of life and they will do well even though they may face struggles. If the person as a child has learned responsibility and hard work a likelihood of success is quite high. If the person decides to go to college, he will succeed because of the ethics and work habits learned at home. The child will also have learned how to interact with people in a healthy way and will develop good, strong, lasting friendships. They will enter adulthood and will begin to look forward to marriage and having a family. If this person pursues a career instead of college, or even a career after graduation from college, she will be prepared to become a meaningful employee, member of society, as well as spouse and parent. When he or she faces problems instead of running from them, or convincing someone else to take care of them, the person will resolve the difficulties on his or her own or seek meaningful help. If on the other hand the individual is raised in a dysfunctional family where healthy behavior and self-control is not taught, life will be difficult and riddled with disappointments and failures. Many such a people either fail in college or drop out because of poor performance. Work is also a difficulty because of lack of self-control and self-discipline, which will lead to frequent terminations. Along with this there are relationship difficulties as well as financial problems, all because of lack of self-control.

If the young adult has not learned responsibility, or has not learned how to interact with people, conflict will result. In many instances this conflict will be manifested by isolation. One young man who never learned how to relate to people became isolated to the point that he had no interaction with anyone except a few close friends and family. Even his interaction with his friends was limited, and by his own admission he kept it as such because the feelings of inadequacy. He of course was showing signs of depression including isolation, poor self-esteem, negative thinking, lack of interest in other people, and no drive to improve. He admitted that his mother always tried to make him feel better by not expecting much from him. She stated that she was afraid of pushing too hard and him becoming worse. The number of young people who isolate and become consumed with video games or the Internet appears to be increasing. It is not uncommon to find several students on any given college campus spending their entire time in the room playing video games rather than going to class or working. One college freshmen said that he attended class because he had to do but after class he would immediately return to his apartment to play his video games. He did not interact with other students for fear of being held back from doing what he wanted to do. Because of the isolation, work performance will typically be less than satisfactory, or schoolwork will be hindered. Typically, these individuals are so consumed by that safe world they have developed for themselves that they have little interest in doing anything else, and when away from home and the video games they are obsessed with returning which keeps them from paying attention to what is at hand. Some young adults will change when they find that living independently requires working and interacting with other people to sustain one's life.

Another problem resulting from isolation of course is a lack of social support and a good healthy support system. Research (Taylor, 2007; Uchino, Cacioppo & Kiecolt, 1996) has shown repeatedly that individuals who have a good support system are much healthier emotionally and physically than those who do not. Some young people very openly and honestly say that they do not need others, and many in this group have learned how to live an isolated life with no social support through the use of electronics. Careers that require little or no interaction with others are attractive to a loner. These may include the technical career path such as engineering, computer programming, and computer design; some areas of the medical field, research, and so forth. Marriage is also out of the question because it requires interacting with someone else on a deep level. Or if this individual does get married, the relationship will typically end in divorce.

Family dynamics that typically teach this type of behavior pattern can be varied. In the majority of cases, the individual was raised by parents who were both demanding and difficult to please, or who were very quiet themselves. When considering the difficult-to-please parents consider the unrealistically demanding parent who is always critical and extremely demanding and lacks emotional closeness with the individual. This demanding behavior from the parent is typically brought about because of anxiety and insecurity. If this is the case the parent will then be critical of the child because of thinking that if things don't go right, he, the father, will be in trouble. One example is a young adult who is successful in school and became a professional. The career chosen required only research. This individual's father was one who felt insecure all of his life and was fearful of others' disapproval so everything around him had to be perfect, including his professional performance, his home, and his family. It was impossible for this young man to ever get any sense of acceptance from his father and admitted that he viewed all people as dangerous and hurtful. As a result, he chose to have nothing to do with people. We also see this from the parent who puts the child in the double bind where no matter what the child does he or she is wrong.

A young lady who was married had difficulties being comfortable with people. She would interact with others, but relationships were always surface-level and business-like. The husband eventually divorced her because she was unwilling to interact with him on any deeper level. Her parents were people who never made demands on the children and rarely showed any emotion. Her parents wanted to establish limits and the majority the children would follow. This woman chose a career in academia and was mostly engaged in research, which is isolated from interacting with others. She would, on the other hand, be very involved with service projects, school activities for children including PTA, as well as community service. As mentioned earlier these relationships were more on a business level which would not require any in-depth interaction. Her behavior was learned throughout childhood, and brought into adolescence and adult life.

A 22-year-old named Karen was very insecure around people. On one occasion she attended a church group for young single adults her age, and instead of interacting with everyone she sat on a rock on the opposite side of the backyard and cried because she was alone. On another occasion she attended a Valentines' dance, but did not interact with anyone there either and spent the whole evening in the kitchen preparing refreshments or running to the store to buy things that she thought were necessary. She would continually complain that she had no friends and that nobody liked her, but would never extend herself to others.

Jennifer, age 21, was a college student who would go to the beauty shop every Friday afternoon and get her hair done in anticipation of being asked out on a date. She never was asked out, and each Friday night at about nine or 10 o'clock, she would call friends over and they would bake cookies and complain about how bad life was. She admitted to going to dances but would always stand with her group of friends; eventually she was told by a young man who was interested in her that he would never ask her to dance because she was always with a group of friends that intimidated him. She would attend the weekly devotional at her school but would always sit alone. Her therapist challenged her to find a young man who was sitting alone and ask to sit by him. She nervously agreed and attended the next devotional where she saw a young man sitting by himself and asked if she could sit next to him. He eagerly agreed. She then forced herself to strike up a conversation that continued after the devotional while walking to class together, and eventually she was asked out on dates, became engaged, and got married to this young man. In too many cases, young adults will choose to isolate and that interferes with their functioning in everyday life and prohibits them from establishing social relationships.

The Demanding Young Adult

On the other hand, some young people are demanding. This is commonly the result of the person acting this way at home while growing up and getting away with it. These are young people who feel entitled and will treat people as such. They typically have few friends and those friends are usually on guard with the individual, so no closeness is established. Such a young person would have difficulty at work because of not wanting to take direction and always feeling like the company owed him rather than feeling obligated to the company for employment. . Not only is this seen at work, but also in social and other close relationships. These individuals typically have a string of close relationships that are usually terminated by the other person because of continual conflict.

One young lady said to a boyfriend she had been dating for about three weeks, that he did not love her because he was not taking her out to restaurants and was not buying her jewelry and other gifts. He decided that she was too demanding and was not worth the effort. He felt he would never be appreciated and ended the dating abruptly. These individuals also typically want to be the life of the party, and when people are not paying attention to them they will get upset and pout, or make a scene until they get attention. Even when the individual gets the attention, the person is never satisfied and is always seeking more. The reason for this, is the need for approval. People who are unsure of themselves continually need reassurance from other people to gain their sense of well-being. If they think that the other person's behavior is negative and directed toward the individual, that person will feel inadequate and try whatever is necessary to get that sense of acceptance or approval. Oftentimes these individuals have learned how to get their way, and by the time they reach adulthood, they have developed quite an array of weapons to get what they desire. Another negative is the feelings of insecurity and guilt because of the way the individual acted to get the attention. Unfortunately, this becomes a vicious cycle which can, if not stopped, become destructive.

As a young adult has learned earlier in childhood that threatening others gets her what she wants, this behavior will be brought into adulthood. As an example, a young adult, aged 23, had a history of abuse growing up and became abusive in dating relationships while in high school. After graduation this young man became involved in drugs and was ultimately a drug dealer. He convinced a young lady to move in with him. In the beginning he was very charming and was able to deceive her. She did not understand his past or his current means of income. Once she became dependent on him for food, shelter, clothing, entertainment, and so forth, he then showed his true colors. He abused her, would always threaten her with physical harm or abandonment, and would work diligently to convince her that she was worthless. This young lady spent over a year literally locked in the house and was treated as a prisoner. She was afraid to tell anyone her circumstances because she was convinced that she would pay for her deeds physically and emotionally. She finally figured out how to get away from him, but was unable to relax and socialize after once she was free for fear of him finding her and hurting her.

A young female college student used suicide as a threat to control her boyfriends. If her boyfriend would not do what she wanted, she would tell him that she would kill herself. She made feeble attempts to make the boyfriends feel frightened and give her what she wanted. One boyfriend stayed in the relationship for over of a year because of his fears that if she committed suicide it would be his fault. Other threatening ploys include exposing someone's weaknesses to other people, causing one to lose his or her job, or even lying about the person to cause legal and emotional problems. These behaviors are also manifested by those diagnosed with antisocial personality disorder. Again, these behavior patterns are learned as children, and there is that sense of entitlement, or also a lack of accountability.

Some people will misbehave by getting others to feel sorry for them. In this case, it is likely to see the individual pretend that he or she is incapable of doing certain tasks. They often have a sad story to tell like never having what they wanted materially, being abused, or never being loved. One common ploy is acting disliked. This can lead to the other person feeling sorry for this individual and making efforts to make him or her feel better. The problem here is that the individual will never feel good enough because if he does then that person has to stand on his or her own. This type of behavior is typically learned in childhood. Parents of these children are weak and unable to set expectations for the child to function in a healthy manner. Most often these are individuals who were either chronically ill or viewed as inadequate, and as a result others feel sorry for them. If this is brought into the workplace, this person will always have an excuse for not performing well, or will act like someone who has been offended or misunderstood; again, this causes the other person to feel sorry for the individual and back away or make excuses for accepting a less than adequate performance.

Relating to Others

If a young adult is either anxious **or** depressed, he will likely withdraw from society due to feeling insecure. Like other problems, when the person acts on these feelings of inadequacy or insecurity, they become reinforced. This then interferes with being able to relate to other people on a meaningful level. If the person was raised in a family where communication was open and this person felt safe as a child expressing his concerns and successes, this will be brought into young adulthood. If, on the other hand, the person grew up in a family where communication was nonexistent, such experiences keep the individual from relating to others. A female college student named Laura was dating a young man who felt anxious when around her. He was used to being open and talking freely with friends and girls he had dated in the past but said that he was always frustrated with her because she would never express her feelings to him. Through observation it became apparent that she was afraid of opening up and letting people into her world because of the way she was treated at home. Her father was a perfectionist because of anxiety and, as a result, was continually critical of Laura. Thus, her fear was that by being open she would somehow get criticized or made fun of. Needless to say the relationship ended and the young man found somebody to whom he could relate, and eventually married the young lady. Laura eventually married a man who was himself not very communicative, but unfortunately they had some very significant difficulties throughout their marriage. One big problem along with those already mentioned, deal with the individual that feels like he or she has to fix everybody and take care of their problems. This interferes with relating to others because the person is always thinking about trying to fix a problem rather than understanding what is really important or needed by the other person.

Adolescents and Young Adult Drug Use

Another difficulty faced by young adults is the use of mood-altering chemicals, including alcohol. This may start in adolescence or when a young person attends college or moves out on her own. Mood-altering chemicals are attractive to young people because it changes how they feel emotionally, and even physically in some cases. If the individual has poor self-esteem, alcohol or a stimulant such as cocaine, could give the person a sense of euphoria or a feeling of not caring about what people say or do. It is not out of the ordinary for people to try using mood-altering chemicals because of friends, or peer pressure. A number of young adults who attended a particular chemical dependency rehab hospital, admitted that their addiction started out of curiosity after seeing friends using them. Young people who have good self-esteem are not prone to use mood-altering chemicals because they feel good enough about themselves as they are.

The patient named Richard was in his last semester of college and was failing his classes because of his use of mood-altering chemicals. He had to return and complete one class in order to graduate. He sought help after consuming enough drugs to cause him to pass out in his car and was found by some passersby. They called the police who had him admitted to a hospital. He sought therapy and was helped for his addiction. After getting help, he no longer used drugs and was able to finish his coursework with high grades. He was hired to a very prestigious position in a major corporation. He admitted that he hoped that by using the drugs he would feel good enough about himself to succeed, but he found just the opposite to be the case. Ronald, on the other hand, started using drugs when he was about 11-years-old because it took him away from the emotional pain he was experiencing from his father's verbal abuse. He continued with this into adulthood and was incarcerated as a young adult.

All mood-altering chemicals are attractive to those who have emotional and mental difficulties because these drugs offer a sense of relief or change in one's emotional and mental state. If the young adult has learned to function in a healthy way and is in control of his or her behavior and emotions, he or she will have no need for such temporary fixes because they are pleased with their lives. Even though this is the major reason young people are drawn to mood-altering chemicals, there are those who start because of needing acceptance from others. Such individuals have poor self-esteem and try to boost their feelings of inadequacy by seeking approval from their friends. This seeking approval may include the use of mood-altering chemicals if everyone else is using them. This need for approval starts in early childhood when a person is not clear regarding his or her position with the parents or other family members, and this insecurity is carried over into social settings. As the individual continues to do what she thinks others want her to do, including the use of drugs or alcohol, her insecurities will increase.

Seeking Marriage

Finally, it is at this stage when young people think of marriage and start looking for a spouse. Although in modern society, to remain unmarried throughout adulthood is becoming more acceptable (Weiten, Dunn, & Hammer, 2015). If the person is secure within herself and has good self-esteem she will likely marry a person who is stable and secure too. If, on the other hand, she feels unsure of herself and struggles with the problems that have been mentioned in this chapter, the person will likely end up in a marriage that will be unsuccessful. First of all, one has to be able to relate to others on a feeling level. If the person cannot do this he will never be able to have an emotional connection with anyone, and it will either keep the person from marrying, or lead to making an unwise choice for a spouse.

Janice was 22 and wanted to marry but was afraid to become serious with anyone for fear of them finding out that she was not perfect and had problems. As a result, she always put on a good front of being concerned for others, being happy, and outgoing. Once the relationship would become serious she would leave it because she feared that if the man she was dating knew everything about her, he would be repulsed, thus leaving her alone. She finally became brave enough to take a risk with one young man. He too had problems and she felt that he could not look down on her. They married, but this union only lasted about 3 years.

Another problem in today's society is the reluctance to make a commitment. This is apparent when young people hang out, but never allow themselves to become intimately acquainted with one individual. Hanging out with the crowd is emotionally safe and no commitments are made. James, at the age of 32, was tired of hanging out and wanted to marry. He met a young lady in a group with which he was involved, and it took several months of pursuing the lady for her to finally become brave enough to leave her safe circle of friends and become acquainted with him. His persistence and her ultimately wanting to get to know him paid off because they were soon married.

Many young adults will say that they do not want to marry because of their fears of having the same type of problems that their parents had. Carly was in this position and felt that she had to defend herself because her parents were always fighting. The result of their fighting left her feeling intimidated and that other's problems were her fault. This put her in a position of trying to defend herself and convince everyone that she was not in the wrong. Jennifer's parents also fought, and she grew up thinking that fighting was normal. Even though she was concerned about this being the case in her future marriage, she dated regularly and eventually became engaged and married. In one of her sessions, she admitted that if her husband was not angry with her, she felt that some unknown problem was lurking in the background and felt unsettled. The problem here was that she was always ready for a fight believing that it was the way marriage functioned. If a young person feels this way because of experiences in her family of origin, it does not mean that the person has to be this way for the remainder of her life. To overcome such a problem one must take a risk by letting down their guard and allowing the other person to emotionally invest in the individual. In turn that individual will invest back on a feeling level. After experiencing success one will want more, which will allow this process to continue.

The difficulties mentioned in this chapter are the result of one's learning. Maturing can be resolved if the person is willing to work and put in the effort to overcome the problems in one's life. Through research, it has been discovered that the more one acts on negative emotions, like anger, the more likely it is that behavior will be repeated. This is because by acting on an emotion or feeling, it makes it easier to act in the same manner the next time. The same applies to acting on positive emotions and thoughts. If one were to manage a behavior by not acting on it, the person will begin to learn that he can control it. Controlling does not mean not having the feelings; it means that they will not dictate one's actions. When the person realizes that these problems are learned, it is then much easier for the person to understand that he or she can change. When the change takes place, the difficulties, conflict, and distress over the problems go away and the person can be settled and calm.

Chapter 5—Worksheet

1. What are several good reasons for not allowing an adolescent to have complete freedom?

2. How are the Mood Disorders often manifested in the young adult?

Chapter 6
Chronic Illness and Family Dynamics

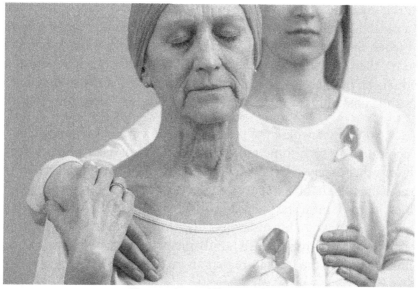

Photographee.eu / Shutterstock.com

How do people manage problems? Every person alive has had problems, and that goes for today's generation and will be so for future generations. Since this is the case it is important to consider how individuals deal with those difficulties presented to them. As has been illustrated throughout, the book behavior is learned and this learning process starts in the home. If a certain behavior is reinforced it will continue. As an example if a young child learns that arguing with mother and father will likely get him his way, the probability is high that he will continue in this unwanted behavior. If, on the other hand, it doesn't work, the behavior will stop. In this case, manipulation leaves the person experiencing an inordinate amount of conflict that is indicated by high levels of anxiety. This anxiety leaves a young person feeling unsettled, and self-doubting beyond what is normal. Along with the anxiety comes fear of pushing too hard and losing one's love or admiration or one's friendship. This again leaves the person feeling insecure, especially because of not knowing what's going to happen as a result of the pushing and manipulation. Finally, the person will feel guilty because of the problems that were created, and the result is poor self-esteem.

Others may feel inadequate and fearful because of being raised by overly demanding parents, or parents that are difficult to please. In this case the individual will be reluctant to take a risk and take a stand with others, and will be easily manipulated. When this occurs, poor self-esteem and inadequate feelings become deeper, and over time the person is convinced that she is worthless and can never take a stance or establish herself as a person. These are individuals who are continually seeking approval from others and when they sense they are not receiving it, they go into a depression. These people also try their hardest to do whatever they think the other person wants so that this individual can have a sense of safety and peace. They are also unable to think for themselves and constantly rely on others for direction, and even how to think and act.

In these cases, and others where the person has not learned to manage life and themselves, it is common to seek some relief with such things as alcohol or drugs, playing continually, or other escapes. Others try to escape from their problems by working on becoming consumed in hobbies, sports, or electronic devices. In this chapter regarding chronic illness in the family, the purpose will be to describe how a chronically ill family member might respond to his disability. Also, how the other family members might typically respond to the chronically ill family member. Mature individuals usually deal with the illness well, but the immature person can bring about a myriad of problems.

Chronic illness is typically defined as an illness that is ongoing with no relief of the symptoms over a significant period of time (Fleshner, 2004). Because of people living longer and having better access to health care, preoccupation with, and a desire to be healthy has become of extreme importance to many individuals. It seems as though almost every family in Western society has someone with some sort of chronic condition. It is important to consider the family as a dynamic, or a continually changing system that can be affected by a number of internal or external factors including chronic illness. Like in times past, a chronically ill family member today will likely have a significant effect on the family as a whole, as well as on individual family members. This is the case with the smallest family, meaning husband and wife through to the family with young children, adolescent children, as well as adult children who moved away from home. The disruptions to the family can include changes in family roles, the parent having to leave the home for employment, one parent being more concerned with the patient than others, or even relocation to a new area. When this sort of problem occurs, adjustments have to be made, and the families who have learned how to work together to overcome problems are far better off than those who fail to work problems through. Those who are unable to work problems through usually blame others or avoid the problem, while others may abdicate the responsibility rather than take it themselves. To understand the effects of chronic illnesses on the family it is helpful to identify the common types of chronic illnesses and disabilities that exist today. These include pain, cancer, pulmonary, digestive, heart and cardiovascular, endocrine problems as well as diabetes (Weiten, Dunn, & Hammer 2015). Also included in this category is the dementia disorders, the most common of which is Alzheimer's (Grundman, et al, 2004).

Chronic pain can be common in adults as well as with children. These maladies typically include headaches, arthritis, chronic back pain, fibromyalgia, and nerve damage. Of these headaches seem to be the most difficult for physicians to treat. They can be the result of stress, poor health of any type, accidents, or some other diagnosable malady. Patients with migraine headaches are often debilitated for lengthy amounts of time and are unable to function because of the severity of the pain. Many have a difficult time tolerating sounds, light, or even certain odors. Along with headaches is arthritis which afflicts people as they age. There are cases though of children who suffer from arthritis. This typically involves inflammation of joints in the hands, feet, knees, shoulders, and elbows as well as in the spine. This can be the result of genetics, years of stress and strain, or the result of serious injury. There are different forms of arthritis, but each type can be debilitating. Fibromyalgia has only been acknowledged as a disease in about the last 20 years. It is most commonly seen in women and can start in the early teen years and most typically among adult women. Before it was recognized as a disease many women were left to suffer and lead to believe that the pain was either not real, or something other than what they were trying to convince the medical profession they were experiencing. Another type of chronic pain is back pain. This is typically brought about by either strained muscles or problems in the spinal column, including bulging discs and stenosis, or narrowing of the canals in spinal column. A large number of people suffering from back pain were injured at work, in auto accidents, or in some other activity.

The Individual

Unfortunately, many who suffer from chronic pain allow it to debilitate them. In one instance a middle-aged male was involved in a car accident that left him with chronic back pain. As a result he was afraid to engage in any activities that required physical exertion for fear of his back becoming worse or hurting again. He either laid on the sofa, the bed, or sat in his recliner. As time went on he became weaker physically and found himself with far less ability to do what he wanted to do, including going to the store, riding in the car, or walking somewhere with his children or wife. He was also out of work and was on disability insurance which gave him a small income each month. All of this left him feeling quite inadequate about himself. Furthermore, to better manage the pain he was given several different narcotics and muscle relaxers upon which he eventually became dependent. Later, after going through in-depth consistent treatment that included physical therapy and psychological help he admitted that he was using pain as an excuse to get the drugs he was seeking. He said he was embarrassed to admit it, but found that the medications took him out of his problems and left him in a safe and dreamy state of mind. Other chronic pain patients have admitted that by being debilitated by chronic pain they were not required to participate in marriage or family, socially, or at work. One middle-aged female admitted that having pain gave her an excuse not to be sexually involved with her husband. Others have said that they began to enjoy the position they were in because they were on vacation from responsibilities.

There are, on the other hand, those who will not give into the pain, but continue to force themselves into activity, but in many instances the patients give into the pain and allow it to affect them psychologically and emotionally. When a person acts this way other family members will report feeling upset and hurt because the patient is not the same. If they feel that the patient is angry with them they will try harder to make the person happy or avoid her. In any case the patient's behavior is not healthy and everyone else in the family develops problems, and family functioning will worsen. One fellow tried to use chronic pain to manipulate the insurance system to collect disability insurance by claiming that he could not walk or function because of the pain. He was lifting his son, driving his four wheeler, doing yardwork, and getting in and out of his car with no problem. He told his therapist at the rehab hospital that he had worked for 10 years and deserved a retirement. Unfortunately for him instead of getting retirement he was put in jail for insurance fraud.

Heart and cardiovascular disease are also common in modern Western society. If the person has a heart attack, or coronary infarction, this can leave him in an insecure state of mind that will affect him both physically and emotionally. A good number of patients who have suffered a heart attack become afraid to do anything or go anywhere for fear of having another heart attack and possibly dying. These problems can be serious which will affect the family. One elderly man suffered a heart attack that was so severe it left him without oxygen to the brain for enough time to cause severe brain damage. He lived as a completely disabled individual without even the ability to talk.

This of course was a very stressful time for his wife, but also for the rest of their children and their families, all of whom lived nearby.

Besides a heart attack is a possibility of a stroke. If a person sustains a stroke, or a cardiovascular accident, the individual is usually left significantly disabled. In one particular inpatient rehabilitation hospital the majority of the patients had sustained a stroke. While in the hospital the family members would typically visit quite often and be concerned, but when the patient was discharged from the hospital and allowed to go home problems quickly arose. These patients often require constant care which is taxing on the family, or they may be able to take care of himself but are unable to return to work.

A 35-year-old married man with two children sustained a stroke in the temporal parietal area on the right of his brain side, and as result was left with paralysis on the left side as well. He was no longer able to comprehend math. Unfortunately, he was an engineer and was no longer able to work. This left his wife with the responsibility of caring for the children and him, and having to work to support the family.

Cancer can be found at any age, and no matter the age the diagnosis is often very devastating to the family. A 19-year-old female was attending college and one evening while attending her social group at school, she complained of a severe headache that came on immediately. Shortly thereafter she passed out. She was rushed to the hospital where a CT scan and MRI were performed and she was immediately diagnosed with brain cancer. She was immediately sent to a major hospital that specializes in cancer treatment and by the next day had brain surgery where a major part of the cancer was removed as well as part of her brain, and it left her with some paralysis on the right side. Her parents were told that she would be fortunate to live six months. This was devastating to her family and friends and the extended family. She had excellent social support from everyone involved, but it did disrupt the family. Mother became completely involved in the care of her daughter, and father did what he could and had to remain employed. The other children did what they could to help but were limited due to age and lack of experience in taking care of ill people. This young lady died a year and a half later. Her parents saw this as a blessing that they were able to have her as long as they did. And although they've missed her, they often stated that there was a sense of relief because of her not suffering, as well as the family being able to continue their lives.

Another couple had a 14-year-old daughter who died from cancer and they were so devastated by it that for the next year or so the father did not work and the parents stayed in the home and lived as hermits. One middle-aged man was diagnosed with cancer of which he was eventually cured, but his wife was so worried about it returning that she would not talk about it nor would she go to visit him in the hospital due to her fears of him dying and her being left alone. Another man in his early 70s died of cancer and his wife went into a depression, and by choice just decided to quit living and died about seven or eight months after his passing.

Because of the prevalence of smoking, a number of people contract pulmonary diseases including chronic obstructive pulmonary disease, or COPD. In such cases the patient is unable to go anywhere, or do much because of the limited ability to breathe. Typically, the patient will reside with one of the children, which can be disruptive for the family. One lady who was a heavy smoker for years decided to quit, and about 3 years after quitting was diagnosed with COPD. One of her daughters lived nearby and helped her mother so she could live independently for as long as she could. About 18 months later she became so ill that she had to move in with her daughter and the daughter's family which became a burden after several months. The mother was finally admitted to a nursing home and passed away after about 2 months.

Along with pulmonary problems are those who suffer from digestive disorders such as Crohn's disease, ulcers, irritable bowel syndrome, and so forth. In these cases, the family often has to make adjustments for bathroom needs, as well as dietary and lifestyle changes, all of which can be frustrating to the family.

Effects on the Spouse

If the patient is married the most significant impact of the illness will be on the spouse. On the spouse lies the responsibility for taking care of the patient as well as the rest the family. Although most spouses will willingly sacrifice to take care of their ill spouse there are a number who struggle with this responsibility. In one particular case the husband was a successful professor at a major university and was diagnosed with multiple sclerosis leaving him completely disabled. He had no use of his body from his neck down. This put the responsibility of not only caring for their children, but also for the support of the family and complete care for him on her. She had to feed him, bathe him, clothe him, take care his bowel and bladder needs, and so forth. On several occasions she very openly stated that she felt cheated. Her husband was making a good income which allowed her to stay home and take care of the family but now she had to work. Fortunately for them the children were in early adolescence or approaching young adulthood so they could, for the most part, take care of themselves. The wife had to go to work and leave her husband in the care of the nurse which was an expense, but fortunately for her and the family, she had a very marketable skill which allowed her to earn a substantial income.

Another case included a husband who worked two jobs so he could support his family. One day while driving a pickup truck for work, he was hit by a semi which left him with severe, permanent brain damage. When he was finally released from the hospital and rehabilitation care facility he was sent home. His wife reported that she had another child on her hands, meaning her disabled husband. With three young children and a husband who acted as immaturely as they did, she was continually stressed. Whether they were in public, at a restaurant, at church, or any other public gathering she had to remain continually vigilant to make sure he did not say something or do something that would embarrass them in any way. As an example, at church he would often make loud comments about different people in the congregation that were often not flattering. He would argue with the children as if he were one of them both and at home and in public. His wife admitted that she felt overwhelmed, but because of her wedding vows she was determined to stay with her husband. In both of these cases the wives did stay with their husbands, but unfortunately in many other cases this was not the result.

In most instances the spouse of the chronically ill patient will, in the beginning, try to do all he or she can to make things better, but may find that the efforts are to no avail. For some it is hard to accept the fact that the spouse will never get better. Oftentimes when this is realized the spouse will have an emotional reaction. This reaction could be sadness, helplessness, fear, or even anger and resentment. But in many cases these feelings evolve from concern and caring to anger and resentment because of the lack of progress with the patient, or the caregiver becomes overwhelmed because of the responsibility now permanently placed on the healthy spouse.

The wife of a middle-aged chronically ill man who suffered from debilitating back pain gradually became involved without outside activities such as community service and social activities with her friends. She admitted that this was her choice because of not getting anything from the marriage. She said that she could not do things with her husband anymore and felt restricted and resentful. She dealt with this disappointment by involving herself in outside activities. The problem with this is the emotional and physical separation from the person who is ill then causes instability in the patient's life because of not understanding what the other person is doing. It is easy for the patient to take what the other person is doing personally and become resentful. One such case was a nurse employed in a military hospital where she met her husband who was a traumatic brain injury patient. She thought that she could take care of him at home and be his wife, but after about 5 years of marriage decided that she did not love him because of the way he acted. He was impulsive and exhibited little self-control when it came to sexual matters. It was at this time that she became involved with an old male friend and decided that he could offer more than her husband. She did decide to stay with her husband because of the money they were receiving for his disability, but after that time there was no emotional involvement on her part. In other cases the spouse may become completely immersed in the children whether living at home or not. If the children are at home the spouse may be completely consumed in the children's school or other activities. If the children are grown and on their own the spouse may spend as much time as possible with of them and their families. In all these cases the negative responses were the result of not having an emotional attachment to the chronically ill spouse.

When the spouse begins to pull away emotionally and/ or physically, the chronically ill patient will typically respond by either seeking the spouse's companionship or will also withdraw. In either case the chronically ill patient will oftentimes become worse because of the stress brought about by the problems in the relationship. The healthy spouse on the other hand will not withdraw but will continue working with the patient and be a part of the solution rather than the problem. If the patient begins to find that the spouse will tolerate the behavior by the patient, manipulation can begin and the spouse could very likely become the enabler of poor behavior. In this instance the spouse will be easily manipulated if she were to feel sorry for the patient or guilty because of the patient's condition. As with the child, if the spouse feels sorry for the patient she will expect little from the patient. This will lead to doubt that what she intuitively knows should be done by the patient. This puts the patient in the position of not having to invest in the relationship because the enabling spouse is doing all of the work. One such case was a lady who had chronic back pain. She claimed to have too much discomfort when asked to do housework or prepare meals, so her husband would take over and do everything for her. The husband had a demanding job which required at least 60 hours a week at work. Then on his one day off he spent it cleaning the house, entertaining visitors if they came by, and doing enough cooking to have meals for an entire week. Although he never complained outwardly, he admitted to resenting the situation and was developing dislikes for her because of the manipulation. Even though she said she could not do housework or help prepare meals because of back pain, she was able to sit up for hours and play bridge with her friends and play golf at least twice a week. Even though this marriage did not end in divorce the husband was so resentful that he almost completely separated himself from her emotionally.

The Effects on the Children

The moods and behavior of the spouse and the patient will have an effect on the children. When children are in the situation where expectations and rules are inconsistent or unclear, they will act in one of several different ways. Most often the oldest child, and most often the oldest daughter, will inherit the role of the second parent. This child will become the one who is continually attempting to keep order in the family. The child will oftentimes be motivated by fear that if he or she does not keep everything in order and keep the younger siblings in line, she will be neglecting her duty. This child will often be the one to keep the house clean by vacuuming, dusting, and straightening things up. She will also try very diligently to help the parents by correcting poor behavior, and to control the children so there will be no disruptions at home. This puts the oldest child in the double bind situation because no matter what she does, the other children are not going to respond positively in most cases. Younger children do not want to be parented by an older sibling so they will rebel. When this occurs the older sibling will become anxious and try harder to make everybody comply. Even if the parents tell the younger children to obey their older sibling there will still be resistance. When the child attempts to keep the house clean the same situation will occur because it is not likely this child will get the others to cooperate and help keep things in order.

One 10-year-old girl felt this pressure after her mother became injured and unable to take care of responsibilities at home. The father told the girl that she had to be the big sister and take care of the younger children because he had to go to work. The girl took this assignment seriously and very soon thereafter started showing signs of anxiety because the younger children would not comply. She tried to keep the house clean but was never successful because the other children refused to help, saying she was not their boss. She felt like she was in trouble and that no one loved her because of the way the other children treated her. It is not always the oldest child who is found in this role. It can be a younger one who is more responsible.

Regarding the other children, one child may withdraw from the rest the family and isolate in his or her room. The child who does this usually feels neglected and unimportant to the rest of the family and as result will go off into his own world where temporary safety and well-being is found. This child will often lay on the bed and sleep or become consumed by video games, reading novels, or any one of the number of different ways children escape problems. Another behavior pattern is a child who will become involved in some other outside activity such as sports, or finding a group of friends to spend time with, or maybe even academics, drama, or music. These children detach from the family and try to find their well-being by being busy so they don't have to think about the problems at home. Many of these children seek the approval that they should normally receive at home but can't get it because of the problems with the parents. These children often become perfectionists with the desire of being perfect and thereby knowing from other people that they have arrived at being a good person. Unfortunately, they never feel like they arrive because people will not respond to them the way they are hoping, leaving them feeling like they are still inadequate.

One adult admitted that his trying to be perfect started as a child when his mother became debilitated and as a result he felt completely neglected by her. Because he could not get acceptance from her or his father he succeeded in school by being the top student, even though he admitted as an adult that he never felt as though he arrived. Another child may completely abandon the family and find a new family with which to become involved. This child will often call the parents of this new family mom and dad and consider the other children as siblings. Usually the family that takes this child in is one who will feel sorry for him, and by keeping the child in their family they may be enabling negative behaviors that will be harmful later in life. In such cases, an individual can easily feel that if the problem gets bad enough he can run away and go elsewhere to find solace and companionship. In all instances because of the disruption in the family due to the chronic illness each member must strive to find balance and equilibrium. If the family circumstances are unhealthy the family members will resort to unhealthy means to fill the void and discomfort because of the disruption in the family system. When a disruption such as chronic illness occurs in a healthy family the members make adjustments to compensate for the family member who is unable to participate in the daily routine. If the father is emotionally healthy he will be able to perceive where problems lie and give appropriate direction to the family members so the problems can be taken care of. Regardless of a family being healthy or not, all families experience problems. Unhealthy families avoid them, argue, or blame others, while healthy families take care of things that are needed to be attended to.

The Chronically Ill Child and the Family

When a child becomes ill this also disrupts the functioning of the family system. Children are unable to take care of themselves so they need someone to help them. This usually falls on the parents. The typical outcome in this situation is one of the parents becomes the primary care provider which is often done at the expense of the rest of the family. The reaction of the other spouse is in many ways the same as that of the chronically ill spouse. In this case though both parents are healthy. As soon as one is taken out of the family system because of the ill child needing constant care, the others are left to fend for themselves. In most cases the parent who becomes the primary caretaker of the ill child is the mother. If she is fortunate enough to be a stay-at-home mom, the stress will be far less than if she is working to help support the family and has to quit to care for the child. This responsibility becomes taxing on the mother or father in several ways. First of all, it is mentally taxing because of the concerns regarding the child's welfare. The parent must make sure the child is safe and comfortable, and getting all the care necessary. It is not uncommon for other family members, whether immediate or extended, to question the caretaker's ability to give adequate care, which brings about feelings and defensiveness on the part of the caretaker. It could be that the grandparents are concerned that the child is not getting well fast enough. Or it could be that they think the course of treatment is unwise and want to take over themselves. One such instance was the young boy with a chronic illness which required a lot of care and time. His mother was continually told by her in-laws what they thought should be done which was not what she thought was needed. As a result, the mother felt slighted and did not want to have anything to do with the in-laws. The in-laws on the other hand felt hurt because she would not communicate with them, and felt they had a right to give input. Both couples remained at odds with each other for several years, but in the end they all just pretended like nothing happened.

The other strain on the parent who is responsible for the care of the child is a physical strain. Usually the mother, who is a caretaker, will not get as much sleep as the rest of the family. The physical strain of taking the child to doctor's appointments, therapies, and possibly bathing, feeding, and all other care needs, can tire a person out rather quickly. If the caretaking parent begins to request help from the spouse and other family members and they do not cooperate, the feelings of resentment will erode the family unity. Even though the mother may feel exhausted and resentful she must continue taking care of the child. This will cause her to draw closer to the child for emotional support, or resent the child for the situation that the family is left in. If this occurs each family member will try to cope with the problem in his or her own way which is usually not healthy.

The Ill Child

The other concern is the ill child. One of the most significant problems is the child being felt sorry for by parents and family. This then causes them to give into the child's whims and desires. As discussed, if the child learns to act in certain ways to get what he or she wants, the behavior will continue even though the behavior is unhealthy or unacceptable. An example might be a young girl being in an accident and leaving her with limited use of her legs. It would be easy for everyone to feel sorry for her because of her limited mobility. She is very likely to learn to be manipulative because, like any other child she may push to get her way and take advantage of the sympathy because nobody set meaningful limits. This happened to a young boy who at the age of eight had a stroke which left one side of his body partially paralyzed. After being stabilized in the hospital he was sent home because of no facilities for children with this sort of problem. Mother and father felt helpless because they thought he could not manage his behavior because of the stroke. If they said no to something he wanted, he would throw a tantrum until he got his way. He was expected to return to school and would refuse to go. His parents would allow him to stay home because they were afraid of him feeling upset. The parents sought help and learned to set limits regardless of his condition and he soon learned how to manage his behavior again.

A young 12-year-old boy was playing and broke his right arm which was his dominant arm. His family lived on a farm and it was his turn to milk the cow daily. He announced that he could not because of his arm, but father insisted that he could take care of his chores. Father said that several days later, after the boy struggled with milking the cow, he proudly brought a full bucket of milk into the kitchen for the family and the cow looked quite relieved also. Another boy about the same age had a broken arm and did not want to go to Boy Scout camp. His parents were wise enough to insist that he go. When he returned a week later, he was very proud of himself because he had earned a good number of merit badges and succeeded in staying at camp for the week. In these instances the parents did not act on their guilty or sorry feelings for the child. They wisely insisted that the child function as he needed to, and the child in both cases learned to overcome adversity by staying with something regardless of the condition.

Another person contracted polio as a child and was left crippled in both legs. He and his parents and his younger brothers and sisters all lived on a ranch. He had to work and take care of chores the same as everyone else. He grew into adulthood being responsible and was in a career that required physical labor as well as intellectual abilities.

A young girl in her late teens sustained a head injury because of an auto accident. Her parents were told that she would never function normally again which was frightening and discouraging to them. After seeking help they told the therapist that they felt that maybe she could recover further than the doctors were saying. The therapist helped the parents understand the need to reteach behavior which they willingly did. The doctor had said she would never be able to work again, nor would she ever be well enough to marry and raise a family. Even though her behavior was childish immediately after the accident, this changed significantly because of the work her parents were willing to put into helping her. They made her help around the house, read, go shopping, and helped her with counting money, planning menus, and so forth. It was not long before she was able to go back to the fast food establishment where she had worked previously and continue with the same job that she had. She was also able to go to school and learn a trade which most people never expected her to accomplish. If the family members coddle the child and feel sorry for him, or they will contribute to the chronic disability or illness. On the other hand, those parents who are wise and willing to put in the effort, and will expect more from the child will, in most cases, see results and go beyond expectations.

The young boy aged 18 who was an A student in high school and was an excellent athlete was involved in an auto accident and sustained a severe head injury. After rehabilitation he acted exactly as the physicians had predicted, which was to be childish and demanding. His mother sought help because he would not do his schoolwork, and would not do any chores around the house. He was always rude to her and her parents who would care for him during the day while mom was at work. The mother felt helpless and the grandparents felt sorry for him which left them in the position of enabling this childish behavior. Mother was helped to gain insight into her thinking and feelings regarding her son which included helplessness, guilt, and feeling sorry for him. She was then in the position to recognize how these emotions and feelings kept her from helping him as her intuition would dictate. She eventually got strong enough to put her foot down and emphatically and strongly state he would not be allowed to act as an immature child any longer. This surprised him, and he began to straighten up. No longer was she or her parents enabling the behavior. The outcome was rather significant in that four years later he was a licensed real estate salesman, licensed real estate broker, and was getting his mortgage brokerage license. In all these cases if the parents, or significant people in the patients' lives, had acted on their emotions these problems from the injuries and disabilities could have been chronic, which would have hurt not only the patient and their families but also would have taken away good contributors to society.

Helping the Chronically Ill Person

When considering chronic illness, which is becoming more prevalent in modern society, the key players in helping the patient get better or improve is the family. Unfortunately, in a number of instances family can, out of well-meaning intentions and because of lack of understanding, worsen the patient's condition. The last subject to consider when addressing chronic illness is the state of the family. One example is a young couple whose first child had a chronic disability. Because of inexperience and lack of ability it was easy for the young parents to act on their helpless feelings and guilt and become extremely indulgent in the child. On the other hand, if the parents have been married for a number of years and had successfully raised other children they would likely be less prone to feeling sorry for the child and be more comfortable expecting the child to function as he or she needs to. This was apparent with the young girl who was engaged and in the car accident and sustained a serious head injury. She was the oldest of six children and the mother and father had received earlier help regarding her rebellious behavior as a teenager. As a result they felt comfortable in setting limits and expectations instead of acting on the urge to protect her. Another situation is the older couple who are empty-nesters. It may be that by this time one of the two is inflicted with chronic pain, or some other disability that not only affects the couple alone but also the extended family.

Dementia

One unfortunate chronic condition that is seen more now than before because of longevity, is the dementias. These can be the result of strokes, earlier drug abuse, head injuries, or can be of the Alzheimer's type. This condition will affect the entire family including sons or daughters-in-law and grandchildren. When this occurs if the onset is immediate it seems to not have as negative of effect on the family as if it is a slow course. Head injuries and strokes occur very quickly, and even though the family has a hard time adjusting to the patient and the changes in personality and cognitive abilities most people seem to accept the injury or accident and attempt to manage the situation. One example was the young man mentioned earlier in his middle 30s who was an engineer and sustained a cerebral vascular accident. After he was stabilized in an acute care hospital he was sent to a rehabilitation hospital for extended help. He was diagnosed with dementia due to a stroke. His wife was shaken by the incident, but had no trouble accepting her husband's deficits and the reality that he would never be able to return to work. The elderly man in his late 70s who had a heart attack and severe brain damage because of lack of oxygen was shocking to the family. His wife and their children and their families did not struggle with him not understanding what they said or recognizing who they were because they could attribute this to the heart attack. He was limited in speech, was unable to walk on his own, could not feed himself, and had a hard time acknowledging the presence of family members. He unfortunately passed away rather soon after the heart attack, but the family was relieved because they knew he lived a good life and there were no ill feelings left behind.

On the other hand, dementias that are slow in their course, such as Alzheimer's, oftentimes have significant negative effects on family members. One such instance is the elderly man who had been showing gradual signs of Alzheimer's dementia for about 3 years. As he worsened, his wife became more and more upset because she felt that his behavior was due to lack of love for her. Even though she intellectually knew that it was the dementia she would expect him to treat her, and interact with her, as he did before the dementia set in. Their adult daughter and son-in-law had to step in to help. The wife saw them as intruding and trying to take over her role as a wife. The son did not live near the family and on his occasional visits would not interact with father and mother as he needed to because of seeing the progression of the disease. As a result, there was significant conflict that interfered with the family in general, and not being able to help the father.

Another example was an elderly man who was in the advanced stages of Alzheimer's and his wife was trying as hard as she could to take care of him by herself. By the time she sought help she was exhausted. She could not sleep very well at night for fear of him getting up and wandering through the house and hurting himself. She had to keep the doors locked from the inside and the keys put away so he could not wander off at night. There were several occasions when she thought that she needed to put him in a nursing home but felt guilty and tried to keep him at home. Her children were not supportive of the idea of him being placed in a nursing home. They thought mother was abandoning their father. However, she did get strong enough to stand up to the children and do what she needed to for her own sake, as well as the health and welfare of her husband.

A man decided to take his father who had Alzheimer's into the home, and over the 2 years they had him in the home his symptoms worsened to the point where they could no longer put them in a daycare program and bring him home at night. He decided to put him in a facility. When he mentioned this to his siblings they became upset and accused him and his wife of not caring about dear old dad. The couple finally had to say that somebody else in the family would have to take him, and the younger brother agreed to do so. It wasn't two weeks before they had father put in a nursing home because they could not handle him. In many such cases people who are not responsible for caring for the patient look at the patient and think he or she is normal because they appear physically healthy. They do not understand that the body may be healthy but the mind is not. Because of this a lot of blaming and accusing takes place because of others feeling that the patient is not getting the care he or she needs.

Another problem deals with family members feeling upset because husband or wife, mom or dad, aunt or uncle, or sibling does not act toward the family members as before. In many instances those family members who come to visit leave upset and in tears because grandma, or grandpa, or whoever does not recognize them does not know who they are. These individuals feel unloved and like they have been ostracized from the person's life or the family. As was described earlier in this chapter the spouse may be upset because of not understanding the disease and taking the neglectful or unaware behavior on the part of the patient as a rejection.

In all of the cases mentioned in this chapter problems occur because the family members act on their emotions rather than their common sense or what they intuitively know needs to be done. It is easy for family members to feel sorry for the patient. If this is the case, exceptions will be made for the patient and will result in little or no progress. Feeling sorry for someone also carries the connotation that the individual is unable to do for himself or herself so others now must do all for the patient. This is demeaning to the patient, and many have said that they don't want to be felt sorry for because of their problems and left to feeling less of a person. There are a number of patients who want to be taken care of and put very little effort into his or her own welfare. Another problem as has been mentioned is misinterpreting the patient's behavior as personal against the individual. It may be that the patient is demanding and might need more help than others assumed he or she would need, and others can feel manipulated or taken advantage of. In other cases, resentment may exist because of the extra burden placed on the caregiver or family members. Participation in activities may be limited which might leave the person feeling neglected or unimportant. In all instances it must be remembered that the family functions as a system and when one element in the system is altered it requires changes from all other elements of that system. In this case the family must make significant alterations to compensate for the chronically ill patient whether that person is a child or an adult.

Chapter 6 —Worksheet

1. What are some of the common chronic pain disorders?

2. Why might a person with chronic pain become addicted to pain medications?

3. How can a chronic pain patient affect the family?

Chapter 7
Mood Disorders and Family Dynamics

Mike Focus / Shutterstock.com

A 57-year-old man had retired from his position in the school system where he consulted with teachers, administrators, as well as parents of at risk children. He also had a thriving practice in family counseling where he specialized in children's problems. His average work week was about 60 hours and he felt fulfilled because of what he was doing. At the age of 57 he had a good number of years in the education system with a significant retirement and his finances were in order. He and his wife decided to take an early retirement. His plan was to continue working as a therapist in a private practice which would supplement his income and allow him and his wife to live comfortably and even have money for any extras they had not enjoyed earlier in their marriage. They sold their home and moved to a new state where they built their dream home and were anticipating a good comfortable life. They moved into the home before it was finished and as a result he could not begin his practice because his office was to be in his home. For the first three months of his retirement his time was occupied by helping his wife decide on amenities for the home, which was not very fulfilling to him. At about two months into the retirement he found himself not having much energy and feeling like nothing in life was interesting. He found himself worrying about finances, fearing that he would not have enough to establish a lifestyle that he and his wife had anticipated. It was more difficult for him to get out of bed each morning and during the day he saw little that would attract his attention. He also had a difficult time sleeping and found himself eating more than normal. After spending some time thinking about his emotional and physical state he finally realized that he was feeling depressed like his patients who he was seeing in his practice were feeling. With this realization he told the carpenter to finish his office and he began visiting those individuals who could start referring to him, and he began writing a book on parenting that he had been encouraged to do for some time.

Depression can affect a person at about any time in his or her life. It is estimated that about 7% of the adult population will experience an episode of unipolar depression at some time during any 12-month period (DSM 5). The symptoms of unipolar depression include loss of interest in activities, lack of energy, and changes in appetite that can include loss of appetite or overeating, problems with concentration, and difficulties with sleeping too much or falling asleep or staying asleep, or both (Weiten, Dunn, & Hanner, 2015). The three main symptoms though to be considered for depression are isolation, poor self-esteem, and negative thinking. To help a person with depression one must first understand the course of the disorder.

Many feel that depression is caused by a neurochemical imbalance. The thinking espoused in this textbook is that the chemical imbalance does exist, but is not the cause of the problem; rather, it is the result of the problem. To understand this, one must understand the fact that the brain will not react unless it is stimulated. An example is a person feeling rather relaxed when the phone rings and then, because of disturbing news, immediately feels tense, upset, and worried. These emotions and feelings do not come from nowhere and make the person worried, but this emotional change is the result of what was learned because of the phone call. Another point to consider is the autonomic nervous system, which is divided into the sympathetic and parasympathetic subsystems. The parasympathetic nervous system is active when the person is relaxed which allows for muscle relaxation, the digestive system to function, the immune system to function, and the heart rate and respiratory rates also slow down. The sympathetic nervous system, which is also called the flight or fight syndrome, is triggered when a person is under extreme stress that will bring about the need to survive, as well as fear and anxiety. This comes about when a person is threatened and will cause the digestive system to stop, the immune system to stop, the respiratory and cardiovascular system to significantly increase in rate, along with muscle tension and an improvement in vision and hearing. These changes are necessary for the person to survive. This occurs when the person is either thinking about a threat that is significant or is actually experiencing one. Some could say that these are the symptoms of a panic attack, and this will be discussed in the next chapter.

Depression is not something that happens spontaneously, or comes from nowhere, but has a predictable course; by understanding the course one will be able to understand the origins of depression as well as how to help the person. Depression starts in one's thinking. The depressed patient came in for the weekly appointment and was excited to report to the therapist that his depression had just lifted. The therapist told him that is not always the case and asked him what his morning was like before he came for therapy. He said that he woke up feeling depressed and did not see much use for life, and needed to come for help. He then said that on the way to the office he was almost involved in a serious accident on the freeway. It was after that his depression supposedly lifted. He realized that the near mishap diverted his attention such that he was no longer thinking about how bad his life was. It must be understood that a person's thinking patterns are learned. This learning can come from childhood experiences in adolescence or even in adulthood. If a child was raised in a home with constant conflict between the parents the child might become frightened and unsure of what to expect. Younger children especially feel that they somehow either have to stop the conflict by siding with one or the other parent, or do something to make mom or dad or both feel better. This puts the child in that double bind position, which means that as hard as he tries, success is never realized because the parents continue in their fighting and arguing. A good number of children feel like this conflict in the home is because of something they did wrong. The child may think that if her grades were better mom and dad will not fight. The child might also think that if she can obey the rules completely and never make a mistake the parents will not argue because perhaps she heard one say to the other "if it wasn't for Susie we wouldn't have these problems." What the parents might be alluding to is the child needing some medical care that will cause a financial burden on the family. The child, not understanding this, would think that she has done something wrong. In this sort of situation the negative thinking is the self-blaming and feeling unsuccessful at being able to help because the problems continue. Another cause for conflict in the family might be the result of problems between another child and the parents. In one case, an 11-year-old girl saw her older sister and parents constantly arguing and fighting. The girl thought to herself that if she could make her sister happy everything would be okay. She tried diligently to make things better with her sister by doing things for her such as writing endearing notes or helping with chores. As an adult this girl admitted that she always felt like she was a failure because her sister never expressed appreciation and continued in the same behavioral patterns.

If a couple divorces and bitter feelings exist between the two it might be that one, or both, may verbalize their ill feelings regarding the other parent to the children. A father consistently spoke negatively of the children's mother when they were with him on weekend visits. He even threatened them with negative consequences if they loved their mother. The oldest child was a daughter, age 15, and she was in constant conflict. She heard what her father said which made her angry with mother, but would also observed mother and, over time, began to think that mother was not the culprit. When she went back to her father and he would verbalize the same negative feelings and thoughts it would cause the girl to once more doubt mother. Eventually she quit trying to figure everything out and just withdrew to her room and admitted later that she was constantly thinking to herself what she had to do to make things better but could never figure out the answer.

It is rare to see divorced parents working together to raise their children. One single mother was trying to teach her three children respect and obedience but was continually undermined by the father, her ex-husband. He would tell the children that mother was not stable and not a wise person and that they did not need to obey her because of her supposed instability. As a result, the children treated mother very poorly which left them in a state of conflict because they knew they shouldn't be acting the way they were, but felt they had permission from the father to do so. It would bother the two older children to see mother cry and they would feel guilty when defying her, but because they could get away with the poor behavior they continued. The youngest child was not old enough to be involved in these problems, although she saw her two older siblings be rude to mother and tried to act the same way. Mother was able to stop that. The two older children were showing signs of depression because of the conflict they were experiencing in the home. Eventually the father wanted to find out what type of therapy the mother was receiving because he thought she was being too harsh with the children, more particularly with the two older children. It took the mother getting strong enough to emphatically state that she would not tolerate the poor behavior of the children, or even the father, for him than to finally admit he could see that they were disrespectful to their mother. He then began to expect the same behavior with mother that was expected when with him. If this had been allowed to continue these children would likely have become depressed as they matured.

Divorce is a difficult thing for children to be a part of and the younger children especially typically think that the divorce is their fault. Children of almost all ages yearn for their parents to get back together so the family can continue as they would hope.

Children who are raised by insecure, critical parents will likely develop depression, especially later in life. One young boy was raised by an anxious father who was never satisfied with anything that anyone in the family did. He was continually critical, which left this boy thinking that he would never succeed in life. He said he barely graduated from high school and only passed because of the agriculture and farming classes that he took. He said that math and history and science were all a problem. He admitted that he actually never tried to do well in classes because he believed his father who said that he would never be able to learn. As a result, he would always give up or would never start anything he was unsure of. This meant not doing homework, not paying attention in class and overall not taking any initiative to learn. As an adult he was depressed because of feeling like he was an inadequate person who never succeeded in life. As a result he would never risk, which held him back at work, at church, and with the family.

Another man who is in his second marriage was acting as he did in the first marriage which was to isolate and at times would spend up to four days in bed doing nothing more than getting up to go to the bathroom or to get something to eat. He admitted that his mother was a person who was always criticizing him and doubting his abilities so he learned as a child to never try. There were several instances in his life where he did follow through with responsibilities, including completing a bachelor's degree in college, although it took several years longer than it should have because of his depression. He was a salesman of office equipment and was continually thinking to himself that he would never succeed so even though he did try he was never strong enough emotionally to stay with the work and make the sales he needed to.

A young college student who was attending a major university in the United States was from England. He was pursuing an education that his parents didn't agree with and were constantly trying to get him to come home and stop stressing himself by going to college. He finally sought therapy because he was not attending to his schoolwork, was feeling overwhelmed, and contemplated returning home. Through therapy he was able to see that his parents were not critical of him by thinking he could not accomplish what he was trying to. It was due to their own insecurities and personal failures in their lives. They did not want their son to have disappointments in his life like they had, so they were always encouraging him to take the easy way and not take a risk. As a result he suffered from negative thinking, which led to the depression. In most all cases critical parents will unintentionally cause insecurities and ultimately the negative thinking which could lead to depression.

An individual may be raised in a loving, supportive home but still be depressed and ask where the negative thinking came from? One young lady was consumed by negative thinking, which was centered on viewing herself as inadequate. As this was explored in depth she revealed that her family was overly positive with everything she and her siblings did. She said she grew up feeling like she was the best at whatever she pursued and in some ways that she could do no wrong. After completing high school and going to work the negative thinking started quite abruptly because no one at work was praising her like her family did. The result was thinking to herself that something was wrong. She did not realize that in the real world praise is rather rare and is not always the best indicator of one's abilities or weaknesses.

When in an abusive relationship most individuals show signs of depression because of negative thinking even though they may not have been depressed before the relationship. They most often say that they don't feel very good about themselves because of what the husband will say to them. If a woman is told that she is ugly or fat or stupid and no one will want her, she will likely believe it, which will lead to depression. Others will face a situation that, to them, is insurmountable, and because of this feeling and negative thinking depression will result. Negative thinking is at the root of all depression and these thought patterns do not come spontaneously but, as illustrated, are learned.

The result of negative thinking is poor self-esteem. Self-esteem in this context means how one estimates his or her value as a person (Weiten, Dunn, & Hammer, 2015). The typical depressed patient is feeling inadequate, like a loser, helpless, overwhelmed, fearful, and so forth. This poor self-esteem is a result of the way the person thinks about himself or herself. If the individual is continually told that he or she is worthless the self-esteem will suffer. In too many cases poor self-esteem comes from seeking other people's approval to feel validated as an individual. Individuals with this problem are constantly judging their worth as a person by how they perceive other people react to or treat them.

An example is a woman who was asked by the women's organization to which she belonged to organize a dinner and program for the women and their spouses. She organized committees for setting things up, cleaning up afterwards, food preparation, serving, and entertainment. She reported that she felt very inadequate because when all was said and done nobody acknowledged her efforts. As a result she thought that she did a poor job, which left her with negative feelings about herself. She was asked to go down the checklist of all that she was required to do for the dinner and she was able to see that all went well. There was enough food for everyone, it was well prepared, and served on time. She did admit that there were a few rough spots in the entertainment part of the evening, but overall it went well. She was then asked why she felt like she did a poor job and her reply was no one said anything to her. She was helped to look to herself for approval and judge her success by the outcome rather than by how she thought other people treated her. She was then able to understand that after the program people were anxious to get home because it was a Friday night and the couples were anxious to return to their families. She also realized that there were several people who were critical of what she did because these were individuals who did it before and felt that she did a better job, and maybe they did.

Others will have poor self-esteem because of not risking. It's obvious that when a person is not willing to risk, he or she will not accomplish anything, which will then lead one to feel less of a person. A favorite saying is "behold the turtle, he never gets anywhere unless he sticks his neck out." The fear of risk starts in the thinking, but by not risking the person will feel guilty or inadequate. Along with fear of risk is the general self-doubt. One's negative self-esteem is, in many cases, the result of not trusting oneself and, as a result, the person never accomplishes much.

The third major component of depression is isolation. The person who is thinking that nothing is right, or that they have no worth will typically not want to be around others. When this happens the person will be left alone and usually end up isolated. The problem is that the person is isolated and there is very little to occupy his or her thoughts, and as a result, the thinking gravitates toward the negative. It then becomes a vicious cycle. One depressed patient isolated for days at a time and would typically sleep at least 16 hours per day. Her problem was being away from other people by choice.

One man's wife divorced him after about 13 years of marriage because he was not willing to get out and work so he could support the family. He remarried shortly thereafter but still continued the same behavioral patterns of negative thinking, which led to poor self-esteem and isolation. When asked what there was in the bed to occupy his thinking he said nothing but the problems and worries he was struggling with, which by lying in bed became worse and more overwhelming. In this and many other cases the patients typically report that this tendency to isolate started in childhood and was tolerated by the family. One adult patient said that he isolated in the woods with his dog. His parents never said anything to him about it, which then gave him permission to continue being by himself. He said that he felt safe away from the family because of fighting and bickering, but at the same time knew there was more to life than what he was engaged in.

It's easy for parents who feel sorry for the child and allow isolation and in most cases the isolation is to the bedroom where the child's thoughts can wander in many different directions, but most will admit that the directions are usually negative. The point here is that as isolation continues the depression worsens until the individual becomes so miserable in that state she cannot stand it any longer and she will decide; to change or will be coerced by someone else to get up and get going. Unfortunately, in one instance, the mother of five children isolated herself in the bedroom for years, which left the children to fend for themselves because father was busy working and trying to support the family. One of the five children received therapy for depression and admitted that he only knew how to deal with problems by withdrawing and finding solace in his own world. Think of a person freezing to death in a blizzard and suffering from hypothermia. The symptoms include feeling warm, having a sense of euphoria, and the desire to sleep. If this person is allowed to sleep, he will never wake up because of being in a coma and then death results. Sometimes it is helpful to think of depression as mentally and emotionally freezing to death. If the person in the blizzard is kept awake even though he may get mad at whomever has tried to help him, eventually the blood start circulating and hopefully the problem will be averted long enough to get help. The individual who is not allowed to isolate and withdraw from the world, but is expected to get out and start functioning, will begin to feel better.

The reason these three symptoms of depression are so important to understand is how they affect each other. If an individual acts on his or her thoughts they will, over time, become reinforced. So in the case of the depressed patient, if she is feeling life is not worth anything she's thinking that no matter what she tries it is ever good enough and no one really cares about her so she will likely avoid others. While avoiding people she is by herself and probably not too busy doing anything because of feeling like nothing is worth it so she sees her world begin to deteriorate around her. The negative thinking will be reinforced. As this cycle continues the depression deepens until the person completely gives up and may even contemplate, or successfully carry out, suicide. By understanding this course of thinking, feeling, and then acting it is easy to understand why the other common symptoms exist.

Depressed people often complain about a loss of energy. They say they have no desire to go anywhere or do anything because they don't feel well physically or are just too tired to function. When a person is isolating he or she will lose energy because of a lack of physical activity. This is not the main reason for the lack of energy; the energy is lacking because of the emotional strain the patient is feeling. Along with this is a lack of interest in most activities. The depressed person cannot see any good in the world, and no matter what positives are pointed out the person will discount the positives because she feels like nothing is good, or no matter what she tries, it will be a failure.

A change in appetite is often a symptom of depression, and in most cases depressed people lose their appetite. This is because of the stressful thinking and the emotional strain placed on the person. Physiologically speaking, because of the person's thought patterns, the sympathetic nervous system is in play and one result is the digestive system either significantly slowing or stopping. The other side of the change in appetite is overeating. Too many people eat as a soothing experience and comforting. A number of depressed patients will act on the desire to eat and say the act of eating was more important than what was being eaten.

Sleep problems are often present with the depressed person and in most cases the individual will have a hard time either going to sleep, staying sleep, or both. The reason is that one is typically consumed in the negative thinking, which is hard to turn off. When this is the case it's difficult to go to sleep because of dwelling on problems, and if the person goes to sleep he will typically not sleep very soundly. When this happens the person will awaken after several hours of sleep and have a difficult time going back to sleep. There are a number of patients, though, who tried to continually sleep because it is viewed as an escape from the depressed thoughts and feelings. One particular patient would sleep for about 16 hours a day and she said that she did this because she did not want to go do things that would cause her to feel more depressed. She had a problem with gambling and if awake and feeling energetic would give in to the impulse to go to the gambling facilities and after losing all of her money would feel like she was a terrible person.

Another common problem is difficulties cognitively. Many patients admit that they are unable to concentrate on anything. Some have said that they would read several pages in a book and not recall what was read or watch a TV program and not remember what was viewed. Others have reported that the thinking is so scattered that they cannot concentrate on any subject. It is difficult to concentrate on something when one's mind is consumed by something else. At the root of all of these symptoms is one's thinking. The thinking then causes the neurochemical change in the brain that is then identified as the chemical imbalance. It is important to remember, though, that the imbalance is a result of, and not the cause, of the problem.

A married woman with two young children presented with symptoms of depression including negative thinking, poor self-esteem, isolation, difficulties sleeping, overeating, and lack of drive and desire to accomplish anything. She said that her husband was always angry with her because of her lack of ambition, and she felt even worse about herself because of his reactions to her. As is typical in the beginning sessions of therapy, her upbringing was explored and she admitted that her father was an extreme perfectionist that left her feeling inadequate because of never arriving at his standard, and her mother was a very permissive person who never expected much of her children. Over the course of her childhood and adolescence she developed a behavior pattern of avoiding responsibilities and giving in to her overwhelmed feelings, which resulted from her negative perceptions of herself as learned in the family. She said that she did well in school and she decided to succeed even though she was told that she would never be able to learn because of a disability but did not see that as a positive because of the way she felt about herself in all other areas of her life. Through exploring further she was able to admit that whenever she would look at a task, whether it to be at home, or in the community, or at her church she would feel overwhelmed and then act on those feelings by shutting down and doing nothing. She also admitted that her parents would never expect her to follow through with things but only either complain and scold, or feel sorry for and allow her to continue in the withdrawn behavior.

Unfortunately, a number of patients have attributed their depression to either the father or mother confiding their problems in the child. When this occurs the child will feel depressed because of not being able to help the situation. Unfortunately for the child he or she will not be able to help because of not understanding adult problems, or where problems really belong. As a result, the individual, whether child or adult, will continually feel guilty and responsible for not only the parents but other people's well-being. In most cases these individuals are easily manipulated by those who are wanting their way because of the fear of being in trouble if they go against what the person wants. In all cases there is self-doubt because of never feeling like he or she has been able to do what this person thought needed to be done.

An individual in his late 30s who was married and had four children had been earlier hospitalized for severe depression and received electroconvulsive therapy, which he said helped for about 6 months. It was during this time that he was suicidal and the ECT helped. He admitted that he always felt like he was inadequate. As a result, he felt he was a failure. He was the youngest of three boys and raised by parents who were continually fighting with each other. The patient being youngest had no way to escape his parents fighting and said that on many occasions they would try to include him in the arguments. Even as a child and through adolescence he had difficulties with sleeping, concentration, and struggled with poor self-esteem and a tendency to avoid people at any cost.

Another example was an adult woman who was depressed most of her life. She revealed that her single mother used the patient as a confidant and sounding board. This left her continually frustrated and overwhelmed because of feeling that she was never able to fix mother. She brought this tendency into her adult life which interfered with her relationship with friends and family although she was an excellent employee because of her need to take care of everything herself. In her family she was easily manipulated by the children who naturally wanted their way and would get upset if mother said no. After the children would beg long enough her guilt to would take over and she would give them what they wanted. Fortunately, her husband was not this way. He was very supportive of her although he would give direction to the children.

One single mother of four children had to work long hours in the medical field to support her family. As a result she relied on the oldest daughter to take care of most family problems including facing bill collectors and trying to keep the younger children in line. The daughter would try to do what she needed to, but because of feeling overwhelmed and inadequate, would usually isolate to her room and read novels. In her adult life she was unable to maintain significant relationships with others. Each of her three husbands had emotional problems that caused the marriages to end in divorce. As an adult she felt that she had to control the other siblings' lives but was unsuccessful because they wanted to live independently. She finally withdrew from the entire family never to be involved with them again. To summarize, it is seriously harmful to the child when the parent confides his/her problems in the child, as has been illustrated in these examples.

If the parent is depressed it is likely that some, if not all, of the children will have symptoms of depression. Because of the parent being depressed he will not have the strength or the capability to meaningfully teach children. The mother who is depressed will unfortunately be so consumed by her own problems and worries and negative thinking that she will not have mental clarity to both recognize the children's problems and know how to help them. It is difficult, if not impossible for a parent to teach a child something that the parent herself is incapable of doing, or at least think she is incapable of doing. As an example, the parent cannot teach a child a foreign language if that parent cannot speak it himself. If the child is to learn a foreign language, she will have to go elsewhere to be taught. This is to say that even though a person might be raised by a depressed parent it does not mean that the child is doomed to depression throughout the rest of her life. If she seeks help she will hopefully get it through the type of therapy necessary to rise above the depression.

One particular mother who had seven children was in and out of depression for the better part of her adult life. She was raised in an abusive home and always felt that she was never good enough and brought this thinking into adulthood. The majority of the children began to show signs of depression starting in late childhood and early adolescence, and most of them continued being depressed as adults. For the most part mother was withdrawn from the family and would isolate in her bedroom and go on drinking binges to self-medicate so she could supposedly cope with the depression. In one instance while the family was either at work or in school she purchased several gallons of black paint and painted her entire room including the windows, the floor, and the ceiling with the black paint and sat in darkness for several weeks. The father did not know what to do to help the wife or the children and spent most of his time at work which required him to be away from home for the better part of each week. This also left the children to themselves and with no guidance to work through their own difficulties. As a result, the older children became depressed as they reached adolescence and early adulthood.

Another mother with three children left the two youngest children to their own devices and failed to give any direction. As a result, the boy was involved in social and political movements designed to destroy society. He said his goal in life was to be left entirely alone to do what he wanted. The girl became withdrawn, but also a people pleaser, and never felt like she was adequate. As a result, she lived a very solitary life. The oldest son married, moved away from the family, and overcame his tendencies to isolate.

The Spouse

Not only will the depressed adult have an effect on the children, but also a significant influence on the spouse. The typical reaction of the spouse is to try his or her hardest to help the other person get better. Many spouses of depressed patients admit to feeling guilty and overwhelmed because they cannot make the other person happy. They find themselves working diligently to do whatever they think is necessary, or whatever the person tells the spouse to do to help alleviate the depression, but nothing ever seems to work. This leaves the spouse frustrated and bewildered, and he could even become depressed himself because of feelings of inadequacy resulting from the interactions with the depressed spouse. When this goes on long enough, the spouse will typically withdraw from the patient and in some way make a better life for himself or herself.

This could be either by becoming more involved in work, a hobby, or another person. The other person could be either the children, friend, or someone of the opposite sex.

One father simply closed down his feelings toward his wife and the children. He took care of the family by both working and earning the money to support the family as well as taking over the role of mother by housecleaning, cooking, shopping, and so forth. But his resentments toward his wife grew to the point where he would just go through the motions at home and not interact with anyone. Unfortunately he did not receive help so he continued in this until the wife finally passed away. He then found a wife who was not depressed and actually awakened emotionally again and lived out the rest of his days very satisfied. Another husband said that he resented his wife because she was not contributing to the welfare of the family. She would spend most of her time sitting in the recliner, or in bed, and not interacting with him when he was home. She would only interact with the children as necessary until he returned home from work. When he was home she expected him to take care of the children while she stayed isolated. He was on the verge of divorcing her when he was referred to a therapist to help himself and the marriage. Instead of resenting her he began to expect her to function, and she found that she felt much better and they stayed together. It is hard for one adult to play either police or parent to another adult, especially when it is a spouse. As a result, most people are reluctant to see what they need to and become the enabler in the situation.

Helping the Depressed Person

In order to help the person who is depressed, one must consider the points made thus far in this chapter. To begin with, the person must be helped with, and stop the negative thinking. Most depressed people think that they cannot control their thinking. They assume that their thoughts are automatic and the individual has no say in what he or she thinks about. This is not correct. The depressed person needs to understand how to control negative thinking. This is accomplished by learning how to focus one's thoughts and attention on matters in a positive way. Positive thinking is not what most people think to be wishful thinking. An example of wishful thinking would be a salesman thinking positively that his phone is going to ring and it will be a customer or client who will mean a great income for the salesman. He sits behind his desk thinking positive thoughts, but the only time the phones will ring is when the landlord is looking for rent payment.

Another example is a therapist who would tell her patients to think positive such as "I'm going to be rich," or "I am wonderful and everything will be in order" with the expectation by the patient that this will come true. The reasoning behind this is that if one thinks positively enough she would set out and make the wish come true. The problem is that the second part of the equation is never addressed. Positive thinking is more along the line of "I can do this." In other words, when a person thinks that he or she can do, or accomplish a certain task and not dwell on the reasons why this cannot be accomplished, the hope is that the person will forge ahead with the determination to do what is intended. An illustration of this is the self-fulfilling prophecy, which purports that if one acts on his or her assumptions that is what the person will see as result of the effort (Madon, Willard, Guyll, & Scherr, 2011). An example is a young man thinking that the girl he met likes him because she smiled at him. He will act friendly toward her, and she will likely evoke a friendly response back. If on the other hand she did not smile, he might think that she was not interested in him and would either treat her rudely or ignore her altogether.

Most depressed people are convinced that they cannot accomplish what they want to, or that they are not good enough. And as a result will not take the risk and by not risking will not accomplish what needs to be taken care of. Then the negative thinking will be reinforced by the behavior. If an adult was told her entire life by her parents that she was overweight and unattractive and nobody would want to be her friend, she would, during childhood and adolescence, likely believe this. She would most likely never risk to establish friendships and ever be close in her relationships. To help the patient overcome this negative thinking a therapist needs to teach the person how to think positively. A person's attention can only focus on one thing at a time. If the individual is dwelling on depressive thoughts this will cause the disorder to increase. If on the other hand the person is taught how to think positively success will very likely be achieved. Thinking positively means looking at the task at hand with a "can do" attitude. The patient has to be taught to keep his focus on what he's going to accomplish and what he needs to do, and when the negative thoughts enter his mind he must dismiss them by again focusing on the task at hand and how to work things through.

As an example, one young man thought that he would never be able to do well at his job and as a result would not risk enough to be promoted. He kept thinking to himself that nothing he did would work and that nobody was on his side. As a result he never tried to establish a friendship with anyone, nor did he attempt to improve his work performance. After seeking therapy he learned to focus his attention on what he needed to do and as he learned this by practicing to focus attention on what he could do, he became more confident in himself and in his ability to do what was needed. As a result, he did exactly what was needed to accomplish his goals at work and was eventually recognized for his efforts and rewarded accordingly.

If the depressed patient is either married or living with family, possibly as a young adult, and does not make an attempt to change, the family members can step in and help. If the family members are strong enough emotionally, they can begin to expect the patient to get up, quit dwelling on the negative, and start functioning in the real world. In some instances a couple may come for counseling regarding the marriage, and the therapist may find that one of the two is depressed. In this case the therapist can help the spouse who is not depressed understand what causes depression and be helped to gather the strength necessary to insist that the other person begin to change the thinking and behavior. Another family member, whether a parent or spouse, may fear setting limits for the depressed person thinking that some other negative outcome may come about. As long as the person acts on these feelings, he or she will be an enabler. It is important that this individual understands that by feeling sorry or fearful of saying anything wrong that individual is actually making the problem worse.

In one instance the parents began to insist that their 18-year-old daughter stop isolating in her bedroom. She would spend hours in her bedroom listening to depressing music and dwelling on how bad the world was and how her family did not understand her. When the parents began to insist that she not go to the bedroom, but be a part of the family, she would get upset and tell them that they did not understand, they did not love her, they were bad parents, and they were just trying to make her worse. They wanted to back off and not cause further distress with her by upsetting her. They persisted in expecting her to be a part of the family and not go to the bedroom. It took close to a month for her to participate without complaining and, over time, she admitted that she felt better being with the family and not dwelling on the negatives that had her so depressed earlier. She also admitted that she thought that because she was a teenager she was supposed to be depressed and in a dark place. She realized that the dark places were not fun, and it was truly hurting her.

Bipolar Disorder

Bipolar disorder is indicated by extreme changes in one's mood from depression to euphoria. Bipolar means two poles, or two different extremes, and in this case the jump from depression to mania, and after a certain period of time back into depression. It is difficult for family members or friends to come close to someone who is always changing moods. A lady in her late 30s was married and had three young children.

Several times during each year she would go into a manic phase where she would have limitless energy and great ideas about being the perfect mother and wife. She would typically start her manic phase by staying up all night while the family was sleeping and bake cakes, cookies, and pies, and when the family would wake up in the morning they would see all this in the kitchen and, unlike most, they were not delighted. They were taken aback and very unsettled. They knew mother was going off again on a manic episode and it frightened them. This was the beginning. She would then do things like try to redecorate the home by buying new drapes, maybe changing the floor coverings, painting, and rearranging furniture. The results were an enormous credit card bill and after several days of this and no sleep she would go with the friends at night to the bars and go dancing. This was great fun several nights, but eventually she would run out of energy and reality would set in. She would also realize that her family was still the same with no changes and she would then, because of these realizations, go into a deep depression.

A man in his middle 50s was diagnosed bipolar, but his symptoms were not grandiose ideas and staying up all night for weeks at a time, but instead would become angry with everyone in his family. This anger would go on for weeks, and his wife would finally get to the point of wanting to divorce him because of the way he treated her and the children. When he would finally settle down, it would become clear to him that he had hurt his wife and children emotionally and then would start thinking to himself that he was a terrible father and very worthless husband.

In both of these cases the family situation wherein they grew up, was explored and what was reported was enlightening. The mother said that she was raised by a single parent who was fearful and anxious and indicated this by always trying to control her. She said that she tried diligently for most of her life to prove to her mother that she was not a terrible person. The baking would start when she started thinking to herself, "I know what to do now to be that perfect mother and wife." Then the excited, euphoric feelings would take over and she would go headlong into a manic phase. The depression would come when she would realize that she was "just like my mother said, I'm no good and I will never be a worthwhile person."

The man, on the other hand, was raised by a father who was extremely demanding and would get angry when this person, as a teenager or child, would not do things the way father wanted him to do. This frightened him, and he grew up thinking that he was always going to be in trouble. Then as an adult he would get angry with his family when he would think that they were not respecting him and would go into a manic phase by also thinking to himself that they had to be perfect so that he would not be in trouble. If they didn't cooperate when he thought they should, he would become extremely angry with them, which was not really anger but fear.

In these cases, as well as many others, people with a bipolar disorder will enter into the manic phase when they are thinking to themselves that they finally have the answer to the problem they are dealing with, such as poor self-esteem. When they get this thought that they can become perfect, they become excited and overzealous in trying to work the problem through so they can get in the sense of well-being and acceptance. Unfortunately, when their success is not realized, they fall into a deep depression realizing they are not what they hoped to be through the heroic measures they were taking. But reality would set in and they could see that they simply made the situation worse.

In the case of the lady, the realization that she made grave mistakes in the manic phase simply reinforced the negative thinking she had throughout her life. The man on the other hand continued to have low self-esteem for two reasons. One because he was never, in his mind, as good as his father expected him to be. Number two, because his wife and family were very disappointed in him and refused to relate to him because of his unpredictability. Again, the point to remember here is that this thinking is learned and, if not treated, will continue. Treatment would likely include medications that would be a mood stabilizer so the patient could be worked with as well as psychotherapy. Without therapy, the patient will revert back to the same problems if and when he or she stops taking the medication.

Children and Depression

Children, like adults, begin episodes of depression when they are caught up in negative thinking. One 10-year-old boy finally admitted while in therapy that he always hated himself because he thought he was not as good as his older siblings. He continually tried to prove that he was as good as they were, but he felt he was never successful. Even though children experience the negative thinking and feelings that result in poor self-esteem, they will often show symptoms of depression different from adults. Because they don't feel right about things, they may act moody and even upset and tearful. Among children, though, isolation is still a common symptom and again the reason is because of poor self-esteem. Other children may complain of physical discomfort typically related to the stomach or headaches. Unfortunately, when children show signs of depression the symptoms are often misunderstood, and the children are scolded or chastised because the parents think that the child is either being disobedient or disrespectful. When this occurs the feelings of depression are deepened because of the child feeling like he or she is at fault for something of which they are innocent.

One of the contributing factors in childhood depression comes back to egocentric thinking (Santrock, 2008). As explained earlier, egocentric thinking carries the theme of the child feeling like whatever happens around him or her, or however he or she is treated by others is a reflection of that child's lack of worth. Young children have not learned that others' behavior is a reflection of that person, not the child. This then leads to the double bind. Here the child is thinking that because something is his fault he must do something to fix the problem. The negative outcome from this double bind (Bateson, Jackson, Haley, & Weakland, 1956) is thinking that "if I can do things perfectly, or fix a problem, I will not be in trouble." When the child discovers that things have not changed, the negative thinking comes back and the child assumes that because things don't change it is his fault, which then creates guilt and more self-doubt.

One young man was depressed because he could never measure up to the expectations of his stepfather. His stepfather was always critical of him and his siblings, and he thought that if he could be perfect his stepfather would settle down and not be angry. The young man was helped to understand that his father treated the family, especially the children, as he did because he was a fearful person. The father's mother was continually telling him that his wife and her children were going to steal all of his money, and that they would take advantage of him every time they could. This made him anxious and on guard, which came across as being critical. The boy was given enough insight to understand that the stepfather's behavior was not the boy's fault, and as a result he relaxed and was able to go about his daily living without the fear of his stepfather's disapproval. He was free from the worry of being in, or getting into, trouble. He was also better able to be cooperative in the family because he was not stressed over what the stepfather may do. He was helpful and even willing to cooperate with the stepfather because he was not feeling threatened by him. This two-part process of depression resulting from egocentric thinking and the double bind continually place the child in a no-win situation. The longer this continues the more entrenched these thoughts and feelings become.

When a child is depressed, it is easy for the parents to misinterpret the symptoms. If the parents know that their daughter is depressed, they might feel sorry for her. If this is the case, they will coddle and protect her because of concern for her well-being and the fear of making her feel worse by pushing too hard. If this is the parent's reaction to their depressed daughter, the daughter will be handicapped further because of thinking that she is either incapable of doing things on her own, or view this as an open door to manipulation. In either case the learning that comes from this is "I don't have to do what others are requested to do." Other parents may become impatient with the depressed child and instead of helping the child they deepen the problem by pushing too hard and too quickly, especially if there is no consideration for teaching. In such circumstances, the parents' pushing will cause further doubts because of the child not accomplishing what is expected, resulting in depression. This then compounds the problems significantly. It is overwhelming to a child to be told in a demanding or scolding voice to do something that she feels she's unable to do.

Other depressed children may be viewed by their parents as being obstinate. In this case, mom and dad will likely become punitive or vindictive toward the child in their attempt to stop the child's depressed behavior. Again this will create doubts in the child's mind. On the other hand, some parents may view this supposed obstinate behavior as something they cannot control and give up and stop trying to help the child. If parents can clearly understand the child's mental state and not act on the aforementioned emotions and thoughts that are destructive, they will likely be in a position to help the child.

Like with any other disorder when a child becomes depressed the situation can very easily affect the functioning of the family. Parents in this situation will likely spend most of their time and effort in dealing with the depressed child, which will leave the other children to take care of themselves. One child stated very emphatically that he felt that he was unwanted in the family because nobody ever interacted with him. If they did, it was only when the child did something wrong and would argue or stay out of the way. In another case the parents of a depressed child noticed that when the child got better, the other children become worse in their behavior, or so they thought. It did not take long for them to realize that because of their time and attention focused on the depressed child the other children were left alone. Because of the lack of parental direction, the children had to make their own way which led to behavioral problems. In many cases, the depressed child will also learn that by being in that state he will get whatever he wants and can feel entitled and that he is more special than the other children. Also because of the feeling of urgency and need to take care of the depressed child some parents may feel more obligated to help the child, which will put their effort into the child at the expense of the rest of the family. It is not uncommon for a married couple to divorce because of one feeling neglected by the other. This can also disrupt communication because of either being unavailable, or unwilling to communicate with the other spouse. It's easy for the parents to argue with each other because of disagreements regarding how to help the child.

Helping the Child

Like any other problem, the parents must look at helping the child by teaching correct behavior. As mentioned, depressed children will usually withdraw from everyone else and by so doing will have too much time to think about the negatives in his or her life. The longer the child isolates the more comfortable a child becomes in that situation. Parents will usually say that they know the child should not isolate. They will also admit that they frequently ask the child to come and participate with the family but will not follow through with this request when the child refuses. When the parents stop acting on their sorry feelings for the child, or their frustration and helplessness, they can then begin to expect the child to come and function like everyone else in the family. In the beginning the child will protest because it is to uncomfortable, or because he is not interested, but when the parents can lovingly and firmly insist that the child come out and engage in the family, the child will eventually obey the requests. This will also occur when a child realizes the parents are not going to rescind the request. Then when the child comes to be part of the family the parents must expect the child to interact and not sit in the corner or quietly exist in the presence of everyone else. In all cases when helping the child to overcome depression, it is important to remember that the negative thinking entertained by the child is at the root of the depression.

In order for the child to change his negative view of himself he must above all else learn to focus on the positive, or "I can do this," type of thinking as well as change the behavior. Positive thinking is not wishful thinking, or telling oneself something positive and it will happen. That never works. A depressed child will say either he can't do what is requested of him or he doesn't want to or it is too hard. The positive thinking, on the other hand, is understanding that even though the task may be difficult it can be accomplished. For example, a 12-year-old girl felt poorly about herself because she could not ride a bicycle. Her parents said that they had tried to help on many occasions and she would go out with the determination to ride the bike, but she would become frightened and act on the fearful feelings and go back into the house. Here the negative thinking was "I can't do this," which would become reinforced when she would withdraw from the bicycle. Her parents were afraid to push her thinking, and that by doing so, she would become worse. Thus, they would leave her alone and sadly watch her become more doubtful of herself. They learned through therapy that their reasoning was actually harmful for the daughter. They admitted that they knew she could ride the bicycle but were afraid that she would not believe it, and thus would never try. They realized they had to say to themselves that she can ride the bicycle, and even though she didn't think she could, they knew this was possible. So after several sessions of therapy the parents proudly reported that their daughter was riding her bicycle. They said they would not allow her to dwell on the negative regarding the bicycle. The next step was to insist that she change her behavior. This meant that they had to be strong enough to insist that she ride the bike with them helping her in the beginning and not allow her to act on her frightened emotions and feelings. They said she struggled for about 30 minutes, but then realized that she had to do what they were asking of her and ultimately started peddling the bicycle with determination and found she could ride the bike without being hurt.

If parents fail to help the child change the behavior, the child will continue into depression. In order to change the behavior the parents must first understand clearly that the child is capable of doing what they expect. Of course, it is not reasonable to expect a child to do something she is physically unable to do. On the other hand, expecting the child to function in a certain manner even though she can't is the first step in teaching. To review the principles of teaching behavior one must first be sure of what is to be taught and that the child can learn. And then let the child know what is expected either by showing or by telling, and then holding the child accountable to that standard expected and correcting mistakes when made until the child is able to do what is required consistently and without mistake. Once the child realizes that he can do what he thought he couldn't, his confidence will increase, and over time he will most likely learn that this perseverance applies to everything he will face in life.

Chapter 7—Worksheet

1. Of all the symptoms of depression which is the root of the problem?

2. What are some of the problems that can negatively affect the family?

3. What type of parenting might bring about bipolar disorder in a person?

Chapter 8
The Anxious Person and the Family

Fabrik Bilder / Shutterstock.com

Anxiety is a common problem in western society and is experienced by adults as well as adolescents and children. It is, of course, a problem that is distressful and significantly uncomfortable for the anxious individual. Like the other disorders, anxiety is learned, and this learning starts in the family, so in most cases the anxious patient was raised by an anxious parent. If the patterns are developed and established early in one's life, they will continue throughout the person's life and will not only affect him or her, but likely all significant people in that individual's life. Anxiety is most apparent in the family with the effect on the spouse and the children. This influence comes as a result of the anxious person verbalizing his negative feelings and thoughts or by simply acting anxious and worried. On the other hand, an anxious child can cause family members to become anxious also if they are not emotionally stable. Regardless of how anxiety is learned, as long as the individual can learn, he or she can change. It is important to also understand how the individual has become anxious, and how the problem was learned, especially if one is a therapist and helps people with this disorder.

Anxiety, like the mood disorders, starts in one's thinking. As with the mood disorders, the person's thinking will bring about one's emotional state and affect one's self-esteem. The thinking and the emotional state together typically have a profound effect on the person's behavior. A news reporter was supposed to do a feature on an expansion bridge. She had to go to the top of one of the two towers. When she stepped out of the elevator onto the platform at the top of the tower, she panicked and would not take a step further but retreated immediately back into the elevator. The fear of heights is not uncommon, and this fear in many instances is irrational because the person's thoughts of falling become the main focus and the emotions set in. The person will act on the fear by retreating from the perceived threat to their well-being. How this thinking manifests itself, and how it is learned will now be considered.

An anxious person is usually caught up in "what-if" thinking, and will typically worry about matters that are unimportant or possibly even nonexistent. This what-if thinking can result from the family environment, life's experiences, or the environment in general. A young mother of two children continually worried about possible problems and admitted that she was always thinking "what if." As her childhood was explored she said that her father was a good man but was continually consumed by worry. If they went on a vacation he would verbalize worries about something happening to the car or not having enough money to complete the trip and so on. At home he was always worried about the bills or something tragic happening to the family. He frequently complained about work and felt as though people did not appreciate him which in his mind could lead to him losing his job. During therapy this young mother discovered how she learned the anxious thinking. She then learned to stop and focus on more positive situations and a healthy, positive future.

If an individual has lived in a dangerous environment this can also bring about anxiety. Imagine living in a country engaged in war. People who live in such circumstances are always on guard and find themselves feeling hypervigilant due to fear of either harm or loss of life. A person might come from a neighborhood where violence such as shootings or robberies are a frequent occurrence. The dangerous environment can also be in the home where abuse is always present. Abuse victims are commonly anxious people because in most cases the victim does not know why the other person is angry. There are a number of experiences people can go through in one's life that will cause anxiety. These include trauma, abuse, frequent disappointments and failures, as well as conflicts at home, work, or with friends.

Generalized Anxiety and the Family

The most common type of anxiety disorder among adults is generalized anxiety. Typically, this individual will be consumed by excessive worry and will spend the greater portion of the day fretting over something (DSM 5). When asked about the worries she will usually admit that she knows the worry is out of control but can't help it. This is the result of difficulties controlling one's thoughts, because of never learning how to manage such negative thinking. An example of this outcome is a man who was raised in a rather inconsistent environment, and as a result became anxious as a child and brought this into his adult life. He seemed to function well but his anxious feelings would take over at times and he would become upset at his fellow employees on occasion. In general, though, the greatest effect was on his marriage and his children. Because of being fearful he was critical and demanding of his wife and children because of thinking everything had to be perfect. If he saw a mistake he would become upset which would in turn cause his wife to become hurt and the children to fear his disapproval. Even though he and his wife stayed married she often said that she wished she had never married him because of his poor behavior.

A single mother with three children is continually worrying about her health, her future, her children's welfare, and the general state of the world. After divorcing her husband she and her children moved in with her parents, which was not a wise decision on her part. Her father was emotionally shut down and had no involvement with the family. The mother on the other hand ran the family and was extremely critical of all that her daughter and the three children did. As a result, the patient was constantly worried about something going wrong and admitted that she worried more than she should but could not help it. In learning about her childhood it became obvious that her anxiety was learned from her anxious mother. Throughout her life she felt that she could never measure up to her mother's or anyone else's expectations. At work she constantly feared making a mistake and being fired in spite of an excellent work ethic that she had developed. Because of her worries about her children she was afraid to parent fearing that she would make a mistake and cause further difficulties for them.

If the person is consumed by negative thinking and worries, it will be seen in the behavior of the family. Usually family members will feel that they can never live up to the parent's expectations which will cause them to either withdraw or become anxious and always try to please the parent. Anxious people typically have a difficult time at work because they are either afraid to to take a risk and go beyond the bare minimum required for the job, or if in a management position will withdraw or become extremely controlling. In either case it will leave the other employees unsure of their standing in their work performance and status. In social settings most anxious people will be quiet and reserved and whenever possible avoid such circumstances because of their fears.

The Anxious Person and the Family

It is important to understand in depth how the anxious adult will affect the family. Instead of considering the family as a whole, first the effects on the spouse will be explored and then the effects on the children. In most cases, the spouse will attempt to do everything possible to help the anxious person feel better. This is because the anxious person expressing her negative thinking will often cause the spouse to think that it is up to him to make the environment, or the situation, better so the anxious person will calm down. The spouse might try to be more attentive to the person, or help more at home and with the family or even try to earn more money. Unfortunately, this puts the spouse in a double bind because no matter what the spouse does the anxious person does not change. This double bind is a result of egocentric thinking, meaning that if the spouse can get the right answer the other person will feel better. Because this never works the spouse will eventually give up trying to help. In this situation the spouse does not understand that the anxious person is that way because of him, not because of the spouse. The anxious person acts on his negative thinking, which was likely learned in childhood, and no matter what the spouse does to make things better the person will still stay in an anxious state. If this difficulty goes on long enough it will erode the foundation of the marriage. It is exhausting to try to make the other person better with no success. A married man's wife was very anxious and as a result she would not allow him to participate in chores around the house. He was only allowed to go to work and come home and be waited on. This was because his wife thought that she could do better job of taking care of family matters. After committing adultery he admitted that he felt as though his wife did not care about him because she was always busy. Because of her preoccupation with the household and family matters she neglected her husband. What he did was inexcusable, but it illustrates the point that an anxious adult can, and will, have a negative effect on the spouse. A woman who was married for over 40 years admitted that she did not love her husband because he was overbearing and controlling, as well as critical of whatever she and the children did. Even though she remained married to him she did not have an emotional connection and they lived as roommates rather than husband and wife.

In some instances, the individual who is married to an anxious person will, over time, develop a negative self-esteem. One example is a young couple who was married for about 7 years when the wife became depressed. In therapy she revealed that she had never felt worthless in her life until she was married because her husband was always criticizing her efforts whether it was her cooking, housekeeping, or parenting. The harder she tried to do things the way he wanted them, the more upset he became, so over time her self-esteem diminished to feeling as though she was a complete failure.

Another instance is an older couple and at the age of retirement the husband went on his own to purchase land and decide on a home to build without telling her. She was in and out of psychiatrist's offices and therapy sessions for years. Her husband was a perfectionist and did not trust her judgment and felt he had to do everything on his own. His assumptions were incorrect, but to him they were reality and he acted accordingly. He would tell her what clothes to wear, he made major purchases without her input, and he generally closed out of his life. Unfortunately the root of the problem, an anxious husband who was impossible to please, caused her to doubt herself, and for years she suffered from depression. No medication she took helped, and no training in communication skills helped either. In another marriage the wife was anxious person and this was indicated by her having to control everything that dealt with family. Her husband said that she decided on the vacations for the family, would determine the budget, housecleaning chores as well as yard responsibilities, and who got to go where and when. Even though it was hard for her husband to admit it, he was showing signs of depression including negative thinking and doubt and a strong desire to isolate.

The Anxious Parent and the Children

When children are maturing, they need to look somewhere for approval. In most cases this begins with the parents. Children are keenly attuned to their parent's actions and what they say and how they say it. Egocentric thinking. An example would be a parent who is constantly in a bad mood. The child may misinterpret the parent's mood as her fault and become anxious because of not knowing where she stands with the parent. Also that the child can never come up with the right behavior or answer to make the parent feel better, which is the same situation with the spouse as has been discussed. When the child is in this position and is anxious she will continue to try to fix things not understanding that the parent's behavior is not a reflection of the child, but of the parent. Another example can be a parent who is very reserved and says little to the child or anyone else in the family. This too can make the child anxious, and egocentric thinking here would cause the child to again think what's wrong with me that mom or dad won't talk to me or won't pay attention to me.

A young 3-year-old boy would become anxious when a particular couple who are friends of the family would come to visit. This began to be manifested when the baby brother was born. Until this time the older brother was the center of the couple's attention when they came to visit. After the birth of the baby brother, their attention was diverted to him and the older boy was ignored for the most part. They complained about the older boy acting strange, running around, trying to sit on their laps, try to get them to do things with him and so forth. The mother reported that she could see clearly why her son was acting this way. He felt ignored by the couple and as a result did not know what to do to get their attention. The mother further stated that she decided prior to the couple's arrival to visit that when they asked why the older boy acted as he did she was going to tell them the reason, even if it meant their friendship. When the couple arrived the older boy started acting out of control again, and they asked why and the mother explained the problem. They felt bad and said they would not do that anymore and began to pay more attention to the older boy but not neglect the baby. The older boy settled down rather quickly.

Besides a parent being withdrawn or difficult to please, is the absent parent. When the parent is removed from the home for prolonged periods of time and returns home the children will likely show anxiety because to them this person is either a stranger, or someone with whom they are not familiar. As with the other examples when the child is not clear where he fits and where he stands the anxious behavior will likely become apparent.

An anxious parent can also contribute to the child's anxiety by continually worrying and verbalizing those worries to the family. One particular elderly lady was anxious all of her life and this had an effect on her oldest daughter who was seen as a patient. The patient reported that her mother continually worried about something going wrong either at home, in the community, or at church. As she verbalized these anxieties to the family her oldest daughter paid particular attention to what her mother was saying and felt that something terrible was going to happen. As a result, she was constantly trying to foresee possible problems. She was hypervigilant and said that she could never feel settled or secure. As a result she had difficulties with sleep, as well as functioning in everyday life. Unfortunately for her the behavior almost destroyed her marriage because she was fearful of going places and doing things thinking that something negative was going to occur.

A young mother of three children ages 5, 3, and 6 months presented with anxiety. She was always fearful of her children getting hurt. She openly stated in the beginning of therapy that her mother had been talking to her over the past 5 to 6 years about this patient being ritualistically abused by the grandmother and step grandfather. The young lady said that she had no recollection of these incidents her mother accused the grandparents of doing. She was not completely convinced it was true, but had no way to repudiate what mother was saying. Not only was she afraid of her children being hurt but was convinced that she could trust no one except her husband, and at that only in certain areas. In therapy she learned to not dwell on frightening thoughts and not act on them. She began to relax with her children and husband. Communication improved and her sense of safety increased significantly. About one year after therapy ceased she called the therapist to inform him of her progress. She told him that she found out from her older siblings and her younger brother who was allegedly also abused in the same manner as her that these abuses never took place. She was unable in the beginning of therapy to see how her mother, who had been anxious all her life, and expressed her anxiety as terrible things happening to her children. A side note is that she was asked how she would have responded if she were challenged during therapy regarding the veracity of her report? Her reply was that she probably would have stopped coming for therapy because of feeling like she was not believed. Her older sisters made it clear to her that mother had worried about terrible things happening to the children as far back as they could remember.

Another case was a middle-aged woman who was extremely anxious and fearful that she would never measure up. She was excellent at whatever she did and was competent at work and at home. Her problem was that she never felt settled and always thought that there was something more she had to be doing. She opened up in therapy, and it became apparent to her and the therapist that her father was the individual who planted the seeds of insecurity and anxiety. He was worried about what others thought of him and as a result always pushed his wife and children to work so they could accomplish all that he thought was expected. One problem was he never felt like anything was good enough, which added to his anxiety and then got passed on to the children. Besides the patient being anxious, she was always fearful of missing something and not having things right. One brother withdrew from the family and suffered from self-doubt most of his life. One sister felt inadequate in marriage and settled for someone who was less than ideal and two other siblings chose never to marry.

A young adult was a fearful child and afraid of risking. As a result, he took jobs that were less than what he was capable of performing. He was also afraid of traveling so never went very far from home. He stated that is father was continually driving the children and his wife to do everything perfectly, but nothing was ever to his liking. The youngest child in this family was most negatively affected by this; she always thought her father was angry at her because he was yelling and very abusive in his language towards her and the rest of the family. As a result this person was so fearful and anxious about things going wrong as an adult that she was mercilessly critical of her spouse and their children. This anxious behavior was so out of the ordinary that her husband and children had nothing to do with her. Because she saw her father get things taken care of by yelling and cursing, she took on the same behavior, which drove her family away. It was revealed that the father had been indulged in his entire childhood and into adolescence. Ultimately he became insecure and fearful of other people disapproving of him. While growing up his mother would let him have whatever he wanted and, even if they could not afford it, his mother would coerce the father into giving in. Most likely if the father had not been involved in getting his way all the time as a child and adolescent, he would have learned self-control, which would have eliminated most conflict and anxiety.

The Anxious Child and the Family

The anxious child will likely have a negative effect on the family. One couple sought help for their 9-year-old boy who was always worried about school and home. He acted out his anxiety by constantly verbalizing his worries to his parents and never acting settled. At school he had a hard time attending to his work because of constantly fearing being trouble. In this case mother and father were not anxious people in most situations, but when interacting with their son they felt unsure about the child's behavior and why he was acting the way he was. They would become unsettled and unsure of what to do when the child acted out his anxieties. This had a rather synergistic effect meaning that the child would become anxious, mom and dad would then become anxious, and that would in turn leave the child in a far less stable state by not knowing what mom and dad were really expecting.

Children have all sorts of fears, which may include being outside, riding a bicycle, getting hurt in sports, and even monsters. A number of anxious children will fear such things as monsters, and the parents typically feed into this fear even though they don't mean to. A 9-year-old girl was afraid of monsters so her parents would go into the room with her every evening and look in the closet, behind the chest of drawers, and so forth to assure her that there were no monsters. They would even take a spray bottle filled with water into her room and spray around the room telling her that it was monster spray. This might sound rather cute for the parents but unfortunately this type of treatment only increases the child's fears. Most children at some time in their early life are afraid of going to bed at night. When the child becomes fearful it usually concerns mom and dad so they in turn try to console the child, but by so doing increase fear by talking about it in an anxious voice that may cause a child to think something is truly wrong. In these cases, one parent may react differently than the other parent, which may result in conflict in the marriage and even negatively affect the other children. One couple sought marital therapy because of arguing about their anxious daughter. He wanted the girl to face her fears and mother feared that doing so would increase the daughter's fears. She said she knew her husband was right but that her fears overrode her commonsense.

It must be remembered that when a child is allowed to act on fears or anxious feelings those feelings and fears become reinforced. The prime example of this is the young boy who was afraid of water and swimming. His parents did not want him to feel upset so they left him alone and did not insist that he learn to swim. He became an adult who did not know how to swim and experienced significant embarrassment and shame because of this inability and his fear. He was also afraid of being away from home for too long, meaning several days. As a young man in Boy Scouts he would often avoid prolonged scouting trips including the annual week-long camping trip each year. He also experienced some health problems, which caused him to avoid anything he thought would make him ill, and because of his mother being fearful of him getting worse, she would allow him to act on his fears. Through his adolescence and into his early adulthood his socializing was very limited outside of his parents and immediate family. When acting on these feelings, the individual gained a sense of relief because of not having to face what he was afraid of. Father finally convinced mother to let go and allow their son to work through his fears. He did so, married, moved away from his parents, and began to establish a new life.

Other Anxiety Disorders

A married woman with one teenage child was working at a gas station and convenience store on a major highway in California. One afternoon a customer came in to pay for the gas and buy some food. For whatever reason the customer was in a bad mood. He became curt and upset with this lady. This bothered her and she tried to forget it, but within an hour this occurred again with another customer which frightened her. After work she went home and had a difficult time sleeping all night because of her fear of people being angry with her. She got up in the morning and went back to work, but because of her dwelling on what had happened the day before, she was only able to last for about two hours and then went home and never returned to work. She and her husband and their teenage son lived in a two-bedroom mobile home in the small mobile home park. There she stayed without setting foot outside for the next 3 years. In the beginning she tried to visit a psychiatrist, but after several attempts was so frightened she quit and never tried to go again. This fear became so overwhelming to her that if her husband was not there she would panic and become so distressed she would not be able to do much of anything. As a result, not only was she put on disability from the state, but he was too for the next 3 years. If they needed groceries their son would go to the store, or they would get friends to buy things for them. For the first of those 3 years she spent most of her time in her small bedroom consumed by fears of people being angry with her. She eventually sought help, and the therapist worked with her over the phone because he did not make house calls and she was unwilling to go to his office. She admitted that she was raised by a demanding and difficult-to-please mother. She was responsible for her younger brother who, as an adolescent, was always in trouble with the law, and as a result she felt responsible for his behavior and him getting in trouble. She learned early in life to fear people being angry with her, and this fear developed over the years and was manifested as panic attacks with Agoraphobia. As she received insight into her thinking, she was able to understand how her thought process affected her mood and behavior. She also learned to not fear other people's behaviors because they were not a reflection of her personally but of something with them. The result was her eventual willingness to risk going outside. She knew that a neighbor woman across the way would probably say derogatory things to her so she was prepared, and when she went outside and this occurred, she understood this was the other person's problem and not hers. After a period of time she had no worries about going outside or out into the community. One big obstacle was traveling in the car which she eventually became able to do. Finally she wanted her husband to return to work. His profession was a long-distance truck driver, and she wanted to travel with him.

A 34-year-old male was self-employed as a diamond salesman and was marginally successful at his work. One late afternoon on his return trip on a major highway he began to think to himself that something terrible could happen such as being robbed or getting in an accident. After thinking about this long enough he became so frightened that he could not drive and had to pull off to the side of the road to regain his composure. He attempted to drive again, but after approximately 10 to 15 minutes had to pull off again and again. This reoccurred throughout the rest of his trip home which took approximately 13 hours for what would normally be about 7 hours. During therapy he admitted that he was raised by an anxious mother who was always afraid of terrible things happening to the family, and especially to him. He stated that he had always been somewhat unsure of himself and fearful about things happening, but for the better part of his life was able to ignore this and continue on with what he needed to accomplish. On this occasion, though, he was unable to change his thinking and experienced significant panic attacks. He sought help because he had to make another long distance trip about 4 hours for a sale and did not want to drive alone but was also unable find anyone to go with him and be his driver. He knew he had to go alone which frightened him, so he sought help to overcome his fear. He was helped to understand his thinking and learn how to keep his thoughts were they belonged and not wander into areas that would be frightening. He made the trip alone and later reported that even though he felt anxious at times he was able to keep his thinking focused on the road, the radio, and the scenery.

A middle-aged woman loved to drive about 50 miles to San Francisco, California. However, her trip would take approximately 3 hours when normally it should take about 45 minutes to an hour. The road she took was north on the peninsula, on the El Camino Real, which had stoplights at about every other block for 50 miles. She admitted that she was afraid of driving on highways but did not know why except that she felt extremely uncomfortable. She learned to keep her thoughts were they belonged and not worry about potential problems. One day she reported that she drove to San Francisco on one of the major highways and had no problems with the trip.

Another lady was afraid of making left-handed turns and as a result had to make three right-handed turns around the block to eventually come to the intersection that she would otherwise have to turn left on. She decided one day to not act on those fears and to take a risk making a left-handed turn. She was successful and realized her fears were unwarranted.

Obsessive-compulsive behavior is also an anxiety disorder. A 13-year-old girl struggled with obsessions and compulsions. Her parents sought help when she was unwilling to go to bed at night and sleep between the sheets and under the covers unless she first washed her hair. The parents said that they often read books together as a family; on one occasion, they read about a Chinese family during late 1800s who struggled economically and unfortunately had head lice. This caused the young girl to dwell on the possibility for having head lice so would not sleep in the bed without washing her hair. Her parents knew this was irrational but were afraid to insist that she not act on her fear thinking that it might make the situation worse. They did say that she would go to sleep in her sleeping bag on top of the bed at night if she could not wash her hair. If she were thinking rationally, she would also realize this was likely to infect the bed if she did indeed have lice. The parents became sure enough of themselves to eventually insist that she go to bed without washing her hair to discover that there were no problems with lice. The parents did say that she had other problems also with obsessing and acting on those obsessions and that they were able to help her overcome them. In this case both parents were concerned about their daughter, but when explored further mother admitted she was an anxious person. Because of this she felt helpless in helping her daughter put her fears aside. Father on the other hand was sure of himself and knew what to do to help their daughter, but he did not want to go against what his wife was struggling with for fear of making the matter worse. The result was the parents feeling frustrated and helpless and the daughter remaining in her fears until the received help.

A middle-aged single woman would not go to bed at night until she removed a large number of hairpins from her hair, which held her long hair up. These pins had to be removed in a specific order and laid out on top of the bureau in a specific order. If she was unable to do this, she became very uncomfortable and put the pins back in her hair and started over again. She never sought help, likely because it did not cause enough stress in her life to want to change. Her family history revealed that most of her siblings were anxious and so was her father who acted controlling most of the time. Her brother was an alcoholic and was married twice. It was revealed that his second marriage was in the process of being terminated because of his verbal and, at times, physical abuse. He was killed in an auto accident before the divorce was finalized. It was apparent that the children carried the need to control matters for their emotional safety. As a reminder, in all of these instances, when the individual was either allowed to or chose to act on their emotions and feelings the problem became more entrenched because of the thinking being reinforced. Only when help was sought did the youngest girl learn to manage her thinking, which helped her change her life for the better.

A number of individuals struggle with traumatic events in their lives, which results in posttraumatic stress disorder. And man in his mid-30s was employed as a truck driver to haul certain materials from one manufacturing plant to another. One morning while traveling from one plant to another he noticed a pickup truck from the opposite direction slowly veering into his lane of traffic. He said that there was another truck in front of him which managed to avoid a collision by speeding up. Unfortunately, though this individual was not so fortunate. He tried everything he could to avoid the accident, and even veered off the road into the ditch, but the driver of the pickup truck did not correct the steering and ran head on into the truck and the driver of the pickup truck was killed immediately. In therapy the surviving truck driver said openly that his biggest fear driving trucks was being involved in an accident and someone being killed. When this happened it was so traumatic to him that he decided he would never drive a truck again. He went to the funeral and was treated warmly by the other person's family, and no animosity was felt. He kept in touch with the widow on occasion and she was always kind and polite, which helped him feel somewhat better. He eventually overcame the PTSD because his wife was so upset that she threatened to divorce him if he did not get back to work. In therapy he learned to manage his negative thinking by first returning to the scene of the accident and getting out of the car and walking around the area. He then decided to go back to the truck yard and at least do office work and clean up around the facility. After about one week of working he saw the truck he drove when the accident occurred and it caused such stress that he immediately left and went home. He knew he had to return, and did, but not without fear. He said he knew he had to overcome the problem so he went to the truck and touched it. Later he returned and opened the door and after about 30 minutes of trembling and sweating he climbed into it and sat there for about 15 minutes. The next day he went through the same ritual, but this time he turned the engine on and eventually drove it around the truck yard. After several days he was ready to start driving again. He admitted that if his wife had not put her food down he would have likely never returned to work. He also realized that the longer he sat at home the more time he had to dwell in his problem and the bigger it was becoming.

A group of teenagers were in a car going home after school and it was later reported that they were enjoying themselves listening to the radio and talking with each other when suddenly they wereinvolved in a serious auto accident. No one was killed, but several were seriously hurt including one young lady. She stated that whenever she heard the song that was on the radio at the time of the accident, she would feel panicky and frightened. Her parents understood that the girl was fearful, but that she had to get back into her life's pursuits and did not allow her to isolate and avoid traveling. She thanked them after a while, but admitted she was angry with them in the beginning. These individuals experienced what would be frightening and traumatic to anyone.

After the Vietnam War was over and the United States left the area, large groups of refugees would get on any boat they could and set-off into the ocean hoping that someone would come by and rescue them. These people were picked by other ships and some were taken to various countries including Canada, the United States, and Europe. Many were not fortunate enough to escape the communist takeover. One example was Cambodia, which was taken over by the Khmer Rouge, and the people who remained in Cambodia were either executed because of being viewed as intellectuals, or driven into the country and forced into labor camps. These camps were brutal where people were fed little and forced to work in the rice fields from almost sunup to sundown. The Khmer Rouge wanted to grow as much rice as possible to pay back their debt for military equipment to Red China. A number of individuals tried to escape from Cambodia into Thailand. Most were successful, but only after great sacrifices including all they possessed in jewelry to pay off the robbers who were in the mountains over which they had to pass to get into Thailand. A number of these individuals arrived in America after being in the concentration camps and spending some time in the refugee camps in Thailand and suffered from PTSD. In this case as well as others, the disorder was not any fault of their own; they were simply trying to survive. When considering war, we have found that a good number of soldiers returning from combat also suffer from PTSD because of the extremely traumatic circumstances under which they had to live as well as what they had to witness. In these cases, not only does the patient suffer, but also family whether a man returns home from war to his parents or someone who is married returns home to a spouse and most likely children. If the person is able to return to a good family structure the likelihood of him or her recovering or at least being able to function as needed is far greater than if returning to a dysfunctional family setting.

Although abuse will be addressed in another chapter, is not uncommon for victims, especially women and girls and children, to suffer from PTSD. Why? Because these individuals have been traumatized in ways that are out of the ordinary and extremely stressful to the individual. Another example is the first responders during 9/11. Through research it was discovered that those who left the scene and went home and tried to get on with his/her life faired significantly better than those who participated in critical incident debriefing. Why is this the case? It is assumed that those who went home were able to keep their minds occupied on other things, whereas those who attended critical incident debriefing sessions worsened because of their continually being reminded during the group session of what happened (McNally, 2004; Bisson, Jenkins, Alexander, & Bannister, 1997).

Chapter 8 — Worksheet

1. What type of thinking typically brings about anxiety?

2. How can an anxious parent affect children in a family?

3. How can an anxious child affect the family?

Chapter 9
Abuse

Sinisha Karich / Shutterstock.com

It is sad to say that abuse of any type exists in our society, but it is an unfortunate truth. Today abuse is defined as any behavior, whether physical, sexual, verbal, emotional, or neglect (Berk, 2007) that is intended to harm another person. It is also identified as either child or elderly abuse. Three types of abuse will be addressed—physical, verbal, and sexual. Each of these is traumatic, and to some degree, the effects will typically be felt throughout the rest of the person's life. It is assumed that abuse has existed since the beginning of mankind, but in this generation is being brought to the forefront, which could be the reason for people thinking it is more prevalent now than before. Abuse is not only parent to child. If an elderly person over the age of 65 is harmed physically by another person, it is considered abuse. It is also not only against women. More cases are coming to the front where women have abused men.

Physical abuse exists when a person physically harms another person whether out of anger, frustration, or the desire to control the other person. It is abuse when the act leaves marks or other evidence when the victim is examined. This can include cuts and bruises and broken bones. One lady reported that her granddaughter was being abused by the granddaughter's husband. In this case the grandmother, who was trained in martial arts, went to the home when the father and baby were there together and the granddaughter was at work. She confronted the husband, he got belligerent with her, and she laid into him. She used a cattle prod on him and led him to the floor where she tied him up with her nylon stockings and held him until the police arrived. They took the young child immediately to the hospital. He was placed under arrest for abuse of a child. The grandmother had no charges pressed against her. At the hospital it was discovered that the boy had a broken limb, multiple bruises, and one other bone that had been broken and healed on its own. This child was only 6 months old when the grandmother saved him from the abusive father, and she was later congratulated for heroism and saving the child's life.

In another instance, a female patient that had been married for over 20 years and had six children was seeking help for her dysfunctional marriage. She reported that her husband had been abusive to her even before they were married whenever she did not conform to his wishes. She said she thought that this would stop when they got married, but it worsened. On one visit she showed the therapist the bruises on her arms and said that her whole back was bruised as well, and the better part of her legs and said that this was not an uncommon occurrence. She decided to leave the marriage, but a well-meaning friend convinced her to stay and try to work things out, but that was to no avail. She did try to escape his abuse one day by getting in her car and leaving. He was so angry that he threw a large wrench at the car and broke the window. The wrench lodged into the windshield, barely missing her.

Another example involves a young girl, age 10, that was taken from her father. Her parents were divorced and she spent weekends with her father. He was physically abusive. He claimed he spanked her to get his point across, but her entire buttocks was one large deep bruise that indicated severe abuse inflicted by a bare hand.

Verbal abuse is the most difficult to detect because there are no physcial scars or bruising that can be seen. As a result, many of these cases are ignored, or not even reported. Even when reported, it is often discounted as being the person's imagination. One example involves a husband that continually told his wife that she was psychotic. For years, she unfortunately believed him thinking that there must be something wrong with her for her husband to continually say this to her. When asked who diagnosed her with this disorder she said a lady in a health food store who claimed to be an herbalist determined her mental status. It was clear that she did not suffer from a thought disorder of any type. However, she believed she had this disorder after years of her husband telling her she was psychotic, and even convincing their children and many of their friends that she had this problem. As a result, when the husband would accuse her of being psychotic she would either try to prove she wasn't by acting in a way that she knew was normal, or she would get angry and try to defend herself by fighting him and resisting his accusations through arguments which gave him the ability to say she was psychotic. She knew she needed to leave the relationship because of what was happening to her and what her children witnessed. She was eventually able to divorce him when she found out that he had been sexually abusing her oldest daughter who was his stepdaughter. Because of that, he was not allowed to be near the family. Typically, the verbally abused person, as in most other instances of abuse, will have poor self-esteem when entering the relationship or because of the relationship, which prevents the person from stopping the poor treatment.

Sexual abuse appears to be the most devastating of all the abuses inflicted on people. This occurs when an underage child is forced into any sexual activity with an adult. This can even occur between children if there is at least a 4-year age difference between the victim and the abuser. In most cases the perpetrator is a family member (father, mother, sibling or other relative), and is rarely a stranger abusing or assaulting the child. Sexual abuse can range from fondling genitalia with the clothes on or off to digital penetration, or rape. Fortunately, the punishment for the crime has become quite severe, which many feel will help curtail the problem. But many others fear that because of the severity, it is underreported.

The Perpetrator

There is no hard and fast pattern or background for a perpetrator, but there are common threads amongst some perpetrators. Like any other mental disorder, or problem, each perpetrator of sexual abuse of any type has his or her own individual history. In most cases one can look to the family history and find where the problem started, or how it was enabled or encouraged. An example is a 42-year-old male who was married and had two children. He did not work but insisted his wife work full-time to support the family. He would do odd jobs and repair people's homes on occasion, or spend his time hunting for lost jewelry in the parks with a metal detector or work on his hunting equipment. He was caught having sexual intercourse with a minor female, served time in jail, and lost the marriage and family. When considering his family background, he had no sense of responsibility or accountability for others. His mother was indulgent and allowed him to do whatever he wanted, especially when he would become upset and have tantrums. As an adult this same thinking carried over because it was allowed, first by family, and second by his well-meaning wife.

A number of perpetrators have a history of being sexually abused themselves. If these individuals resort to sexual abuse as adults, it is usually because they had the idea that it was acceptable because of what happened to them. One male perpetrator admitted that he was molested as a teenager by a male neighbor. He said that at the time he was disgusted with what had happened, but later allowed himself to dwell on the incident that eventually led to an obsession which was acted out by molesting children. A number of children have admitted that they knew what was happening to them was wrong, but at the same time it felt good physically. The result was seeking the same pleasure again later in life with minors. In most all cases when a child is molested it will have a negative effect on the child's self-esteem and interfere with feeling comfortable enough around other people. Thus, he will not learn how to relate to them and will become a loner.

The poor self-esteem amounts to the negative thoughts and feelings a person has about him or herself. Most perpetrators have a poor self-esteem although many will not admit to it because then they will have to also admit that they were wrong and be held accountable for their actions.

One middle-aged man had been incarcerated twice for sexual assault or molestation. His mother was a bitter person and miserable with her life. He stated that he never felt good about himself because of the things his mother used to say to him. Several years after his second incarceration, he married a woman with a 7-year-old daughter. The wife knew about the husband's history but felt that she could trust him. When the girl reached puberty he sought help to learn how to deal with the daughter who was asking for more affection than he could afford to give her at that time. He stated that this was the age that he was most attracted to, but because he had resolved never to act on that again, he had to completely avoid any physical contact with her. He said that she would beg him to wrestle with her, or let her sit on his lap and it made him feel bad that he could not accommodate her wishes. He knew what could possibly happen if he did. After working this through, his confidence in himself increased significantly which in turn helped him with his self-esteem.

Another man was caught molesting his 4-year-old granddaughter and later admitted that he had never felt like he amounted to much. Because of his poor self-esteem he married a woman who lacked maturity and stayed with her because he felt he could do no better anywhere else. His wife divorced him because of the molestation, which once again substantiated his worthlessness as a person in his mind.

A number of perpetrators lack the ability to relate to others on a mature level and will seek the intimate companionship from someone who the perpetrator thinks will not be able to resist him or her. One perpetrator molested his oldest daughter from the time she was 8-years-old until she was close to 17. She never said anything to anyone for fear of causing problems, so nothing was ever addressed until later. His 3-year-old granddaughter told her parents that he had touched her inappropriately, which then brought to light the other history of molestation. He said he attempted to molest his next younger daughter when she was 12, but because she put up a fuss and resisted he left her alone. This was an individual who felt as though people rejected him if he tried to talk to them and develop a close relationship, and this was even apparent in his marriage. Relating on a mature level is a demanding exercise, and he admitted he understood that and it would give him what he wanted. Unfortunately, the molestation destroyed his self-esteem. He was sentenced to a minimum of 10 years in prison with a possible maximum sentence of life. His entire family, meaning his wife, children, and grandchild, completely severed ties with him and left him a lonely person.

Another man and his wife had three children of their own, and then decided to adopt more children. Eventually they adopted seven children. On the surface they appeared to be a happy family. On one occasion one of the adult children asked her 14-year-old sister if the father had been molesting her. Initially the 14-year-old sister denied the accusation, but later admitted to it and the older sister said that he had molested her also. When this was reported to the authorities it was revealed that he had been molesting almost all the children at some time in their lives. He could relate to his wife, but not maturely because she was the one who "ran the show." He spent very little time interacting with and relating with family members except through molesting the children. He later admitted that he was raised in a family where communication was always on a business level with no emotional closeness encouraged at all. Unfortunately, he was never incarcerated, but was also never allowed to be near the children again until they reached adulthood.

In all of these cases the perpetrators felt significantly inadequate as adults, even though on the surface they may appear to feel confident. As a result, they would seek intimacy from small children who would not be able to say no.

Abuse as a Type of Manipulation

When considering physical and verbal abuse, and the pattern is explored in depth, it becomes apparent in most all cases that the abuser is manipulating to get his or her way. This pattern of manipulation is almost always learned in childhood wherein many instances the person was abusive to his or her parents while at home. If he learned there that it worked, that he could get his way, he will bring this behavior pattern into his adult life, including marriage.

A young woman mentioned in a previous chapter, who been married for about 6 months, reported in therapy that her husband was abusive to her. One example that she gave was when she asked him to help her with cleaning the house. When she made the request he became upset and started yelling at her and threatening her physically saying that she was lazy and did not care about him, and that he was going to show her who was the boss. She immediately walked away and did the housekeeping herself. He was a prime example of not only seeing anger in his own home growing up, but also that acting on his own anger toward his parents, as well as others, now including his wife, would get him what he wanted.

Several cases will be revisited to illustrate this point. The first is the husband who become physically abusive to his wife who did not want to have sex with him. He knew very clearly that by getting upset she would become intimidated and ultimately give him what he wanted. The longer she put up with the behavior and caved into his pressure, the more entrenched his abusive behavior became. Unfortunately, her children saw this behavior and thought that they could manipulate mother by treating her the same as their father. The second case is the husband who refused to work. His wife reported that on many occasions when she would not do what he wanted, he would become violent and abusive. One time he wanted to go hunting and she asked him to stay home to help her with a repair on the house. She said he immediately became angry and began to strike her until she finally backed down and told him to do what he wanted. In this case their only son treated mother the same way starting in early adolescence and continuing into his adult life. Not only was he verbally abusive to his mother, he was also verbally and physically to his wife.

There are a number of different ways that one can use abuse to manipulate the other person. One method is to place the blame and accuse the other person of being at fault. A middle-aged man was accused of infidelity by his wife. When she confronted him he became rather angry and then turned the accusations back on her saying that if she were not such a poor excuse of a wife, he would not have done what he did. In many instances the abuser will demean the victim to justify their own behavior by telling them that they are of no worth. In these cases, the victim will believe it and spend a great amount of time and effort trying to become the person that, in this case, she thinks her husband wants her to be. One particular wife reported that her husband told her she was undeserving of his love because she was such a loser. As this was explored in therapy she was able to see that she was not a loser, but actually a very good wife. To his surprise when he said this to her again her reply was, "if I'm that bad of a person you must be pretty sorry yourself or you wouldn't stay with me because you don't think you could do better." When this type of behavior is seen as a manipulation, it is much easier for the victim to stand up to the other person and not be intimidated. Threatening the other person is also employed to manipulate through abuse. When the abuser wants his way he will threaten the victim with either physical harm, threats of telling others about the victim's weaknesses or problems, withhold money, love, or even the children.

A woman married to an abusive husband finally found through good sources that her husband was committing adultery. She eventually found the strength to confront him and he manipulated her by accusing her of the problem and saying she was the one committing adultery, not him. She felt as though she had no way to disprove his accusations even though they were not true. So with a helpless feeling, she dropped the subject. Accusing other people to manipulate them is abusive and cruel. To hear the husband say to the wife "it's your fault that I do what I do" is often seen with drug addicts and alcoholics, telling them that it is the spouse's fault that the person has to drink or use drugs. Others will accuse the person of not loving, or not caring about them, which will create self-doubt and feelings of helplessness, shame, and guilt in the victim. In other cases, anger is a form of abuse. One man admitted that he had to come up with a good reason to be angry with his wife so that he could justify leaving her for several days to go off and be with a girlfriend and use drugs. He would accuse her of not taking care of the money and not caring enough about him to take care of the household as she needed to. He later confessed that he did admire her and she was a great wife, but by being angry and accusing her of not being good enough, he could get his way. His wife's self-esteem was extremely low, and she was in therapy for long period of time to regain a sense of worth.

The Victim

As has been mentioned in this chapter the victim is an easy target because of accepting the blameworthy intimidation and thereby caving into the wishes of the other individual. The general feeling is that they have done something wrong or deserve the poor treatment. In most cases the victim has poor self-esteem that was likely learned in childhood. The double bind can have a significant negative effect on the person. Here the individual is continually thinking he or she has to do something to make the other person happy, but because the person is never happy, the individual is found in a no-win situation. Many victims of abuse readily admit that they always felt as if they were at fault and deserved the abuse they received. Because of this thinking, as has been mentioned before, they spend all their time and effort trying to please the person so the individual will not be hurt again, even in childhood. This thinking, if not corrected, will likely be carried into adulthood. In adulthood the person will typically choose relationships that are destructive and unhealthy because of the constant idea that it is this person's duty to make the other person happy. The abuser sees the victim as weak and will use this weakness to get his way, because it works. This type of thinking is especially present in victims of sexual abuse. Furthermore, the victim will think that the sexual abuse is her fault because this only happens to bad girls, or boys, and those who are bad and dirty.

The young girl who was admitted for treatment in an inpatient adolescent psychiatric unit eventually opened up and talked about her abuse and openly admitted that she felt it was her fault. A perpetrator once stated in therapy that he could not help himself from molesting his young daughter because she was so cute. He would say this to her repeatedly, which left her thinking that if she were not so attractive she would not be hurt. This is the case with many victims and is shown by them deliberately keeping themselves unkempt and always wearing unattractive clothing.

When a person, but particularly a child, is abused in any way, but specifically sexually her or she will behave in ways that are not typical for the victim. Most often the victim will withdraw. Also a change in personality will appear because of the trauma. In all instances this change is abrupt, and parents will typically say that within weeks, their son or daughter changed from a very happy, outgoing child, to isolating in the bedroom and not wanting anything to do with people. Other individuals will become provocative. One female patient who was a victim of molestation for a number of years as a child said that she always got in trouble with her mother for being too "sexy." She said that she figured being sexy was the only way people would like her because of the way she had been treated. As a result the desire for affection and acceptance was strong, and the only way she knew how get it was to be provocative. This opened the door for further sexual abuse throughout childhood and adolescence, and when she became an adult she was constantly promiscuous.

These changes occur because of the conflict the person, in this case a child, is experiencing as a result of their abuse. The child does not understand why he or she is being mistreated, especially sexually, and will try the very best he or she knows how, in order to cope with the traumatic experience. This conflict includes feelings of shame and self-doubt and as a result the child will feel uncomfortable in the presence of others, especially parents. One female patient said that her older brother married a woman who had been previously married and had a son who was about 4 or 5 years older than the patient. This abuse started when she was about 9-years-old when her brother and his wife and the boy would come to visit the parents. She said that the adults would leave to go shopping or run errands and leave the children home alone. While alone, the boy molested and raped her over the next 4 years. Needless to say she was traumatized by what happened, but also felt as though it must be her fault. She said that she was afraid of telling her parents what happened fearing that they would be upset with her and blame her. The trauma was carried into her adult life. She had no desire for any type of sexual intimacy with her husband even though they had two children.

A 14-year-old girl revealed her history of abuse by saying she and her girlfriend became friends with a young married couple down the street from her. Over time the husband began to show an interest in the patient, which to her was very flattering. Not too long after the relationship was started he began to molest her and then engage in sexual intercourse. According to this young girl, the wife divorced her husband because of other problems and had no idea what was occurring between this girl and the husband. He then encouraged her to dress extremely provocatively and walk around the mall so he could take pictures of her. While all this was occurring she felt frightened and guilty and quickly began to show signs of a psychiatric problem, but no one knew why. While in treatment at a psychiatric facility she revealed the history of her abuse which explained her behavior.

The Lifelong Effects of Abuse on an Individual

It is not uncommon for an adult who seeks help for emotional or mental problems to have had a history of abuse of some type. Unless a thorough history is taken in the initial visits, and the patient is honest, the abuse history will not be addressed, and it will leave the patient in a negative position. Usually the patient will admit that he did not want to reveal this for fear of being thought less of as a person. In most cases the abuse victim will show signs of PTSD (Cutajar, Mullen, Ogloff, Thomas, Wells, & Spalaro, 2010), which can go undiagnosed because of too much focus on the symptoms and not talking about the root of the problem. As a result, the patient may be diagnosed with anxiety or depression, or even bipolar disorder. The symptoms of PTSD are the same in this situation as one would see in someone who was a combat veteran or an individual who had been in a traumatic accident. The patient becomes hypervigilant and always on guard, which is usually interpreted by others as being aloof or stuck up. This is not the case. The person is afraid of getting hurt by someone else. Also because of the hypervigilance the patient usually has a difficult time establishing or maintaining relationships on a deep-feeling level.

A married man who had been molested as a child by his babysitter had been married previously, and his second wife was threatening to divorce him. She felt as though she was not important to him because he was never home for very long periods of time, and when at home he engaged in activities that excluded her. She naïvely thought that it was because he did not love her. He had never revealed the history of abuse because of shame, but when he finally did, he was able to relax. Through help in therapy he learned how to relate to his wife on a feeling level and the marriage was saved.

Along with the hypervigilance, is a startle response that is beyond normal. Abuse victims will often be on edge and unsettled. One adult victim said that even in her safe home with her husband and children, if she would hear the bedroom door open in the night she would panic. This was because of her stepfather opening her closed door at night when she was a child and coming in the room to molest her. Other problems such as self-doubt, mistrust of others, mood and anxiety disorders, and thought disorders along with dissociative disorders are often found in victims of abuse.

ozguroral / Shutterstock.com

A woman was raised by an alcoholic and abusive father and said that she always tried to be on his good side. Her mother was continually saying to her and her older brother that they had to be quiet and keep dad happy so he would not drink. When he drank he became belligerent and oftentimes abusive with the mother and the children. Unfortunately, no matter how quiet the family was and how congenial they were with the father, he would continue to drink and be abusive. This lady admitted that in late childhood and into adolescence she was everybody's best friend and was always available to help whenever help was needed. She said she felt as though she was the fixer of others' problems, and by so doing she would get their approval.

An adolescent boy who was a victim of physical abuse by his stepfather was always being the class clown and tried to make things humorous. He said that when he was able to make people laugh he thought they liked him, which gave him a sense of comfort he did not get at home. On the other hand, many live in continual fear of upsetting the abuser which was the case with the mother just mentioned. She was fearful of upsetting the father and him becoming abusive.

One couple had four children, and all four were timid and withdrawn. They would not say much to anyone, and if they did it was only brief conversations. They would spend most of their time either by themselves or huddled together as siblings. The oldest boy admitted that he acted on his fear by spending most of his time in the backwoods of their neighborhood with his pet dog. Another man said he dealt with his fears of being abused by being aggressive himself, thinking that if he was tough enough people would leave him alone and not hurt him. As a result, he became very successful at work because of his demanding behavior which drove people to perform their tasks, even though they were motivated by fear. This had a negative effect on his marriage because he felt that he was always being attacked by his wife so he had to keep her at bay by being angry with her. In most cases, though, the individual will act timid and shy thinking safety will be achieved.

Even though PTSD is likely present in most all abuse victims, mood disorders are not to be ruled out. As was mentioned in a previous chapter, depression, as well as all of the thought disorders, are rooted in one's thinking. In this case the individual is often in the double bind position, or feeling guilty for everything and as a result constantly suffering from poor self-esteem. Also, when the person thinks negatively, the result is poor self-esteem. With the negative thinking and the poor self-esteem comes the unhealthy behavior that will serve as a reinforcer for the problems that exist. If the victim is again feeling worthless because of what has happened throughout childhood, that individual will either not risk, or if she does, the risking will be very limited, and in many cases unsuccessful because of the negative thinking. In most instances, isolation is a common behavior. Even if the person does not isolate, his interaction with other people will be limited to only safe topics such as the weather or sports. If there is an involvement with the family, it is most commonly seen with the children because children do not judge adults like adults. Unfortunately, when the child matures, the parent will have the same feelings and eventually cut off the relationship.

People with anxiety disorders continually think about getting in trouble, or doing something wrong, or something bad happening. This was the case with a lady whose husband was an alcoholic and even after she divorced him and moved far enough away from him to not be traumatized any longer, she still suffered from generalized anxiety disorder. She was always thinking that something bad was going to happen. She said she was raised in a healthy home. As it was explored further she revealed that her parents were kind and loving people, but were not very effective in teaching her, her brother, and her sister how to stand up to people. She married the man who showed interest in her, which had never happened before. She thought that he would take good care of her. When he began to reveal his true personality after they were married, she became fearful which brought about the anxiety disorder. Others will feel that they need to always be on watch and have to be ready for anything that may happen. These are individuals who have likely been traumatized in childhood and can only feel safe when all safety measures have been met.

An 18-year-old girl was brought to therapy because of her strange behavior. It was apparent that she was experiencing a psychotic episode because of not understanding reality. She would laugh inappropriately, have conversations with herself, many of which did not make sense, and would always respond inappropriately with people. Her parents were looking for something to make her better and would only visit those who could help her on brief occasions. They admitted to one therapist, that they thought she had a vitamin deficiency. Even though the lady could not talk about what had occurred, it was apparent that she had been traumatized by some sort of abuse while at college. The onset of her symptoms were immediate and the progression was rapid. Brain damage and any other type of neurological disorder were ruled out, but unfortunately her parents persisted in looking for some reason other than the suspected trauma to explain her disorder. The result was a long-drawn out process of trying to find help, but not ever succeeding, and the girl was finally admitted to a mental institution.

Others may experience auditory hallucinations because of being abused. In many cases the individual will have conversations in his or her head because of the conflict experienced in life. As a result, these voices would be people saying negative things to the person such as "you are bad," "you're in trouble," "no one can ever love you" and so forth. This of course is a result of feeling that he or she is to blame for the abuse that occurred, and the voices and so forth are a reminder of their guilt.

For years the dissociative disorder had been misunderstood. It was assumed that the person was either psychotic or had some sort of a brain dysfunction. Recently, though, it has been discovered that many women suffering from the dissociative disorder, earlier known as multiple personality disorder, are victims of abuse, especially sexual (Putnam, Guroff, Silberman, Barbon, & Post, 1986). A young single woman had been repeatedly admitted to a psychiatric unit because of her dissociative disorder. She eventually revealed her history of sexual abuse. While probing her dissociative disorder in-depth she stated that she had a strong feeling that when she was abused by her father it was happening to a different person because she was not that type of individual. First, the person being abused was a bad person who was not worthy of anybody's loving treatment. As a result, when she felt threatened she would leave her present personality and go back into this other personality where she could keep her sense of herself safe. Over time she developed a number of other personalities that would fit given situations.

Another young lady, age 17, was given a diagnosis of dissociative disorder. Her parents were divorced, and when she told her mother that she had been molested by her father when she visited him, her mother became upset and blocked visitation. The girl was raised in a religious home, but because of what happened, felt that she was a bad person. And like in other cases, other personalities began to be developed.

Helping the Victim

When abuse occurs mental disorders are often the result. A number of methods have been tried in helping victims, but many have been unsuccessful. If the victim is encouraged to continue to relive the experience, the trauma will decrease, but actually, the patient typically gets worse. If the patient is coddled and people try to make him feel better, the problem will worsen. When a child is abused, the fear response is quite marked, and in this case when the parents find out about the abuse, they will become frightened and unsure about how to help the child. In most cases the parents and other family members will feel sorry for the child. As a result, the child will learn unhealthy behavior patterns. If the child withdraws, which is most likely the case, the parents will leave her alone for fear of making things worse by talking and asking questions. If the child is allowed to isolate, the problem will become worse because of having too much time think about the trauma, as well as negatively about herself. A number of children become shy and do not interact with others, and again most parents will then allow the behavior to continue for fear of causing a child to become worse. In these cases the necessary path to take is to insist that the child come back and act as he or she did before the abuse took place. Many well-meaning adults would say that this is wrong because they don't want to make the child feel any worse. The problem is that by leaving the child alone, or indulging child, the unhealthy behavior continues and even worsens. The loving parents who want to help their child will put aside their fears and insist that she begin to act in a normal way.

One such instance was an 11-year-old girl who was molested by a neighbor. She became tearful and frightened and would not talk to anyone. Her parents eventually found out what the problem was, felt bad about her trauma, and tried to do what they could to make her feel better. They bought her new clothes, they did not insist that she participate in family activities if she didn't want to, and eventually she quit going to school. The parents finally sought help, and treatment was given along with the direction they needed for their daughter. They learned that they were reinforcing her fears by allowing her to act on them. As a result, they stopped feeling sorry for her and started to expect her to get out and play with friends, interact with the family, and go back to school. In the beginning she would resist and get upset, but she finally realized mother and father were not going to allow her to act the way she had been, and she reluctantly started doing what she needed to. After a time, she found that she was okay and could continue living the way she did before being hurt. Another couple felt that they would do more harm than good so they allowed their daughter to persist in her behavioral patterns resulting from the abuse only to see her deteriorate significantly.

This is the same for helping adults. When they stop acting on the emotions and feelings they begin to heal. One man who was severely abused by his father when he was a young boy developed signs of PTSD and hyperactivity. When he sought help as an adult he learned that the abuse was not because he was a bad person, but because his father had problems. As that was clarified he then had to learn to not dwell on his fears, and to not act on them. Over time he became comfortable with himself and the circumstances, and even though he was successful at work, became more so because of his new learned confidence in himself. Until he sought therapy he dealt with his problems through self-medication by using drugs and alcohol.

The woman who was abused by her brother's stepson when they were children stated that she wanted nothing to do with sexual intimacy. She said her husband was upset for being shut out and was going to divorce her because he lost love for her. When she revealed her history of abuse, her thinking was explored, and it became apparent that sex to her was something that was traumatic and bad. Every time her husband wanted to engage in sex she would have recurring flashbacks of the abuse. As a result, she avoided it at any cost. In therapy she learned two principles. She first learned to not dwell on sex in a negative way. She also learned that by acting on her fears she made them worse. She then began to risk sexually with her husband and while engaged in sexual activity focused on the pleasurable aspects of it. Over time the problem was resolved, not only with sex, but her life in general. She was open with her parents and told them what happened. To her astonishment they were not angry with her but felt sad the she did not tell them what happened so they could have protected her. As a child though she did not know what to do so she acted in a very negative and withdrawn way.

Chapter 9—Worksheet

1. How is abuse defined?

2. What is the most common reason for a person to abuse a victim?

3. What is the typical behavioral pattern of a child who has been sexually abused?

Chapter 10
Chemical Dependency and Family Dynamics

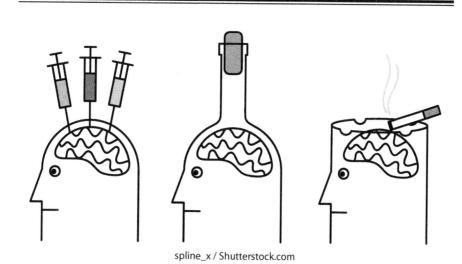

spline_x / Shutterstock.com

To understand chemical dependency it is important to have an idea of the various mood-altering chemicals that people consume. These various chemicals are called mood-altering chemicals because they alter how one feels emotionally, mentally, and even physically. They include depressants, stimulants and hallucinogens. Dependence is defined as the physical and mental need for the mood-altering chemical, and the drug is considered physically addictive if there is tissue tolerance, or the need to increase the dosage to get the same effect that was originally experienced with lower doses (Weiten, Dunn & Hammer, 2015). Also, withdrawal symptoms are consistent and predictable. Not all mood-altering chemicals are physically addictive. However, whether physically or not, the psychological addiction is the one that keeps people coming back. If one is dependent upon a physically addictive drug the person will not have the physical cravings once he or she has gone through the withdrawals. The body is healed and there is no longer a need for that mood-altering chemical to feel normal. The psychological addiction is more difficult to deal with. Because the drug gives the individual a sense of well-being, or some sort of euphoria, or even an escape from current problems, the desire for this feeling lingers long after one has gone through the physical withdrawals. People who are dependent on mood-altering chemicals will often admit that the real desire to use them is present when they want to change their mood, or deal with stress or other difficulties. There may be a genetic component to addiction, and research has been conducted in this area for many years, but until now little definitive data completely supports this being physiological only. Even if the person has a genetic predisposition to being dependent on mood-altering chemicals, he or she has a choice whether to use them or not. Some will say that they have no control, whereas others will say that they choose not to control it but to continue in their dependency.

It is interesting to observe and find out what types of people are drawn to particular mood-altering chemicals. In general, those who are dependent upon mood-altering chemicals experience emotional and mental problems of some sort. The drug-dependent individual is typically insecure and because of a poor self-esteem feels as though the drugs help him feel good enough to function in everyday life. In most cases the individual will feel that he or she can only be normal when under the influence. One man with a long history of drug dependence admitted that when under the influence of cocaine he felt "10-foot tall and bulletproof." He was raised in a rural community and always felt that he was somewhat less than his peers because of his family circumstances. He was drafted into the military during the Vietnam War and was trained to be a sniper. He said that he was so frightened when sent out to protect the troops that he would find some sort of a mood-altering chemical to calm his nerves, which typically was the morphine in his first-aid kit. After being discharged from the military he developed a good career, but all the while felt as though he was not as good as others. When the pressures of work would become strong enough, he would leave work and spend several weeks alone consuming cocaine and whiskey. This pattern of drug use was of the binge type. He would go for months without using drugs, but then because of certain circumstances he felt he had no control over, he would resort to cocaine to feel better.

A 40-year-old housewife admitted herself for inpatient treatment to withdraw from Valium. She was active in her church and tried to be as good in other church member's eyes as she thought they were. She also felt inadequate as a mother and as a wife. Valium was initially prescribed for back pain, which also gave her a sense of calmness and serenity and was a relief from her doubts and poor self-esteem. While in treatment she was reassured on many occasions by her husband and children that she was a good mother and that no one thought ill of her, but because of how she felt about herself she had a hard time accepting this.

Because of the dependence, the individual will become a very good manipulator, and some manipulation schemes become quite elaborate. This can include guilt, intimidation, blaming, accusations, and in many cases elaborate promises. It's easy to make a person feel guilty if that individual is insecure and then cause the person to doubt himself. The husband kept telling his wife that it was her fault that he drank. He told her that she put too much pressure on him and expected more out of him that he was able to give, which caused him to want to drink. He sadly stopped for a while, but had a job that paid less than he needed to support his family, so his wife had to work which gave him an excuse to return to the drinking.

A wife who was addicted to alcohol blamed her husband and children for her dependence. She would tell everyone in the family that she could not stand them because of the way they treated her. She always felt like she was not good enough. Along with guilt, like with the abusive person, the addict or alcoholic will use blame to get people to leave her alone so she can do what she wants. "If it wasn't for you always nagging at me, or always demanding from me things I can't do, I wouldn't have to leave." In most cases these individuals know how to use guilt and blame to their advantage and will admit that they really don't feel the way they say they do, but it gets them what they want.

Intimidation is a common ploy which is harmful to the spouse and family. This typically comes from threats of leaving or violence. When the person feels frightened enough she will leave the other person alone and let him do what he wants. Threats appear to be a powerful tool because it always leaves the victim not knowing what to expect, and because of always being on guard, the victim will cave into the pressures of the intimidator. In most cases the threats are of physical harm to the other individual or someone close to the person. One man, after being married for two weeks left his wife for about five months. He felt he was entitled to do what he wanted and used intimidation as a weapon. He worked as a welder and said that his bosses liked his work so much they kept supplying him with drugs including cocaine and marijuana so that he would keep working. He said that after being gone for about five months he decided to return home and came in the house on a Saturday morning. He was greeted by his wife asking where he had been. He said he looked her in the eye and told her that if she were to keep up the questioning he would leave and not come back until he was ready. He told her to go make breakfast, which she did, and she never questioned him after that.

Other people will intimidate by cutting the spouse off, leaving her feeling like she will never be in the good graces of the manipulator. Others will threaten to leave, or never talk to them, and so forth. Physical abuse and threats of physical violence are also common with this population. One man would beat his wife if she told him she did not want to go drink. He would come home later drunk and continue to beat her. For the most part the threats of violence cause the other person to be quiet and not challenge the addict.

Accusations are also a tool of manipulation. As with the abuser, the chemically dependent individual may accuse the other person having the problem. This is to take the focus off of the addict so as to never be questioned about what he is doing. The person might say "I know you were drinking," or "I know you're doing drugs, you're just hiding from me." In that case the one being falsely accused will put forth a great effort trying to disprove the other person's suspicions which keeps that person from then blaming or questioning the guilty party. Another ploy that is common is making promises. This can either come about before the person leaves to use the mood-altering chemicals, or after the incident. If the person wants to go out and drink or use he may promise his wife that he will not drink and will be home very shortly. When the wife agrees, then he is free to go do what he wants, or so he thinks. In many instances the dependent person will make great promises after being caught, or after something serious happening as a result of the abuse of drugs or alcohol. Typically he will promise to never do it again and beg the other person to trust him. Sometimes these promises are kept for a period of time, maybe even several months, but in most cases the promises only last one or several days. The person might truly feel remorseful in the beginning, but when the cravings take over, or the pressures are enough, the person will forget the promises and go off and do what he wants.

In all of these cases these behaviors are typically learned in the family. It could be that the person is the victim of abuse or neglect like one young man who was introduced to methamphetamines at the age of 11. He said his stepfather was extremely abusive and his only escape was to consume the methamphetamines that were given to him by his friends who told him they would make him feel better. He found out that it worked and continued pursuing this throughout the rest of his young adult life. It could be that the person sees adult family members using mood-altering chemicals to deal with problems so the individual grows up thinking that's how one deals with life. In other instances, the person may start using drugs to fit in with the crowd because of needing approval that is not received at home. Because of poor self-esteem, a person will likely gravitate to those people who are not very upstanding in their own lives. If this is the case, the person's self-esteem eventually becomes worse because of who she is hanging around with and what she is doing. It could be that the person was raised in a drug-free home and circumstances later in life will cause the person to want to drink or use. This often occurs in the military or young people going to college. Unfortunately, many who are drawn into this and reach early adulthood, lack a sense of self-control because of being overly controlled at home. When they're on their own they let go and indulge in things like mood-altering chemicals, which become a thrill to them as well as an escape. Unfortunately, as the addiction becomes strong enough, school and grades and all else are ignored, or work takes second place to the addiction and the person's life is in the early stages of being ruined.

The Spouse

In most cases the spouse of a drug-dependent individual is one who constantly wants to please other people. The spouse oftentimes is one who was raised in a family where rules were either inconsistent or difficult to understand, which would leave the person wanting to know where she stands. In other cases the person might come from a family where a parent is difficult to please. The person who is difficult to please might be one who is critical of others and will come across as never satisfied with what anyone does. This might also be a form of manipulation by the parent to get people to do what he or she wants. In any case, some children are affected by an insecure feeling that would leave them trying to please the other person so that this individual will not be in trouble. Some parents do not communicate very well, and as result keep quiet or to themselves. In this case the child will be left wondering what the rules are or what is expected. The child may feel anxious and again try to make that person happy so that the person will feel safe and secure. Some children are raised in a home where the parents are always pleasing everybody and as result talk to the children and manage the family in ways that come across as the child needing to please others. In such instances, the child, who then later becomes an adult, is left feeling anxious and insecure. This individual will now likely be an easy target for the manipulator, which is a typical behavior pattern of an addict or alcoholic. This is where the seeds of enabling are planted. Remember that the drug-dependent person is consumed by the need for the mood-altering chemical and thus will do whatever is necessary to get what he wants.

One of the driving ideas of the spouse that keeps him enabling is that if he can do well enough by pleasing the person, or keeping everything in the family in control, the person will not go off and use or drink. The result is the person continually trying to make the addict or alcoholic happy. One particular mother was always trying to keep her son quiet because her husband would get upset and said he could not handle the noise and would leave. He used the noise as an excuse to go to the bar and drink with his friends. In another case a female patient in an inpatient chemical dependency unit asked her therapist and the group she was attending why her husband was never satisfied with her. She said that he would always complain about her and the children and was always leaving. When asked what she attributed his behavior to she openly said that it was her fault because he would tell her it was.

The male members of the group were asked if they acted this way toward their girl-friends or spouses, and they all admitted to the same treatment. When asked why they treated their significant others this way they became quiet, but eventually one man raised his hand and said that he might be thinking to himself at the beginning of the work week that Friday would be payday and he would want to spend the weekend with his friends drinking and using cocaine. Even though he admired his wife who worked full-time to help support the family, was a good housekeeper, and also did a remarkable job raising the children, he said he had to find fault with her to justify what he wanted to do. He said he could not tell her how much he loved her and was appreciative of the fine work she was doing, and then turn around and say he wanted to go off with his friends and not come home until Sunday or Monday after work with the paycheck spent on drugs and alcohol. He also said that on occasion he would even commit adultery on these weekend binges. He admitted that each day of that week he would become angrier by looking for things that would upset him, and by Friday afternoon would be very angry. He said he would come into the house and yell at his wife and children and tell them that they were not good people and he did not want to be around them, and then get in his car and leave. He would be thinking to himself about a block away from the house that he accomplished what he wanted to and now could go and have fun.

In other cases the spouse might try to cover for the person's addiction by making excuses for her. This is often done because he wants to avoid any turmoil or get in trouble. A prominent MD in his town was an alcoholic and his wife spent most of her time and energy trying to cover his bases so that he would not lose patients and not lose face in the community. If he was unable to get up in the morning and work because of being hung over, she would call the office and tell the staff to cancel his appointments because he had the flu or some other illness. Her children said that she would always tell them that dad had had a hard day and wasn't very happy when asked why he was alone in the back part of the house. Unfortunately the children knew better and did not believe mother.

One wife would call work and tell the boss that the husband could not come in because of being ill when actually the person drank too much at lunch. A husband did not want his family to think ill of his wife so when she missed activities because of being inebriated he would say she had things she had to take care of and was too busy to come. On other occasions when she would become drunk and act inappropriately, he would say that she was under a lot of stress and she didn't really mean what she said or mean to act the way she did. One alcoholic man had a good system working for him. He was self-employed and had a solid crew working for him and so they, along with his wife, were always able to cover for him when he was unable to work which gave him the freedom to drink whenever he felt like it.

Some spouses may act out their insecurities and fears by being overly attentive to the person. Because of fear, and in many cases thinking that it is his or her responsibility to make the other person happy, the spouse will attend to the spouse's every need. It could be that the spouse is told that the person has to go on drinking because he's upset with the family so the spouse will do everything possible to make sure the children are in line and everything he wants or needs is taken care of. This is usually at the expense of the welfare of the rest of the family. Other individuals will almost act like slaves and be there for the beck and call of the individual no matter what. This comes back to doing everything right so the person will not use or drink. One wife took great pride in the idea that she could know her husband's wants and needs even before he knew what they were. She boasted that no matter what he needed it would be there for him immediately.

One anxious husband of an alcoholic wife tried his best to keep his profession intact by doing whatever she wanted him to do, which might even require him missing work. At home he would do almost everything from preparing meals to helping children with homework and putting them to bed at night. He was raised in a family where the father was quiet, and as a result of not saying much left the family guessing what he wanted. His anxiety and fear of disapproval was so strong that it interfered with him being a meaningful husband and a good father. He was not able to let his wife know what he expected of her and help her put a stop to her drinking. Because of his fears of the children causing problems, he catered to them anyway he could. In these instances the problem worsens because the person is trying to do everything, which leaves the other person not responsible for the welfare of the family. It also leaves the spouse in a position of self-doubt and never achieving that standard that is supposedly expected.

The insecure spouse of the chemically dependent individual will, in many cases, never question the person. Many spouses have said that they knew something was wrong but were afraid to say anything for fear of making the problems worse. One wife admitted that she was told by friends that her husband was destroying the family financially because of his addiction to cocaine. She admitted that she could sense this also, but rationalized by saying that he meant no harm and as result she would never challenge his behavior. She was raised by a controlling father who was always right and would never allow anyone to question his authority so she grew up with the idea that men were never to be challenged on anything.

In most all cases there will be a point in time when the spouse of the addict or alcoholic will become frustrated and upset enough to make threats of divorce or never talking to the person again. One example was a wife who threatened to leave her husband about once or twice a year because of his abusing drugs and hurting the family. He would ignore her and she would then feel helpless. She hoped that the threat would cause him to change, but it never happened. Empty threats are usually made with the hope that if one puts enough fear in the other person it will cause him to stop the destructive behavior. Unfortunately, most addicts do not care about much of anything except getting the drugs they want which leads them to serious manipulation. It doesn't take long for the person to realize that the spouse does not mean what she says so the addict continues in the addictive behavior patterns. In this case the behavior, manipulation by intimidation, or ignoring is being reinforced. Even when the spouse finally means what she says and severs the relationship, the other person will not take this seriously and continue acting the way he has in the past. Finally, when the addict realizes the other person means business, he will either give up trying to get the spouse back, or stop the addiction and begin the act in a healthy way.

One cocaine addict was married and had five children. He was part of a very lucrative family business so he never had to worry about money. His wife was afraid to say anything for fear of him divorcing her, so he had an open door to do whatever he pleased. After a number of years of being neglected and the continual turmoil, she became strong enough to file for divorce. He decided that he did not want to lose her or the children and immediately stopped using the drug. He said that one evening he was trying to be a good father and husband by cleaning the kitchen. He was proud of the fact that he put the dishes in the dishwasher, cleaned the pots and pans, the countertops and the floors. He then started the dishwasher only to find out that the kitchen floor was totally covered in soaps suds. He panicked and his wife got upset and he learned to not use dish soap in the and dishwasher. He eventually learned how to be a father and husband and overtime his wife was able to let down her guard and trust him.

The final outcome with those who fail to do what they say and continually enable, is a history of mood and anxiety disorders. This is because the spouse is continually in a state of uncertainty and fear because of the unknown, or at least what the person perceives is the unknown. Also, in most all instances, the person feels completely inadequate because of, in her mind, never getting things right. It is only after the spouse realizes that she is being manipulated, and what she was told is incorrect that the victim can begin to get better.

One instance is the wife whose husband came home from work every night and started drinking and would not stop until he passed out. This individual was not verbal and rarely said anything to his wife. She was always seeking help from doctors for her depression and was constantly told she had a chemical imbalance so they would try to regulate her neurochemistry through medication. Unfortunately, she never solved the problem although she would feel better physically when medicated and not find herself worrying as much as when off of medication, but every time she stopped taking the meds she would go back to the same depressed mood.

A woman who had been married for about 27 years had a history of alcohol abuse and dependence. She would get upset and depressed and start drinking for months without being sober. Her husband was at his wits end because he did not know what to do to stop the problem and became depressed, would place blame on himself, and would avoid the problem by spending an inordinate amount of hours at work. Other spouses can become anxious because of the constant thought of something bad happening and not knowing what to do to deal with whatever problem is presented.

The Children

As has been mentioned throughout the text, the family functions as a system, and this system does not only include the spouse, but also the children, and in some instances the extended family including grandparents, siblings, and so forth. Dealing with an addict, or alcoholic parent is significantly difficult for children because they do not have the mental capacity to understand the problem, and because of their egocentric way of viewing themselves with the other person. Unfortunately for most children the other parent is unable to help them because the parents are so consumed by problems in the marriage and with the spouse that they do not have enough well-being and strength to work with the children. The result leaves the children making their own conclusions, and in most cases they fault themselves and believe they must do something to fix the problem. The difficulty with the situation is that a child never feels successful because of the way the parent acts.

A 16-year-old boy presented with symptoms of depression, including a poor self-esteem and negative thinking, along with the desire to isolate and not socialize. He told his parents he wanted help and they were glad to get him in psychotherapy. About six weeks into therapy he finally revealed the source of his depression. He said his father was an alcoholic. Because of his drinking the young patient concluded that he could not trust people and was always afraid of rejection. He said that his father would embarrass him in public trying to make him talk to other people when he did not want to. At home the father was always critical of the boy and could not figure out why the boy never wanted to be with him. The result was his poor self-esteem and his desire to isolate for fear of being ridiculed or rejected by peers and his family. Children in these situations will interpret the parent's behavior in a particular way and act according to the perceptions which can be manifested in one of several different general behavioral patterns.

Because children often have a hard time explaining their thoughts and emotions, it leaves parents and others wondering why the child acts as he does. Because the family has a person, in this case a parent, who was chemically dependent, instability exists and continual conflict whether blatant or subtle. The behavior patterns of the children may be manifested as one trying to become a second parent, or as a child who might withdraw, who becomes immersed in an outside activity, be taken in by another family, or resort to using mood-altering chemicals to deal with the problems in the family. Where there are several children in the family, the oldest child, especially if a daughter, will likely be placed in the role of a second parent, or at least attempt to assume the role out of a sense of duty. This child will make sure the other children behave and will be the one who takes over household chores and even cooking. The child may also become the parent's confidant, which has been discussed in earlier chapters, and will likely lead to the double bind situation and result in emotional problems. This is the child, especially if it's a daughter, who will prepare meals so that the parents will not be stressed and will also try to keep the house in order by cleaning and trying to get the other children to clean also. The problem is that no matter what the child does, the parents will still stay the same, and the younger siblings will more than likely not cooperate.

A husband and wife who were both alcoholics would leave their children in cheap motels for several days at a time while they would go off and drink. The oldest child was a daughter, and as an adult she was continually anxious and depressed because of the fear of something bad happening and being her fault. As a child she felt responsible for caring for everyone and would try to keep the children quiet so they would not cause problems and get kicked out of the hotel or taken by the state.

A 16-year-old girl could sense her mother's insecurity because of her alcoholic father. She would come home after school and clean the house and often start dinner because mother was working. She was fearful that they would be angry with her and fight and that dad would leave and go to the bar.

If there are multiple children in the family one might feel so uncomfortable that he will withdraw into his own world. These children usually will resort to the bedroom or some part of the house to keep away from the rest of the family. If in the bedroom, or somewhere else, they're putting themselves in a position to become depressed because of idle time to think negatively. These children may likely retreat to a depressing type of music and read books and so forth. One child's parents complained that he never interacted with the family which left him feeling upset and discouraged because of his isolation. It became apparent that the boy withdrew because of the way his father acted after drinking. The boy felt completely vulnerable, helpless, that he had no control over his life, and that he had no one to support or protect him. He said his best friend was his dog and that if he was not in school or required to be in the house, he was in the woods in the back of his property with his dog exploring, talking to his dog, and enjoying the safe feeling of being alone. In such cases there might have been a sense of safety, but the end result leads to depression and discomfort when relating to other people.

Another child might become the perfect student in school. This child, like any other, will try to do whatever she can to get a sense of acceptance and well-being. Here the child will find solace and comfort in academics. This child is typically a straight A student and is usually at the top of the class. She will be at school whenever possible, or studying someplace that is quiet, such as her room or possibly even the library. She will also likely be involved in a number of school activities, clubs, or social organizations. The reason for all of this activity is because by being a good student, and being a member of a number of organizations, she will have the sense of acceptance not realized at home. Unfortunately, this is a child who even though she is involved in school will lack people skills.

A young man aged 15 was one of these children. He tried to be perfect in school because he knew that he would never get any recognition at home. He was one of the top students in his class and also the president of several organizations on campus. He was only home to sleep at night and to have meals when required. The rest of his time was spent in the pursuit of academics. He had no friends and according to him his reason for not having friends was because it took too much time. On further exploration he revealed that people frightened him, especially young people his age. He was not treated very well socially by his peers because he did not know how to relate to them.

If he was in a social setting, he would spend his time talking to the adults because he felt more comfortable with them. He would try to engage in academic or intellectual conversations that were of no interest to his peers. This problem was even perpetuated in his family knowing they could not relate to him, and he had no interest in them. A number of young people who are top students are in this position because they feel inadequate in other areas so they put all their effort into the academics.

It is not uncommon for a child in this type of a family setting to find comfort with another family. Several young people have stated in therapy that the other family was more loving and accepting and they felt safer there than at home. These are children who will end up calling the parents of this new family mom and dad, and the siblings, brothers and sisters. The family may be well-meaning and want to help. In many cases they do because of protecting the child from the chaotic home of his origin. One family in particular took in several children from dysfunctional families, one of which was from a family of an alcoholic father. The parents took great pride in being able to give the children help so they could have a home. The problem though may be inadvertently encouraging resentment toward the biological parents and ultimately have a difficult time relating to others on a feeling level. One young adult on the other hand said that if it had not been for those that allowed him to be a part of their family, he would have ended up either a derelict or criminal. He was raised on an Indian reservation and was one of the younger of a large number of children, and his father was an alcoholic. Unfortunately for him on one of his visits home, his father in a drunken state, committed suicide in the presence of this person. At that time he was about 11-years-old. If it had not been for this other family who took him in, he likely would have had no one to go to for support, comfort, and ultimately good healthy direction.

There are other avenues children will choose to deal with the dysfunction in the family due to drug and alcohol abuse. One high school student was an excellent athlete. He was average academically, but excelled on the sports field. He played football and basketball and was the starting catcher for the baseball team. He spent all of his time working out and practicing for the particular sport he was participating in at the time. He received a significant amount of praise and recognition from people, but at home he was ridiculed by his alcoholic father. His father said that he was wasting his time and should be working and told the son that he would never amount to anything. Another person found solace in music. She was an excellent pianist because most of her time was spent practicing the piano. She received accolades for her ability to play the piano which gave her the sense of well-being and importance that she was not receiving from home. Like many of these other instances, she did not know how to relate to people on a feeling level. She said one of her boyfriends complained that he did not want to be with her because she was always too busy and was never very affectionate. She married a man who was rather meek and had a difficult time establishing himself as a person.

The Drug Dependent Adolescent

Young people becoming involved in drug abuse is common, and many become dependent on mood-altering chemicals. This usually starts in middle adolescence when children are increasingly exposed to more temptations. Most young people will say that they started using drugs or drinking to fit in with their friends and to become popular, and had to work hard to get used to the taste of alcohol or even overcome the uncomfortable feelings from using tobacco. In many cases children start with what are labeled gateway drugs. These are typically the drugs that are available to the general public and are easily accessible. They include alcohol, tobacco, and marijuana. Even though it may take some work for young people to become accustomed to using these drugs, they do admit that in most cases the emotional result was far more important than the taste or the discomfort from it. A number of young people have admitted that their first cigarette gave them a feeling of strength, comfort, and solace. Vaping, or using vaporized cigarettes to smoke, is also becoming rather popular with the young people because there is no odor and it's easy to get. A 14-year-old boy was caught by his parents vaping and admitted to his therapist that he did it because it made him feel better and less stressed. He was feeling stress at home and school because he was not producing well academically. Another young man was introduced to marijuana and said that it took him away from all of his problems and left him feeling like he was okay and that he could handle everything. The problem was he did nothing.

One young adolescent male used drugs and he became very destructive to the family. His father admitted that after trying many different ways to help his son stop using alcohol and marijuana. He started in high school and within a short time dad discovered that he and his wife were always arguing with each other and that he almost destroyed their marriage. He went on to say that not only was he destructive to the marriage, but also led his siblings to feel that it was okay for them to misbehave because he was getting away with it. In other instances parents might spend all their time and energy trying to keep the child away from drugs or alcohol by sending the child off to private schools, to camps, and so forth. Other parents send their children to treatment facilities and in some cases the survival-type treatment programs. Siblings can also become a part of the problem by covering for the child who is drinking or using drugs. One young child said that she felt afraid for her older brother so she would always lie about him and back of his stories when questioned by the parents, but she always felt guilty for doing so. Unfortunately, as in the case just mentioned, the child who is addicted to the mood-altering chemicals will become manipulative and then have a very negative influence on the other children in the family. Because of this problem most parents feel helpless and frightened because of the potential consequences for the child's poor behavior. They try to help but usually report it is to no avail.

A person will not change unless she sees the need to, or has the desire to. Most young people will say they have no desire to quit but that they can whenever they want to. Unfortunately for them they are too immature to understand the strength of an addiction. Parents who seek help will most likely admit that they have no idea what to do to help the child. Most talk about unconditional love and feel that maybe that will win the child over. They do not realize that unconditional love is actually making the problem worse because a child is getting the idea that no matter what he or she does it is okay. Unconditional means that "I love you no matter what you do, it is up to me to show you enough love and caring and tell you I love you so that you will then have a change of heart."

One couple thought this was the answer to their son's drug problem. They would never scold him for what he was doing, mother always tucked him in bed at night when he would come home under the influence. Unfortunately, the behavior became so destructive that the father finally had to dismiss the young man from the family. He told the boy that as long as he was doing this he could not be part of the family as he was hurting everyone in the family. He said that his family members got mad at him for doing this thinking that the boy was going to become worse. He said that his friends at church disagreed with him and told him emphatically that he would never see his son again. The boy was gone for about a year when he finally called home one day and told his father that he had been in rehab for the past three or four months. He told his father he was sorry for what he had done and was trying to straighten out his life. He asked the father to come visit him and the father did on several occasions and found out the boy was sincere in his desires to change. After about three visits the boy asked the father if he could please come home to be with the family. This surprised the father and he said that he thought about it for a brief period of time and finally said he would love to have the boy home but could not have him back the way he was before. The boy agreed wholeheartedly and said that he would never go back to that, was allowed to come home, and a year later was still living according to his understanding of what was right as well as the desires of his parents. He was going to school, attending church, and became the model big brother that he should've been in the beginning.

Parents must learn to be strong enough to stop the poor behavior in the beginning. The longer they put off establishing the rules of the family for the patient, the more difficult it is to stop, and the more it destroys the family. Unfortunately, in our society we were encouraged to be loving to our children. To the contrary, children see this as weakness and see the love as permission to continue on their destructive path. Only when they realize they cannot be a part of the family and as long as they are doing what they are will they be in the position to make a choice of what they really want. This may sound harsh to most people because of the fear of the child getting worse when the line is drawn. The question to ask is what is there to prevent the child from doing the things that they fear the child doing while living at home, and in most cases is already doing? If the child is in sent off to a treatment facility the parents must be involved in the process and must make it clear to the child that she will not be released from the facility until she has decided to live according to the family rules. These rules include no use of mood-altering chemicals. In the beginning the child will rebel and get upset, but when she realizes mom and dad are not going to change, she will eventually come around like the young man just mentioned. Sometimes a child needs to be dismissed from the family, but this has to be when the child is within the adult age range. Sometimes children are told that because they are unwilling to manage themselves the parents have to do it for them. The parents may have to take complete charge of the child's life until she is able to consistently show that the destructive behavior is no longer present and understand that it will not be tolerated. In many cases children will use mood-altering chemicals to change how they feel. They do not understand that the more involved they become in the drug use the more conflict and trouble they feel emotionally and mentally. The kind person is one who will help the child stop so they can have the peace of mind that comes from living according to family rules, as well as her knowledge of what is right.

Helping the Person

The question of how to help the person is always foremost in the family members' minds. The person will not change until he or she is uncomfortable enough to do so. In most cases this requires cutting the person off and dismissing the person from the family until he decides to change. This is frightening to a number of families and more especially spouses because of the perceived ramifications from this decision. They fear that the person will become worse, retaliate, find somebody else, or even commit suicide. The spouse needs to understand that that is the individual's choice, but that the person needs to know that this will not be tolerated. In most cases when the line is drawn the person changes because he realizes the loss of the family, job, money, or all is too great of an expense. If on the other hand an enabler is always trying to help, the person prolongs the problem and makes things far more difficult to deal with in the future. Kindness is not permissiveness because permissiveness encourages poor behavior when the person is immature. Kindness is helping the person stop the poor behavior that is so destructive by not allowing it in his or her presence. If the person wants to change his life badly enough he will change. This is not to mean one tells the person to be gone forever, but when the changes are sincerely and honestly made he is welcome like the flowers in May.

Chapter 10 — Worksheet

1. Describe the chemically dependent person, and explain why he or she uses mood-altering chemicals?

2. How does the enabler act toward the chemically dependent spouse?

3. What is one way a dependent child might respond to an alcoholic parent and the family situation?

Chapter 11
Personality Disorders

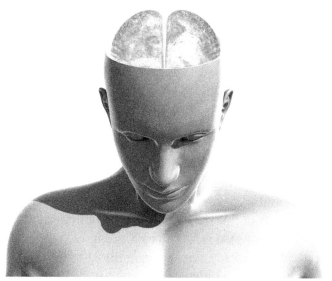

imredesiuk / Shutterstock.com

Definition of a Personality Disorder

A personality disorder needs to be thought of as a long-standing disorder that is so deeply entrenched in the person that it becomes his or her personality (DSM-5). As a result, most individuals feel that they don't need to change, or they don't have a problem. If they do seek treatment, they usually don't stay very long because they think that the requirements to change can't be accomplished or require more than they are willing to do. Most therapists do not want to work with personality disorders because it is almost a thankless job. When a person changes, it is usually because they have suffered enough discomfort, and have gone through a long period of therapy. Personality disorders are divided into three categories. Cluster A is odd and eccentric and includes the odd personality disorders, which are paranoid, schizotypal, and schizoid. Cluster B is the dramatic personality disorders, antisocial, borderline, histrionic, and narcissistic. Cluster C is the anxious personality disorders, including avoidant, dependent, and obsessive-compulsive. It must be noted though that most people who have personality disorders have symptoms that do not typically fit just one category. A borderline person may also have symptoms of histrionic and dependence problems. In another case, one who is obsessive and compulsive may also show signs of schizoid behavior patterns.

The Disorders and How They Are Learned

The Odd and Eccentric Cluster

The Odd and Eccentric group includes those who act in ways that come across as either bizarre or eccentric. The first point to consider is that each of these stem from a fear of, or discomfort with, people. The schizotypal individual show signs of schizophrenia but not to the point of one with the actual diagnosis. This individual has little to do with people and chooses to live in his or her own world, which in many cases is somewhat of a fantasy world. These are people who have bizarre thoughts and ideas about themselves and about their surroundings and can often have hallucinations and delusional thinking. In spite of this they are still able to function well enough in society to support themselves, and in some cases marry and have families. For the most part, though, they again tend to stay to themselves. In most cases they would not be seen as schizophrenic, but as people with some strange ideas about life. These individuals are often raised in families that are chaotic, with no consistency, and are difficult to predict. Thus, the person develops his own world to survive.

One such case was a 17-year-old boy who was raised by very withdrawn and defeated mother who never put her foot down with anyone, and an alcoholic father who was often passed out on the couch drunk, would not work, and thus, would be in constant conflict with the wife. The young man didn't have friends, but said that if he did, he would never have brought friends home from school because he would be embarrassed when his father would be found naked and passed out on the couch. This young man had developed somewhat of a fantasy world, thinking about science fiction stories and reading bizarre, scary books.

Another young man 19 years of age was attending a university in another state from his parents and was referred for evaluation in therapy because of his bizarre thoughts. In therapy he revealed that he was the youngest of five boys and unlike the other brothers, he was more like his mother's stature than his father's. His father was an airline pilot, was athletic, and his brothers were also athletic. He, on the other hand, had a slight build and did not do well in sports. He said that his father and brothers teased him and made him feel like he was less of a person. He also admitted that he was often picked on by the other children in the neighborhood. His way of dealing with the problem was retreating to his room and summoning his friends from outer space. In his mind he would rally them together and they would go and beat up the people who hurt him, and of course, he was the leader. Through the years it became such a pattern with him that this became his personality and was interfering with him succeeding at the university. It was recommended that he return home and seek psychiatric help, which he did, and he was later able to return to school.

The paranoid personality disordered individual is one who is consumed by fears and discomfort as well as distrust of people. In many instances they think that someone is out to get them so they develop elaborate schemes to avoid those threats they imagine. One particular father was always late getting home from work. He finally admitted that he had to take a different route each night to avoid people who were following him. In another example, a young male adult was raised in a somewhat unstable family where mother and father were always disagreeing with each other and this frightened him. He was continually fearful of doing something wrong and getting in trouble. He developed thoughts in his mind of people spying on him, which made him frightened to go anywhere. He worked in a job that required little contact with the people, which was acceptable to him.

The schizotypal and paranoid personality disorders are not as common as the schizoid personality disorder. This is an individual who is perfectly okay being alone, has no bizarre thoughts, but has no use for people. One example is a man who did not like being around others, and even though he was married, he left his wife and family to be a hermit. He lived in the mountains with his dog and survived off of the land. He would come into civilization about twice a year to trade furs for coffee, salt, and sugar. He admitted that he decided to return to his family when he realized that he was losing the need for language. He said he had not forgotten how to speak but said he had no use for it by himself and away from civilization. Another example refers back to the married man introduced in Chapter 2 who would leave home for work at approximately 6 AM to avoid speaking with the family. He was a bank auditor, which allowed him to be by himself during the day. . He would return home late enough in the evening for his wife and children to have already eaten dinner. His wife would make a plate for him, which he would heat and take to his study where he spent his time during baseball season figuring. Most individuals with this disorder will choose careers that exclude them from interacting with others.

In all of these cases each individual was, for whatever reason, unwilling to engage in the people-world, and the result was isolation and as little contact with other people as possible. Because of their tendency to avoid people, they give others the false impression that they do not like people. When this is the case, they are in turn rejected by others, which leave them feeling like nobody likes them. This often starts in childhood, when these individuals learn that interacting with other people brings about discomfort and even pain. If the young boy is continually ridiculed by his father or mother, he will assume that his parents, along with others, are not safe and will be avoided.

Another example is a person being raised in a family where communication is limited. One individual with the diagnosis of schizoid personality disorder said that he was raised on a farm, and the nearest neighbor was about 5 miles away. He said his father was not a man of many words, and his mother was a quiet person. As a result he also pursued the career of farming because it meant he could be alone with his equipment and the animals he was raising. He sought help briefly but decided after two sessions not to return because he thought that he was being pushed to become more involved with his wife, children, and others.

The Dramatic Cluster

The dramatic cluster includes people who typically have a difficult time interacting with others because of their overbearing personality traits. It is important to understand that with this group of people, for the most part, are in constant conflict with others. The first group to consider is the antisocial personality disordered individual. As was mentioned, in childhood disorders, this diagnosis cannot be given to persons under 18 years of age. Males make up the majority with this diagnosis, and most are found to be in trouble with the law. Although not everyone who was incarcerated has this diagnosis, a good number are. This person is one who is found to lack any consideration of rights of others and has no regard for the laws of society.

Many abusive spouses are antisocial. The reason for this is because they have the idea that by being aggressive they will get their way. One man in his mid-20s was attending a university and proudly stated that he coerced one of his teachers into changing his grade. He walked into the office on a Saturday afternoon with his rifle in hand and requested that the teacher give him a better grade than he had received in the class. This man proudly said that the teacher got frightened and immediately granted his request. When he was a youth he shot a friend and was never held accountable for it.

In another instance a man was raised by a single mother who owned a bar and also ran a brothel. He was taught from an early age to have no regard for authority or the law, and as a result did not care about anybody's well-being but his own. Even though he was never incarcerated, he was in continual opposition to the rules of society and was void of any caring for other people. In many cases this disorder starts in childhood when a child is given a diagnosis of conduct disorder. Because there is either no, or limited accountability, the child has a false sense of not having to the answer to the law or any other authority. A prime example of this is a man who was on trial for murder, and during jury deliberations one member of the jury felt that she could not find this individual guilty because she could not hold him accountable for his behavior due to a poor diet during childhood. She was convinced otherwise by the others, and he was convicted and given the death penalty. At the end of the trial, the judge told the jury that he was grateful for the decision and then revealed to them information that could not have been brought up in the trial. He told the jury that this person had been in trouble with the law since he was about 13-years-old and was always able to somehow get away from responsibility and accountability until his final crime.

The borderline personality disordered individual is typically found with women, and most therapists either dread working with this clientele or will refuse to do so. This is the person who is quick to start relationships with people, especially with the opposite sex, but for a very small reason, or maybe even no apparent reason, will become upset, mad, and sever the relationship. In many cases these are women who seek relationships that will make them happy, will be the answer to all their desires, and after meeting a man, will immediately assume that he is the person. The relationship starts rapidly and is deeply emotional, and as soon as the man says or does something that the person does not appreciate, the relationship is over because the man is viewed by the woman as a deceiver and terrible person. When this occurs, the other party, in this case the man, will be left standing and wondering what went wrong? Often the person will do whatever he can to make her happy and when she does come back; he will be walking on egg shells and living in constant fear of doing something to upset her.

A young single man initially sought help with his fiancée. She was always very moody and demanding, and almost impossible to please. He went ahead and married her anyway and then came for therapy because of the severe strife, arguing, and fighting between them. They were asked to leave the apartment complex where they were living because of the noise they were causing from fighting. She was always accusing him of being with other women, or at least lusting after them. She did not trust him and checked his phone continually. Even though she was accusing him of flirting, she saw nothing wrong with her talking to other men whenever she felt like it. Because she was afraid of not being attractive to him, she had breast implants thinking that would make her feel better, but he found out that she was then even more flirtatious because of her new breast size. In therapy she admitted that she acted this way as a child because she always felt like she was not measuring up. As a result, she would get upset with her father and mother and accuse them of not loving her, and they would do whatever they had to do to make her feel important. This behavior pattern was carried into adulthood, which ultimately led to divorce. Again, these are people, typically women, who have learned that by acting upset, demanding, and emotional, that they get their way most of the time. The problem is that they are continually in conflict and can never understand why no one likes them or why they cannot keep friendships.

The histrionic personality disordered person is one who has to be at the center of attention in most situations. They achieve this by either dressing flamboyantly and far beyond what is expected or they are loud and do whatever is needed to get people to pay attention to them. One example is a lady who was the center of attention in every social gathering because of ingratiating herself with everyone. She attempted to get them to give her approval so she could feel okay about herself. Simply put, this is the person who has to tell the most stories or whatever has happened to him or her is far worse and more tragic or extreme than what happened to someone else. Also, at a social gathering the person has to make the grand entrance so that everyone knows that he or she is present. One individual always had to be the funny one and would do whatever was necessary to get people to laugh. His dress was average, but his demeanor was extremely outgoing and loud. If he felt he wasn't getting enough attention he would either pout or get louder and more aggressive.

The individual with the narcissistic personality disorder is one who feels that he or she is entitled and can do nothing wrong. This person has the mistaken idea that if everyone did things the way she wanted things would be okay, but if they didn't do what she wanted, a heavy price would be paid. This person has little tolerance for people who challenge him and his authority. Also somewhat like the antisocial personality disorder, the narcissist feels as though he does not have to answer to the rules of society. One example was a prominent attorney who always had to let everyone know he had all the answers. If he was in a leadership position complete obedience and conforming to his wishes was demanded, and he would not stop until he had what he wanted. On one occasion he bought a car and had the mistaken idea that he could work his way around the contract for payment and not pay for the car. When he was taken to court he was surprised to find out that the judge did not agree with his logic and ordered him to pay the debt he owed.

A woman was raised by a very controlling father who continually demanded obedience, and if others did not cooperate, he would yell and carry on until they would finally give in and do what he wanted. This was a constant pattern of his, and his youngest son picked up on this and carried this tendency into his adult life. He married a woman somewhat younger than him and always felt as though he had to control the family, and she needed to be a good wife, follow his directions, and never question him. They had three boys and not one could ever measure up to his standard. Saturdays were miserable because he had to make sure everybody was working and everything had to be perfect. As a result, he lost his marriage and the children have very little to do with him.

In another instance a married man was successful in law enforcement and felt comfortable at work because his position required everyone to follow his orders. He was not given the same courtesy at home and as a result almost lost his marriage because his wife was finally strong enough to put her foot down and not be involved with him and his poor behavior. It even got to the point where he did not think she was good enough for him and he became interested in another woman. It was only after she put her foot down that he realized she was an excellent wife and he would be the one who lost the most if they divorced. Another elderly man had been narcissistic most of his life and almost lost his family. No one could ever question him, and if they did they paid a heavy price, which was his wrath and extreme disapproval of them.

In all of these cases the individual was not raised in a situation where rules and limits were consistent. They also learned that by acting selfish and demanding, they would get their way. This unfortunately leads to isolation, poor self-esteem, possible depression, and a very negative outlook on life because people do not want to be around them. What is lacking here is accountability. This is shown by their feeling that they are different than everyone else, and as result don't need to change.

The Anxious Cluster

The anxious personality disorder cluster is indicated by behaviors manifested by one who is fearful. These individuals are insecure and unsure, but unlike the other disorders mentioned, these individuals are afraid and anxious, and therefore act in a way that appears to most as meek and timid, and in many cases, easy to manipulate. The dependent individual is one who suffers from the fear of abandonment. Oftentimes this abandonment was learned in childhood being raised by parents who were negligent or otherwise rarely present. This person comes across as needy and clingy. He always worries about pleasing others so he will try to become whatever the other person wants him to be. This person has no sense of being a whole person and as a result is always trying to do what the other person wants. He has no opinion and when asked what he wants to do, he will say something like, "it doesn't matter, whatever you want to do." This person becomes burdensome in a relationship because most people do not want to be the one making all the decisions and having to always take the lead. In a healthy relationship people give-and-take whereas the dependent person will only give and never take which keeps the other person from being able to invest.

A wife was dependent and always did whatever her husband wanted her to do. This was great during the brief engagement of about two months because the husband thought that she would always be there by his side and support him. After about a year of marriage he expressed frustration because he was not allowed to invest back in her. She was there at his beck and call. By not allowing him to invest in her, he was beginning to lose interest in the relationship. Even when he tried to explain his feelings to her, she would only feel guilty--thinking that she was doing something wrong and would then try harder to make him happy by doing more for him.

In another example a woman had been divorced for about 18 months and had a young son about the age of 4. She started dating a man who was there to please her any way he could. If she needed something he would buy it for her, if she wanted to go somewhere he would take her. He would often surprise her with gifts and never expected anything in return. He said it brought him great pleasure to take care of her, but he also privately admitted that he was afraid if he expected anything back, that she, like other people he had known throughout his life, would leave him. She eventually broke off the relationship because she did not respect him. He once again was left with the thought that he was not good enough and could not please anyone, which made him even more dependent.

A woman in her mid-40s never married and was afraid of close relationships with people, but on occasion found someone with whom she could be friends. She stated that the friendships would not last and she felt this was because she would become too dependent on that person and almost smother the individual.

Anxious people are consumed by worrisome, frightening thoughts, and the obsessive-compulsive personality disordered person is no exception. This individual will typically feel that she has to go through certain rituals to feel calm and safe. Unlike the OCD diagnosis, the person with the personality disorder is not as burdened by the problem in most cases, but will still have a hard time functioning in a number of settings.

A middle-aged man who is well-educated and employed in a high status position was afraid of germs. He would work and wash his hands, but not as frequently as someone with OCD. Because of his fear of germs however, he would get upset if anyone coughed or sneezed and would try to remove himself from the area. The fears that the person experiences are unrealistic and usually unfounded, but the person will still act on the compulsion. This is often learned in childhood, and in most cases, the person as a child found certain behaviors to give him a sense of security.

A married woman with two children was raised in a family where the father was always obsessed with appearances and had to have everything perfect. Because of the way he treated the family, the patient felt as though she had to be perfect in all that she did. If something was not right with her she would get angry and cause a commotion until the problem that existed in her mind was resolved. She admitted that she had this tendency since she was little and would only feel comfortable when she thought things were in order according to her standard. Her behavior was so troublesome to the rest of the family that she was eventually left alone and not included in family activities. Her husband found a sense of well-being in several hobbies that he was pursuing, including woodworking and model building.

An individual with the avoidant personality disorder acts on his or her fears by avoiding social situations that are uncomfortable. To illustrate this, a single mother with a 9-year-old daughter was attending a university to become an elementary school teacher. She attempted to be a part of a social group in her church that was comprised of single adults and would attend all meetings and activities, but always stayed by herself. On one occasion the group sponsored a Valentine's dance and she was in charge of the refreshments. When asked if she enjoyed herself, she said she was so busy she didn't have time to think about anything. When questioned further she admitted that she did not talk to anyone unless they approached her, never danced with anyone, and spent most of her time either in the kitchen preparing food, or running to the store to buy refreshments. She said that she did this because of her discomfort with other people. On another occasion the group met at the home of a married couple who was friends with one of the group members. It was in the summer and everyone congregated in the backyard, including her. She did not socialize with anyone but said that she sat on a large rock in the back corner of the yard that was somewhat secluded by bushes. She sat there and felt lonely and cried for a while.

Another single lady who felt uncomfortable around other people would also socialize and acted much the same as the person just described. If she would talk to people at a social gathering or even casual visits, she would carry on a polite conversation but would not let it get past surface conversation. She admitted that she wanted a close relationship but avoided them because of her feelings of inadequacy and fears of people hurting her. This problem started in childhood. Because of her weight, she was picked on and teased incessantly by children at school and church. The result was isolation in school and ultimately convincing her parents to be homeschooled, which reinforced her negative feelings about herself and her tendency to avoid people. Another woman was divorced and had three adult children. She was so entrenched in her avoidant personality that she would go to work if it was a job that did not require much interaction with other people. For the most part she spent her time caring for elderly people, and many of them suffered from Alzheimer's. She admitted that she was somewhat insecure as a child. Her marriage was abusive verbally and physically, and as a result her doubts about herself became so strong that she felt that no one would ever appreciate her.

The Family

Throughout this chapter brief mention regarding the family has been made; however, it is important to consider this in greater depth. As is understood of the family, it functions as a system where each family member has his or her own roles, whether positive or negative. Each is expected to stay within that role. When considering the borderline personality disordered person for example, the young lady who almost destroyed her marriage because of her continual fighting and her husband's distress said that her parents were negatively affected by this. She indicated her father always tried to cajole and appease her. Mother, on the other hand, was afraid of her temper and outbursts so she treated her with kid gloves and would do all she could to avoid a confrontation. This usually meant giving into the desires of the daughter. As a result their inconsistent and inadequate treatment of her reinforced her behavior, which she carried into her adult life. An example of the family of an antisocial personality disorder was a single mother who raised three boys by herself. Her husband was in prison and left her both financially distressed, and embarrassed. She had two sons who were in their late teen years and a son who was in middle childhood. The two older brothers were constantly in trouble with the law and the younger brother idolized and wanted to be like them. As a result when he left elementary school and entered junior high he was showing the signs of conduct disorder and, by the time he reached 18, he had the same antisocial disorder as his father and brothers. The mother was fearful of saying anything to the boys because she did not want a fight or confrontation so they were allowed to come and go as they pleased and were never held responsible for their behaviors.

A young boy in his middle teens started showing signs of conduct disorder at the age of 11. He continually got in trouble at school by not doing his work and defying authority. When older, he felt more comfortable with breaking the law by destroying others' property, breaking and entering, and stealing school property. On one occasion he stole the school money that was earned by the students from a candy sale. Both parents were unable to set limits because of physical and emotional problems. They would try to keep him in control but unfortunately were unable to hold him accountable. Because of the lack of accountability he had the mistaken idea that he could get away with whatever he wanted. He once said that he felt that he could always "beat the rap." It was not until he was 17-years-old and put in juvenile detention for the second time for 9 months that he decided to stop breaking the law with the exception of using illegal drugs.

In many instances the histrionic person has not ever felt sure of herself and her value as a person, so she will typically attempt to be the center of attention. This often comes from parents who are inconsistent in their teaching, or parents who are demanding but never clear in letting the child know that he or she has arrived to the standard expected by the parents. One case was a mid-30s male who was married but had a long history of conflict including being tossed from family to family, parental discord, and no consistency in his education. He was finally sentenced to a training school but admitted that he never felt as though people approved of him so he was always the class clown and the comedian as an adult. Because of his problems he was unable to maintain a job, which also left him feeling inadequate.

Those who fit the anxious cluster are people who, in many cases, have been traumatized by family in childhood. This could be anything from sexual to verbal or physical abuse, or even neglect. One single lady who was avoidant was raised in a large family by an immature father. She was constantly fearful of upsetting people. Her father would not come out and say he was upset but would act disappointed or pout, which would leave the family on edge and fearful of disappointing him. She said that she had to be excellent so people would not recognize her or have any reason to question what she was doing. Even though she was excellent at work and wanted relationships, she was always isolating. On the other hand, the dependent person is typically one who was either raised in a family that was extremely demanding and never satisfied or a family where the lack of success is ever present. Here the example is the young man who was always told by his father that he would never amount to anything and tried to please his father and everyone else. He became a dependent person who was always anxious to please and never feeling that he was acceptable.

Those individuals who are in the odd personality cluster for whatever reason choose to be alone. In many, but not all cases, these are individuals who were raised in families where emotion was never expressed and social involvement was not encouraged, or may even have been discouraged. Many were raised by a parent who has the disorder and as a result have not learned how to function in society. One such case was a man whose father was a loner and his mother was very distrustful of people. He grew up wanting to be by himself and was reluctant to trust people. He said that as a youth he spent most of his time with his dog either in the yard or in the vacant land around his subdivision where he found comfort and safety. He said that as a child he wanted to interact with people, but eventually gave up because he only saw them as potential hurt and pain. He excelled in athletics, but only had to interact with people there on the sports field. He married and struggled for the better part of the marriage because of his tendency to avoid confrontation. He learned in his family that fighting was the best way to get people to leave him alone which left his wife and children constantly feeling like they were in the wrong and that he was not pleased with them. His wife finally became strong enough to put her foot down and tell him his behavior was not allowed to continue. He wanted the marriage badly enough to work on overcoming the problem. Because of this entrenched thinking and behavior he was in therapy for a number of years before working through his difficulties.

Another adult male was allowed to act on his withdrawn feelings as a child. In the middle of his seventh grade year he decided he did not want to go to school any longer but wanted to stay home, and his mother allowed it. His father disagreed but did not have the fortitude to insist that the boy return to school. He sought help when he was in his middle 50s, stating that he was tired of being lonely and wanted to change. The problem with him, as with most of those with a personality disorder, was that he did not stay in therapy because it became too uncomfortable. He admitted that the changes he knew he had to make were too much so he quit and went back to living a very isolated life. It became so bad that not even his family would have anything to do with him.

Those with the dramatic personality disorder, regardless of the specific diagnosis, are people who do not trust others and feel insecure around people, but in this case their discomfort is manifested by trying to take control of situations. One example is a man who was in a drug rehab facility to accomplish two things. First of all, he knew that as long as he was in the rehab hospital, he could not be approached by the law. He also said he wanted to stop using drugs and in the beginning of the program was enthusiastic about recovering. He admitted in therapy that he had been unfaithful to his wife, had stolen from people to get what he wanted, had no regard for the law, and that he had a troubled adolescence. As an adult he felt as though people did not mean what they said because he had never been held fully accountable for his misdeeds. In his case, the lack of accountability was apparent, which is also present with most individuals who fit into this cluster.

A middle-aged housewife was raised in a family where rules were inconsistent and there was a lot of emotion expressed openly by both the parents and the other siblings. She admitted that she felt the only way to get a sense of acceptance was by acting flamboyant and to be the center of attention. She said that all her life she wanted people to say that she was okay but never felt their acceptance so she had to be the life of the party. When all of the attention wasn't on her, she would go into depression thinking that she once again was a worthless person.

The next question is how does this person affect the family itself? As has been explained, family dynamics have a profound influence on the child's learned behavior patterns. When this individual then becomes an adult and tries to establish his or her own life either as a single person, or married, these behaviors begin to affect the other person or people negatively. Most spouses will admit that their love for the person has diminished because of the continual conflict. This oftentimes leads to divorce, which hurts everyone in the family. In the beginning the spouse will likely think that it is her fault so, as has been pointed out, the spouse will try harder to make things work. This will not only interfere with the marriage, but also with being a parent. When the parent is so consumed by the conflict created by the other spouse, there is no energy, or time, or wherewithal left over to care for the needs of the children. This typically leaves the children floundering and not sure what to count on, or expect, so they will react much the same way as was explained with children raised in chemically dependent families and other dysfunctional families. Unfortunately, a number of these young people will grow up with the same disorders as manifested by the parents. Even if this is not the case the dysfunction will continue because of the insecurity and distress that one develops after having been raised in a chaotic environment.

One example is a young lady who was raised in a chaotic family by a single mother who despised being a parent. The mother did whatever she had to do to stay away from the discomfort of the children and the problems of home. As a result the youngest of these children developed a dependent personality disorder. She was one who always sought approval from other people and was easily taken advantage of because of her willingness to please them. The only boy in the family developed an antisocial personality disorder because of his disregard for his mother's authority, and ultimately the authority of society. He was involved in drugs to include selling and transporting and eventually had to move away from his hometown never to return for fear of retribution from both the drug community and the law. The oldest of the children was a daughter who eventually indicated signs of the avoidant personality disorder. She had to be the second parent and could never live up to the expectations of her mother or other family members. She was also resented by her siblings because of her controlling behavior with them. She resorted to crafts and hobbies to occupy her time and was always uncomfortable around people. The one daughter in the family who did not develop a personality disorder said that she had other extended family members that she would gravitate to as well as people in the community who were stable and trustworthy. Of the four children she was the only one who had a successful marriage and did well raising her family. In this case the personality disorders were developed because of the dysfunction of the mother.

A schizoid personality disordered individual was married and had two children. He was successful in school as well as in athletics, but in both cases these were activities that did not require much interaction with others. He was an excellent student because he spent most of his time studying. The sport he participated in required individual performance so he did not have to interact with teammates. Even when the sporting events required travel he spent his time in the books which kept him from relating to others. He was highly successful as a professional in the medical field because his field of expertise did not require interacting much with people except in the position of authority with the patients. His wife dealt with her husband's emotional and physical absence by involving herself in spending money. She was often busy shopping for clothing, or children's items, and decorating the home. The children developed a strong relationship with mother but literally had nothing to do with father because they never knew him except that he would come home and retreat to the television or books.

In all these cases, the individuals stay in their personality disorders and their behaviors because others are afraid of saying anything, or sense the individual will not change anyway so why try. When people do complain, the individual will either overpower them or ignore them, which leave the person feeling disarmed and unable to do anything to help. On the other hand, those few people who are able to withstand the resistance and not back away can be of great help to the person. The reasons the person will resist this is because first this is a reinforced behavior, and second not wanting to, feeling insecure about changing. For the most part people tolerate the individual and eventually go about their own lives ignoring that person. People can change when they want to, but typically the want does not come until all else has failed and the discomfort is significant.

Chapter 11—Worksheet

1. What is a common reason for an individual to manifest the schizoid personality disorder?

2. When considering the borderline and the antisocial personality disorders, what is a common theme or thinking?

Chapter 12
Therapy with Children and Parents

Image Point Fr / Shutterstock.com

Typically, when a child presents with a problem or disorder, parents will want the child to receive help so they send him or her off to a therapist. In extreme cases, the child may be sent to a treatment facility or treatment program. Unfortunately, in most cases little if any progress is made. This becomes discouraging because the parents want their child to do well and will do all that is necessary to get the help needed. This may also include the medical profession where medications are prescribed with the intent of helping the child function in a healthy way. Success may be seen while the child is on the medication, but when off, the behaviors typically return. In most cases, the child will be seen by a therapist or psychologist while the parents sit in the waiting room and are left out of the loop. This is frustrating because the parents want to help but are left not knowing what to do. If the parents are not involved, most therapy with the child will be to no avail.

A child and adolescent psychiatric facility had several types of programs including a day program where children would come during the school day and return home in the evening. The week program has the child in an inpatient facility during the week. He would go home Friday afternoon and return Monday morning. In both cases, it was noticed that the children would do fairly well when in the facility. When the child in the day program returned home and came back the next day it was noticed that the progress that had been made in changing the behavior was undone. This was most pronounced with the children in the week-long program. When the children would come in on Monday morning it would take most of the day to settle them down. These problems would carry over into Tuesday and by the afternoon they would be back in the routine. Wednesday and the better part of Thursday would be a good day, but Friday would be difficult because the children were anticipating going home. It was noted by the staff that when the patients returned on Monday what was accomplished during treatment was nonexistent. It was apparent that the parents were not included in therapy so they had no idea what was accomplished and the progress was not continued at home. Unfortunately according to the staff a number of these parents did not want to be involved to begin with. They just expected the staff and medical doctors to correct the child's problem, much like setting a broken bone or curing a bacterial or viral infection. In other instances, children who are sent to treatment facilities for at least a year will do well in the facility, but because the parents are not involved the child returns home and the old behaviors typically reappear within about 2 to 8 weeks. This again is because of the parents not receiving help in teaching their children and not continuing the facility program at home.

The goal of therapy should be to bring about change that is long-lasting or even permanent. The question to be asked is, when does change occur? People, including children, will not change if there is either no need to or the current behavior is not uncomfortable enough to bring about a desire to function differently. This desire only comes when the child understands that the unhealthy behaviors are no longer tolerated or allowed. The child may understand this in a controlled environment such as the therapist's office treatment facility, school, at church, or others' homes. If the change is not expected at home, no change will occur. As has been pointed out in previous chapters, children misbehave to either find out what the rules are, or if those in authority mean what they say. The child may think that the limit testing has gotten him his way in the past so why not now? If the rules are consistent everywhere, including the family, the behavior will change. This change may not come about immediately, but as the parents remain consistent with the rules, changes will be seen. The point to be made is that behavior is learned and is taught. Thus, the parents, or the primary caregivers, are the most important people in the child's life and have the responsibility for the child's welfare and are thus the primary teachers. If the child learns that the parents are meaningful and consistent in their expectations and rules, the child will find security and obey. On the other hand, if the parents are inconsistent, or teach out of coercion or anger, the child will become confused and not sure what to count on or expect. Again, consistency is of utmost importance.

How to Help Parents

This chapter will begin with several case histories that illustrate how a parent's emotions and resulting behavior can interfere with teaching a child. The first point to be made in providing help to parents is the understanding that the therapist is not to become one who coaches and tell the parents what to do step-by-step. Many therapists unwittingly get caught up in this tangled web and find that they are not accomplishing what is desired. If the therapist feels it necessary to control the situation and tell the parents what to do, the problem ends up resting on the shoulders of the therapist. The therapist cannot fix either the parents or the child but can only assist those responsible for the problem to understand what to do. Also, if the therapist tells the parents want to do and the parents do not feel the same way, nothing will be accomplished, or if it is, it will be somewhat insignificant. Therefore the therapist must help the parents decide on their own what they need to do. If the therapist does all the work and tells the parents what to do and things don't work, the blame will come back on the therapist. Again, it's important to understand that the therapist is to help the parents by helping them learn to help themselves not the therapist doing it for them.

This point can also be viewed as helping the parents determine where they stand on any given problem. If they don't know where they stand they will become inconsistent by acting on their emotions and feelings. Parents cannot teach correct behavior when they are emotionally entangled with the child. Also parents cannot teach something they are not sure of themselves. An example is parents who are depressed cannot teach the child how to avoid depression. Also a parent who has difficulty with anger and temper problems will have a difficult time teaching the child to be in control of his or her behavior. The therapist is to help the parents not act on those emotions and feelings that keep them from being effective teachers. These emotional reactions are, in most cases, the carryover from childhood experiences or may be acquired later in one's life.

As an example, if the parent was raised by abusive parents she will either be abusive and aggressive with the children or afraid of hurting the child. In either case, the parent will not be able to set limits and teach healthy behavior. On the other hand, the parents may not want to invest in the child because of discomfort with people in general. If this is the case the child may find that pushing the limits gets her what she wants. A father had difficulty teaching his children. Although they all matured into competitive and successful adults in their professions, they did not love their father and in fact many avoided him. He was an only child and as a result of that and his competitive spirit he always had to prove to everyone that he was better than they were. This was carried over to his children who felt like they had to be better than everyone else. In many instances he was argumentative with them and would leave them feeling like they had to fight verbally with him and ultimately they learned to distrust him. A good number of his children had emotional problems as adults.

Some individuals may have been raised in a healthy family where they were loved and had effective and meaningful limits but maybe did not learn how to act socially. One couple decided they did not want their children to be involved with the outside world so they homeschooled their children and kept them on their property of about 6 acres. The only social interaction the children had was with friends at church for about 3 hours on Sunday. The father and mother were both socially awkward and had difficulty relating to people. As a result, they were unable to teach their children. A parent who is timid and shy might also have a hard time teaching the child to be outgoing. In many cases the home atmosphere can keep a person from learning social skills.

An example might be allowing children to fight with each other without any parental guidance, or belittle each other because the parents are afraid to stop it. Why is a parent afraid to stop children from fighting? It might be because that parent was picked on and hurt growing up and would feel fearful of any type of confrontation. If this is the case, the fearful feelings might interfere not only with teaching their children how to act at home, but also with peers. The mother who wants to be her daughter's best friend is, in most cases, the woman who as a child and adolescent never felt popular or accepted and so vicariously gets this feeling from her daughter. By being the daughter's friend, the daughter does not learn respect for others and also does not respect boundaries because "friends never tell friends no." There are myriads of examples, but the point to be made is that parents' feelings toward the child are not something that happened randomly but are the result of how the parents think about themselves as well as the child.

The most common feelings that parents have that interfere with teaching are feeling sorry for the child and feelings of helplessness. A single mother was raising two young boys and felt sorry for them because of the living circumstances. Since the ex-husband was not paying child support, the children and wife were deprived of many things in life that other people were enjoying. Mother also had to work, which kept her from being with her children as much and she wanted. She also felt sorry for them because they did not have a father, and on many occasions they would complain about feeling left out because of other children having a father. The result of these feelings she had toward her children made it almost impossible for her to set limits. When a person feels sorry for the child he will become indulgent and will try to do anything necessary to protect the child from any situations or things that may cause hurt. In this case the mother tried to be both father and mother by playing catch with the boys and involving them in sports. She tried to have men at both church and on the boys' teams help out by being a surrogate father. Since she did not find many who would volunteer for the job she felt even worse for the boys.

A group of parents with young blind children were attending a therapy group to become better parents to these children. They all felt sorry for the children because of the disability but overtime all but one of the parents realized that by feeling sorry for their children they were further handicapping them. They were not expecting these children to function in a normal manner. The final holdout, a father, said that he felt it was his duty as a Christian to feel sorry for his daughter and as a result did not see her progressing like the other children. By the end of the 8 weeks of therapy the father realized that feeling sorry for his daughter was detrimental.

Feeling helpless is a common problem with parents because they have convinced themselves the child is unable to do things that the parents want him or her to do. One couple said that their young daughter would refuse to help with family chores and would say she couldn't because they were too much. Mother and father felt helpless because no matter what they tried, the daughter would resist and not cooperate. Another couple felt helpless in helping a child stop lying. They both said that they could see him actually doing something he shouldn't and he would smile and then continue in his misbehavior. They would try to get him to confess to the wrongdoing, but he would always say he did not do it. They could even say they saw him do it and he would deny it, so the child learned to manipulate in this way.

Another example of people feeling both sorry and helpless was mom and dad helping their 12-year-old girl who had cerebral palsy. Neither parent felt sorry for her, nor did they feel helpless and as a result she was able to dress herself, feed herself, walk with the aid of a walker, and was learning to live an independent life. One day when she came home from school she announced to her parents that she wanted an electric wheelchair. To this they said no because they could not afford it and she did need one. She said she saw a boy at school with one and wanted one just like his. Because they would not grant her wish she began to shut down and refuse to dress herself and refused to walk. On one occasion when she refused to dress herself she was taken to school in her pajamas. The people at school became concerned and called in child protective services. It was decided by the authorities that she would be better off living in a foster home. She was removed from her home, was given an electric wheelchair, and over a very brief period of time lost the ability to take care of herself that she had developed at home. When she turned 18, she was released from foster care and because of her disability was placed in a group home where she eventually married another disabled individual. He was both physically and mentally disabled. She became pregnant and had a baby girl. Because of hers and her husband's status, child protective services immediately took the baby from them and placed her in foster care and eventually adoption. It was at this time she reestablished her relationship with her family and was able to admit to her parents that her situation was her own choosing and that she knew that her parents meant well and were helping her more than anyone else. The result of her choices placed her in a position of being dependent on someone else for her care for the rest of her life.

Some parents will take the child's behavior personally. This is often the result of ego-centric thinking wherein the parents assume that the child is misbehaving and defying them because the child does not respect them. In most cases when they feel disrespected they will become angry and when this happens parenting stops and intimidation and even abuse will likely be the result. They do not understand that the child's behavior is because she is a child, not because of disrespect or a desire to hurt the parents. Some parents will say they will make the child respect them no matter what, and as result will become controlling and almost punitive in demanding the child's respect and admiration. The goal of therapy with parents is to help them not act on their emotions but to gain the strength to act on their own wisdom so they can teach effectively.

Therapy with Parents

When providing therapy to parents the initial interview should begin with the all-important question of what the parents' concerns are. Once this is been clarified a thorough case history of the child's development starting with pregnancy and delivery is to be reviewed. It might be that the pregnancy had complications, and if so were there any resulting effects on the child? Along with this is the delivery and whether there were complications that could have occurred during delivery, including anoxia. Next the developmental history needs to be explored. Here the therapist needs to ask if all developmental milestones were reached within normal limits. These milestones include the age at which the child was able to roll over, sit up on his or her own, and when he or she began to crawl and ultimately walk. This is commonly achieved within the first year of the child's life. Rolling over often starts at about 4 months and by 6 months the child should be sitting up because of proper muscle and skeletal development. Crawling will usually start at around 7 to 9 months and walking by about 12 to 13 months. Next, verbal development is considered, with children beginning to use one word sentences by 9 to 12 months and by 18 to 24 months being able to identify objects and speaking in small sentences. Toilet training is important to consider, and this usually starts when girls are between 2 ½ and 3-years-old and boys typically from 3 to 3 ½-years-old. Girls are usually trained earlier than boys because of the sphincter muscle, which develops about 6 to 10 months earlier in the girl than the boy.

Social behavior is important to gather data on. Most children have others to play with at an early age, and in our society a good number of children are placed in day care in infancy. It is important to determine if the children learned to get along with others, share, and if he or she tests the limits to an extreme. How does the child interact with mother and father, siblings, and with friends? Last of all it is important to get information about the child's general health and possible past illnesses or injuries. The reason for inquiry and history is to get the information needed to determine if there are any deficits. For example, were the pregnancy and birth without complication? If no, there is no need for concern. However, if the pregnancy was complicated and even though the child may be healthy, a difficult pregnancy could cause the mother and or father to feel differently towards this child than with the other children. Was mother bedridden during the latter part of her pregnancy because of threatening an early delivery? If this is the case do her and her husband feel this child is special and are so grateful to have him that they gave him whatever he wants? Perhaps there were complications during delivery that might involve neurological problems that have to be addressed. A child may be on track with rolling over, sitting up, crawling and walking, but slow in language development. If this is the case this needs to be assessed. In a good number of cases, though, there are no problems with the ability to produce speech. The problem is the family's understanding the verbal grunts or hand gestures and not requiring the child to speak. Toilet training can be a concern and if the child was either late in bowl and bladder control, or is having problems with this, a physical exam needs to be conducted. If no problems are detected by the doctor, it is most likely a behavioral problem. Social interactions at home as well as at school and elsewhere might be a good indication of the child's maturity and ability to relate to others. It is also important to understand the relationship between the child and the parents. If the child is testing limits at home he will likely continue this with his friends and elsewhere.

After the history is taken the therapist needs to then return to the parent's concerns about the child's behavior or presenting problem. During this time the therapist should be listening for the feelings of the parents toward the child and their feelings about being parents as well as their interactions with the child. Because of this the therapist needs to ask several probing questions such as "when you talk to your child how does he or she respond?" Another question would be "if you tell a child to do something will he or she cooperate for will there be resistance?" This part of the interview in the initial session should not be glossed over but should be explored in depth. As the parents talk about the child their ability to work together as parents will become apparent rather quickly. If they disagree with each other it will become clear as to which parent feels sorry or helpless and which parent wants to take charge and teach. One parent may be dominant and the other one quiet and submissive. This observation will help clarify the relationships with each other and with the child. Again, the therapist is looking for clues to the family structure and dynamics and what may be interfering with the parents being effective teachers.

Next the parents need to understand the child's behavior and behavior in general. This understanding seems to be lacking with most parents and as a result they have a difficult time knowing how to teach the child. The parents should be taught in the beginning about teaching by example and by precept, with the emphasis on precept. When parents understand that they are teaching laws or rules to the child, it becomes easier for them to remain consistent. With this in mind they need to understand that the child's testing, or misbehavior, is not because he doesn't love them, but because he is trying to find out what the rules and limits are and where the parents stand. Along with this is the need for parents to have a clear conceptualization of conflict, which is a result of inconsistency and chaos in a family. They need to understand that when the rules are not clear or are inconsistent, it makes the child feel anxious and unsettled, and fearful of getting in trouble and oftentimes guilty. These feelings together can be detrimental to the child's growth and development. Taking care of this step may be accomplished in the first session but will usually be addressed starting in the second session. As parents understand this concept they're prepared then to explore the crux of the problem, which is not their lacking understanding of the children's needs for consistency, but the parents' emotional entanglement with the child. This is a point that will have to be made repeatedly because many parents think they are not acting on their emotions. Others may say they are willing but have no understanding of how to stop the unwanted behavior. Furthermore, parents need to comprehend the concept of meaning what they say. All this is accomplished through helping them understand their emotional involvement with the child.

Regarding meaning what one says, most parents confuse this idea with knowing what they want. Unfortunately, knowing what one wants and accomplishing it may be two different matters. The couple who adopted a boy at the age of 4 was struggling with him at the age of 12 because of not following the family rules. He did well in school and athletics, but at home he was continually sneaking food, riding vehicles he was not allowed to without adult supervision, and playing with electronic toys that could only be used at certain times. When this matter of not meaning what they said was addressed, both parents looked confused. The mother said she did definitely mean that she did not want him to disobey, and after several moments of contemplation the father said that he could see the point. He also wanted the boy to conform, but he had not been holding the boy strictly accountable to the expectations. With this understanding the parents were able to monitor the boy's behavior extremely closely for an extended period of time. Eventually when he was able to convince them that he would manage his actions they began to gradually allow him to have privileges and he managed the freedom well. When a parent means what he or she says, that parent will need to explore the feelings and thoughts that keep him from meaning what he or she says and staying with the rule until the expected behavior is consistent. This requires work in the office because the therapist is spending most of the time helping the parents explore their doubts or misunderstandings until they feel comfortable enough to become 100% definite that the behavior that is being targeted will stop or change.

It must be remembered that the real help with the parents is in helping them free themselves from the emotional entanglements that keep them from parenting and teaching. If this point is neglected or forgotten the therapist ends up back in the same problem mentioned earlier of taking upon herself the responsibility of "fixing" the problem. To this point the preliminary steps have been established in providing therapy, and there's one more element to be introduced to the parents. This is discipline. In the early stages of therapy, most likely in the first session, parents will ask what methods or techniques need to be employed to change the child's behavior. Most commonly they're looking for consequences. Unfortunately, many parents have this misconception that consequences will be severe enough to coerce a child into submission. Unfortunately it's a very weak method of disciplining because children will often become accustomed to negative consequences and not be bothered by them which in turn leaves the parents feeling defeated. Consequences do exist, such as if one fails put gasoline in the car, the engine will stop. But in therapy parents want the therapist to tell them exactly what to do and what to say with a hope that the child will magically change. Once again the therapist has to go back to the emotions or feelings that are keeping the parents from meaning what they say and not depend on some outside force or coercion to bring about change. With this in mind the therapist must help the parents differentiate between punishing and teaching. In most cases, punishment is viewed by children and adults as paying a price for one's misdeeds, and when the price is paid the person can go back to what he or she was doing, and in most cases change is not seen.

One example was a patient who said while in high school she would weigh out the options. If her friends wanted to stay away from school one day to go to the reservoir and swim, she would think to herself, "is there anything tomorrow that is more interesting or important to do then wanting to go with my friends?" If nothing was of importance the next day she would go, understanding that if she got caught she would be grounded for a day and then it would be over. If on the other hand something the next day was more important or fun, then she would decline. Many adults who have been incarcerated feel the same way. Even though a good number will say they will not go back to what they were doing, a good number will say that they have paid their debt to society so the slate is clean and then they can go out and do what they want. They do not see the incarcerations as an opportunity to become a better person. Research has discovered that punishment is ineffective. In most cases the subjects will obey in the presence of the punisher, but when the punisher is not present the subject will go back to what he or she was doing. Also if the punishment stops, the child may begin to think that the problem is over and she can go on about her business.

An effective method of discipline is, as was explained in Chapter 3, the bench or timeout. The first point to be emphasized with the parents is that timeout is not a punishment and that the problem is being placed upon the shoulders of the child. In other words the parents must decide where they stand and then enforce timeout until the child is willing to conform, not only for the moment, but to make it a permanent change. Mom and dad also need to understand that it is not likely that the child will change immediately but will require reminders and trips back to the bench until the problem is fully resolved. The caution here is that some parents will get anxious and let the child out of timeout too soon and unfortunately will not see the progress wanted. This might be because of time constraints, or fear that the child may sit there forever and not want to come out, or it just becomes too much of a nuisance to leave the child in timeout until he is ready to change. In many instances parents will struggle with timeout for a period of time until they become clear on what they're expecting and comfortable with being definite and sure about their position and expectations. The parents must once again work through those feelings that interfere with the bench being successful. They must be reminded that the child is not to be sent to his or her room and the child is not to sit in timeout for a specific amount of time but to leave the child in timeout until she is willing to change.

Therapy should be weekly in the beginning because the parents need to return home and work on what they're learning. Also, they will have questions and need to come back soon to get the guidance and help they need. During this period of time many points will be repeated frequently until the parents are comfortable with what they need to do. Also, the therapist expecting accountability is helpful because the parents know they must report back at the next session on how the week went. During these therapy sessions the therapist must be patient and help mom and dad work through their difficulties so they can become the teachers. As therapy continues and progress becomes consistent and changes become more permanent, the therapist can then stretch out the time between sessions. In the beginning they can be every other week and as progress remains they can eventually go to once a month, and when the changes are solidified treatment can be discontinued. With this in mind, though, the therapist must remind the parents that she is available if they need to return for further insight. If the therapist has been successful, the parents will have the tools to deal with any problem that will be presented as the child matures. As children mature, new horizons are opened and children must learn how to manage them. For example, when a child learns to ride the bicycle, mobility is greater, and the child can go further distances from home. He then must be taught rules of where to go, or not to go, and when to return home and so forth. Children may test these rules in the beginning, or may forget, or not pay attention, but with repeated help and even possible timeouts from the bicycle or freedom in general, the child will learn to be responsible. The same goes for the driver's license and other opportunities that present themselves as a child matures.

Therapy with Children

As has been emphasized throughout this chapter, most work must be with the parents. A general rule is that children under the age of 12 benefit little from talk therapy. This is because they are not cognitively mature enough to comprehend the abstract concepts taught to an older child. The child may be agreeable to what you're saying, and at least appear to be, but due to lack of cognitive maturity and understanding, that same problems will continue. If a child is at least 12 years of age, therapy can be provided with the understanding that the child is willing to change. As with any other situation, if the child is unwilling to change, time and money is wasted. This is when the parents are to become involved again. Several rules need to be established with the child in the beginning including limitations of confidentiality and the need to be open and honest during the sessions.

Regarding confidentiality limitations, one must remember that the parents are the responsible parties for the child. The child needs to be informed in the beginning that even though what is said in the session will, in most cases, be confidential; there are things the parents need to know. The child needs to be reassured though that if the therapist is going to tell the parents something about the child that the child will be informed before this takes place. When presented this way, children will likely not resist because they are reassured it is only to help. Also, when working with the child separately from the parents, it might be an opportunity to get a different view of the family dynamics and the dynamics of the parent-child relationship.

When the rules are established, it is important to begin a therapeutic relationship with the child. This begins by showing an interest in what the child is saying and not jumping to conclusions. Most children will be timid in the beginning, but in most cases they warm up to the therapist in a rather brief period of time. Along with showing interest, it is most important to be a good listener. This does not mean that the entire therapeutic process is the therapist listening and the patient talking. As with any other situation, one cannot help if he or she has no idea what the real problem is.

A young 14-year-old boy was brought in by his parents who wanted him to stop being argumentative with the stepfather. He was seen alone and because of the therapist understanding the parents' dynamics, he was first able to allow the young man to speak openly. As he began talking he stated that he felt as though his stepfather did not trust him and that his mother was taking the stepfather's side, which left him feeling alienated. As a result he admitted that he would oppose almost everything they would say, but because of feeling hurt he was more defiant toward his stepfather than toward his mother. In this case he was mature enough to understand insight into his stepfather's and mother's behavior and as a result of the insight he did not take what they were doing personally. The stepfather was anxious, which caused him to be guarded and controlling with the family. The mother sided with the stepfather out of fear of him leaving her and the children financially destitute. This insight was handled appropriately by the young man and as a result he stopped feeling defensive and acting defiant.

Some therapists become emotionally entangled with the child, which will cause more harm than any good that will be accomplished. The therapist cannot afford to allow his or her objectivity and judgment to be clouded by emotions toward the patient. Two examples should help to clarify this point. The therapist was new to the field and became involved in a child custody case where abuse was well-established, and the father admitted to abusing his daughter. The therapist began to feel sorry for the girl, and she became manipulated by the grandparents who pressured her to side with them regarding the girl's custody. They wanted the father to be completely out of the picture and to never have contact with her again. The father completed his sentencing, lost the marriage because of this incident, and spent several years trying to establish a relationship with his daughter. After a drawn-out battle in the courts, large legal fees, and hurt feelings it was decided the father could slowly begin to reestablish his relationship with his daughter. He was required to receive help from a separate therapist, and it was concluded by the therapist and by a court-ordered psychological valuation that the father was no longer a threat to the daughter's safety. Because of the girl's therapist being emotionally entangled in the girl's situation, as well as being afraid to go against the grandparents, she caused the separation from the father to be extended for over a year longer than it should have been.

The second example was a male therapist working with an adolescent boy who was diagnosed as oppositional defiant. The therapist admitted on several occasions to his colleagues that he felt frustrated with the boy because he was not willing do what the therapist wanted him to do to resolve the boy's difficulties. He was taking the young man's behavior personally and finally in his last session with the boy the therapist became so upset with the boy that he hit him. Of course the boy was assigned to another therapist, and this individual temporarily lost his license to practice. Becoming emotionally involved in any situation is unhealthy and will likely lead to serious problems.

When helping a child, the therapist must understand that he or she is there to help the patient, in this case the child. This is accomplished by understanding where the responsibility for the problem lies and by holding that person accountable for helping the child get better. As the parents become less controlled by their emotions and feelings toward the child, they will relax and be patient and consistent with establishing the limits and rules. When the parents are emotionally drawn into a situation, they either become too indulgent in the child or too upset and possibly controlling. In all cases this will result in inconsistency and confusion. The child is confused because he does not know clearly what the expectations are, and the parents are confused because they cannot figure out why the child will not obey. Children thrive with consistency and will relax because of the emotion taken out of the situation, and they will become more open with the parents and hopefully more willing to follow the rules. Again, if the therapist takes it upon himself to correct the problem, he will become responsible for the success or failure. This will likely lead to failure because the parents will not feel the same as the therapist, and if they don't the child and therapist will become frustrated. It is a primary responsibility to teach the parents how to help the child, not to do it for them.

Chapter 12—Worksheet

1. With whom should a therapist work when providing therapy for a 4-year-old child and why?

2. Why is it important to help the parents decide where they stand when setting limits?

Chapter 13
The Foundation for Therapy with Adults

wavebreakmedia / Shutterstock.com

To provide effective therapy to an adult, the therapist must first of all understand the root of the problem. In all cases the problem presented in therapy was learned. Because the behavior is learned, it stands to reason that as long as a person can learn he or she can change. It is unfair to the patient to inform him that his problem is set and he has no way of changing. There are circumstances where a person must accept the problem, but also she can learn healthy ways to work around the problem. Because behavior is learned one must understand where it began, which in most cases was childhood as has been explained throughout this book. There is no need to spend a large amount of time exploring childhood while in therapy. The purpose is to help the person understand how the thinking and behavior were acquired. With this in mind it will become apparent why the person is acting as he is as an adult. If a child is allowed to act on her fears of the dark she could likely carry this discomfort and fear into her adult life. If a person learns as a child to pester the parent until the parent caves in, this tendency could very easily be brought into adulthood.

These behavior patterns that are started in childhood can be the result of various family circumstances and situations. One is to be reminded that the behavior will only continue if it is reinforced. Consider for example the child who continually tests mother and father, and the odds are in his favor of getting what he wants. He will not have learned impulse control and not believe people in authority. The child will likely take this behavior to school, to church, and in friendships.

One middle-aged man who had never married admitted that as a child if he cried long enough his mother would cave in and give him what he wanted. He said that she was an easy mark and unfortunately he did not respect her because she was easily manipulated. He had been in multiple relationships, but none were sustained because of his continual testing of the limits. In another example, one young lady was on the verge of losing her engagement to a person she truly loved because she was always questioning him. In therapy she admitted that she was never sure as a child where she stood with her parents and had to continually pester them for clarification. She dealt with others in the same way. Her fiancé was in love with her and wanted to make her happy so he constantly attempted to please her. Every time she questioned what he was doing to find out where she stood, he would assume she wanted something. He would try his hardest to give her what he thought she needed, but she was always questioning him. He finally tired of the behavior and was threatening to end the engagement, at which point she asked why and he was honest in his reply. He said her behavior was extremely frustrating and left him feeling empty. It was then she decided to seek help and eventually learned to not question what he did or said. She had to learn to know for herself where she stood so that she would not have to seek direction from others.

Regardless of the reason for the limit testing those who engage in it are never happy because they are continually in conflict. They are fearful of losing the other person's love, or some other negative consequence. It also leads to anxiety and even depression. The depression is often the result of loss of friendships and no one being there to help when help and support are needed.

Others have learned through the relationships with parents and siblings, as well as peers, that people may not be trustworthy. Many patients will admit that they could not go to their parents for comfort or direction or even companionship because the parents were too stressed or busy to pay attention to them. Children raised by a single parent will likely feel that they cannot burden the parent with their problems because the parent is stressed by life's circumstances. Others may learn that if they attempt to get close to a parent or sibling that they are ridiculed.

One adult male patient tearfully admitted to this when describing his circumstances. He said he grew up feeling that he was less than normal and would never be worth anything because he could never get close to his mother emotionally. She was busy working and trying to take care of all at home and he thought she had no time for him. When he did try to share his feelings with her, she would listen while being busy taking care of other family matters. As a result, he quit trying and withdrew into a reclusive lifestyle for a number of years. He got a job working for a computer company where he was employed on the assembly line installing computer chips. He said he liked the job because it was not demanding and he could avoid interaction with people. In some instances, the parents may attempt to be too positive with the child leaving the young person with the impression everything he does is great and wonderful. This type of behavior from the parents is well intended, but ill guided. This child will likely enter adulthood feeling that he or she is worthless because in the real world praises are rarely given.

In other cases, as with the 40-year-old male mentioned in a previous chapter, some are raised in a tumultuous family and constantly asked to side with one of the parents. As they mature and reach adulthood they feel they have to fix everyone. This is unfortunate because this tendency will put the person in a position to be manipulated by others. These individuals are typically victims of abuse and are taken advantage of by others continually. A young lady who had graduated from college a year earlier was frustrated at work because she was given a great number of responsibilities and was never compensated, or even acknowledged. She thought that the harder she worked the more people would appreciate her. What she hoped was that by being quiet about her feelings and always ready to do whatever was asked, she would be liked. Because this never happened she became depressed, which allowed health complications to increase and she eventually had to quit work for a period of time. In another case a young college student was raised by an anxious mother who always feared doing something wrong. This fear was verbalized so often to the young girl that at an early age she started viewing herself in the same light. By the time she made it to college the fear was so strong that could not drive anywhere without immediately, upon her arrival home, calling the police department to ask if there had been a hit and run accident reported. After several weeks of this the police finally insisted that she get help. She admitted in therapy that this fear of doing something wrong, like hitting another person while driving, caused her to be afraid to leave her home to go to class.

Some individuals learn early in childhood to be incapable of accomplishing anything and learn to feel helplessness (Seligman, 1975). These are individuals who are raised with the notion that nothing ever works and that they have no control over their lives. This can be the result of being coddled and never learning how to accomplish anything. Such problems are often seen with children suffering from a disability. This disability can either be physical or mental, but in either case the helplessness comes from feeling that the odds are against the person. No matter what she does she will always assume she will fail.

An older man had been on disability for most of his adult life because of hearing loss. This loss came when he was about two-years-old and contracted a high fever. Because of this his parents felt sorry for him and never expected him to accomplish anything in life. He never tried and as an old man regretted his life and his lack of accomplishment. In most instances the person will either refuse to try to improve, or if he tries he will give up before ever accomplishing the goal. This was because staying with the task was never expected. As has been mentioned, behavior will not continue into adulthood unless it has been reinforced throughout the person's life.

All adults will have problems regardless of their status in life, age, or other circumstances. The mature person will know how to work problems through, whereas the immature person will not. Maturity is indicated by completing a task when started, the ability to give-and-take without wanting his half out of the middle, and being able to relate to others on a genuine, honest, and feeling level. Immaturity on the other hand is indicated by a person's unwillingness to consider the other's needs and as a result will not be able to give-and-take, but will take from others and if required to give back will do so begrudgingly. Others who are immature may constantly give with nothing expected in return. In either case the relationship is lopsided. The immature person will very likely be willing to start tasks and in the beginning implement a new idea whether at work or home, but when responsibility becomes the least bit stressful will drop it and go do something else. The immature person will have many projects started but nothing completed. These individuals lack self-discipline and thus do not follow through with completing tasks. Finally, the immature person will, for whatever reason, not relate to others on a genuine, honest, and feeling level. These are individuals who do not risk, but keep things to themselves which leaves the other individual not knowing where he stands with that person.

With the foregoing points illustrated it is important for the therapist to take a thorough history in the first or several sessions. During this time the therapist will be able to get a clear picture of what difficulties may cause the person to seek help. This information will likely include such areas as the family of origin and the relationship this person had with the parents. It may be that the person was able to be open with both parents and feels comfortable relating to others openly. On the other hand, the individual may have been raised in a family where communication was either discouraged or never engaged in. With this information the therapist will begin to get an idea of the individual's ability to relate to others. Next, it will be important, and helpful, to understand the person's relationship with siblings. It might be that there was a healthy relationship, or the possibility of fighting between the siblings which would cause the individual to be guarded. In another instance it might be that the person learned to rely on one or two siblings to the exclusion of parents and others.

It is also important to explore social relationships to get insight into the person's ability to interact with other people. If the patient is shy and timid, social relationships will likely be lacking. Perhaps the individual is social and outgoing and learned as a child how to be social. This person will have a healthy outlook on life and can relate to others. School and education history is important. Here the therapist will learn the individual's ability to work and to follow through with responsibilities. Even though the person may have had excellent grades in school, it does not mean that he will be without problems. In a number of instances this may indicate the lack of social skills because she spent most of her time in the books. Many find comfort in academics and in the books to avoid socializing. It also helps the therapist understand the cognitive abilities so that he can better understand how to interact with the patient. The last two points to be considered are work history, which can reveal significant insight into the person's abilities, and problems. One may need to consider the type of work the person pursues as well as length of time spent at each job. Finally, it is important to explore the individual's relationships, whether in the marriage or as a single person. When this initial part of therapy is accomplished therapy can begin.

The first question of course to be asked is why the person is seeking help. Many will be honest, but there are those who will not be for various reasons. Those who are sent for therapy by the courts, or must seek help to maintain their welfare status, will very likely tell the therapist what the person thinks the therapist wants to hear. There are those who genuinely want help and will be open about their concerns. A number of patients who attended a certain clinic that catered to those on government assistance for a disability had little success. In this case many of the patients knew they had to continue therapy or they would lose their benefits. They attended meetings but would not invest in therapy. Those who are court ordered will, in most cases, not invest in therapy because they either see it as a punishment and something they have to put up with, but they think they don't have a problem. One couple in particular was ordered to seek therapy for parenting and spent all their time in the sessions trying to convince the therapist that it was not their fault the children were taken away. Many who are ordered by the courts to receive help for addictions will not see themselves as having a problem or lack the desire to change. They will put in the time but not the effort to make necessary changes. On the other hand, people who have to pay out of their own pockets to receive help will most likely invest in the therapeutic process because it is their choice to be there. It becomes apparent rather soon in the therapeutic process whether the person wants help or not. Those who want help are willing to listen and work on changing by implementing what they are helped to understand. Those who are not will agree with the therapist in most cases, but will never change because they don't invest in the process and do not practice what they are taught.

The therapist's primary goal is to focus on the patient's thinking and resulting emotional state. Most patients are consumed by negative thinking and fail to realize how damaging it is. It is important then to invite the patients to explore this negative thinking and to determine the validity of it. An example is an adult male who struggled with depression that was interfering with work and his marriage. In the initial sessions it became apparent that he felt worthless and unable to change. The root of his thinking was explored, and it was revealed that his mother was a very demanding individual especially regarding school because she worked in the school district. He said that he was never able to feel like he had worked hard enough because she was always questioning his grades, completion of assignments, and his overall school performance. He said he was almost an A student but struggled with several subjects where he earned B grades. Even with this, his mother was dissatisfied to and accused him not trying hard enough. He was helped to recognize the thinking pattern he developed as a child and how it affected his adult life. He felt that he was a failure in his marriage because his wife was constantly complaining about him not investing in the relationship. He began to understand that he did not communicate with her for fear of her being angry which caused him to feel disinterested. After his negative thinking was identified and explored, he was ready to understand positive thinking. There are number of techniques used to apply positive thinking, but most of them appear to be ineffective because they do not address the root problem but only try to change the symptoms. This patient felt that he could never accomplish anything or live up to people's expectations, and as a result of this perception he often did not try or risk, and if he did it was with a lack of determination to succeed. The focus has to be changed from what a person is unable to do, to what one needs to do and begin to develop a "can-do" outlook. He felt that he was unable to succeed at anything but was willing to try acting differently.

The point to be understood in this and in similar situations is the need to change both thinking and behavior. The person might think that he or she is able to do better at work or complete a difficult task. If this is never acted upon the person will continue to revert to the negative thinking. As in the previous example not only did the patient try to change his thinking to focus on the positive, but he also had to act on the thinking. Communicating with his wife was one activity that frightened him, but when he began to risk because of thinking that he could, he saw the results which bolstered his confidence. In the beginning he was unsure about talking to his wife and was frightened, but he said later that he continually focused on a positive outcome and would open up and share with her. When he did, he discovered that his wife was pleasant and willing to listen. After several weeks of open communication his fears almost completely dissipated. He was then able to apply this principle of changing thinking and behavior to his work where he put in a greater effort to complete his responsibilities. Finally he was given several promotions over the next year.

Another example is a truck driver who was mentioned in Chapter 8. He knew he had to go back to work after the accident but felt as though he could not. His thinking was considered in-depth and he admitted that he feared driving again because of another accident occurring. He was helped to rationally think this through and decided that the possibility of another accident like the previous one was very unlikely. When he went back to the scene of the accident, he had to practice keeping his focus on the scenery and remember that the accident was in the past. He quickly realized that the negative feelings he was anticipating when visiting the scene of the accident were manageable. He still had to continue working on changing his thinking and behavior by going back to work in the capacity of an office helper, before eventually driving again. During this time his attention had to be on his work and not on what happened previously.

There was a woman in her middle 60s who presented with depression and was, by her report, always crying. She said that she loved her husband, but that they did not have a very close relationship. She had two adult children, both of whom were married, and she was closer to her daughter than her son. She became severely depressed when her daughter informed her that she and her husband were moving out of state for employment and that the mother would not be able to visit as often as she wanted. What further complicated the problem was the daughter being pregnant with the first child. The patient feared that she would not be able to help her daughter with the pregnancy and birth and that she would be estranged from the grandchild because of the distance between the two. As her thinking was explored she was able to reveal a troublesome relationship with her mother since the patient was a young child. She said her mother always felt like she was put in a less than ideal position by leaving Europe and marrying the patient's father. Thus the mother was continually depressed and was critical of the patient because she did not see her as being physically attractive. The patient felt lonely as a child because of being pushed away by mother and as a result she felt unsure of herself in public and had few friends during her school years. She said that she hoped her marrying at a young age would help her feel better about herself. She soon discovered that she still felt the same even though she was married and had a husband who was kind to her. Because of her fear of rejection from her husband she did not invest in him which caused them to drift apart emotionally. She felt that she could only get solace and well-being from her children, but the son was not very affectionate so all of her energy and time was directed to her daughter. She overcame her depression by realizing that she could visit her daughter, although not every day, and that she would still be a part of the grandchild's life. She also knew she had to keep herself busy and her mind occupied so she would not have time to dwell on the negative. She joined an exercise group that met three times a week. She also took up art that she had enjoyed earlier in her life and received positive feedback for it. She signed up for an art class and began to socialize with other class members, and she returned to activity at church and became involved in the women's auxiliary. As the depression subsided she felt more comfortable in the marriage and begin to risk being open with, and caring about, her husband which she discovered brought positive feedback from him and the relationship flourished. As has been illustrated each of these cases were successful because the patient was willing to be open about the problem, to work on identifying the negative thinking that was at the root of the problem, and to risk by changing behavior and acting in a positive direction.

There are instances where a person begins to make changes but will begin to experience resistance or disapproval from family members because of the change. One must remember that individuals belong to some sort of a system whether in the family, with friends, or even at work. If this person is in a dysfunctional family the parents may constantly attempt to exercise control over the person and mount significant pressure hoping the patient goes back to the way he or she was.

A young man sought help for anxiety. It was revealed that his mother used him as a confidant since he was about 10-years-old. He felt that he had to fix her as well as the rest of the family so that she would be happy. He was in the double bind because no matter what he tried to do to help nothing changed. He said that he was the same at work where he was continually trying to help other people. He often felt bad because people would either reject his offer or take advantage of him by having him take care of their problems for them. In therapy he gained the insight and strength to not take upon himself the responsibility for other people's well-being. In the case of his mother he stopped trying to help her and placed responsibility for the solutions to the problems on her. She became upset and accused him of not loving her anymore, and when she found out he was seeking therapy she demanded that he stop seeing the therapist because he was hurting her son. She mounted the pressure that she thought was necessary to bring him back into line and continue in the family system as he had been for years. On several occasions, he was ready to stop therapy but was able over time to realize what mother was attempting to do and stayed with his decision to not become involved. The result was him becoming independent and finding that mother could take care of problems on her own.

In another instance, both the mother and father were controlling. When the oldest child decided to marry the parents told the fiancé that they would have to live in the same neighborhood with the family and that the father should manage the couple's financial affairs. The soon-to-be husband was strong enough to insist that his soon-to-be wife ignore her parents and establish their own life together away from the family. This was frightening to her, but she could see the unhealthy relationship her parents were trying to maintain and followed her fiancé's wisdom and against her parent's wishes married and they moved to a neighboring city. Over time the parents stopped pushing and accepted the marriage as it was and actually begin to respect both their daughter and son-in-law because they knew they could not be manipulated.

There are patients who will resist getting better because they fear losing that relationship with the therapist. As a result they continue to come up with new problems or resist changing. One such case was a middle-aged woman who had never married and suffered from social anxiety that she struggled with since childhood. She finally found the therapist with whom she felt comfortable and tried to stay in the therapeutic relationship for as long as she could. She resisted socializing with other people, would always say that she did not know why, and needed to figure out the reason so she could get better but never faced the problem head-on. The therapist finally had to tell her therapy would no longer continue because of the lack of progress. This upset the patient, but because she wanted to continue with the therapist was willing to do what she had to. She eventually developed a close relationship with several friends and no longer needed the therapist. In such a case the therapist has to be strong enough to set limits and resist the temptation to try make the patient not feel upset when expected to improve. In most instances the patient will become upset, but it is not the therapist's fault. It is because the patient is frightened and does not want to change, or does not feel that he can, change.

In some cases, helping the individual requires family therapy. There are individuals who refuse to change because they are being enabled and do not want to have to stand on their own. This is often the case with those who are drug dependent. In such instances the addict will do all he can to get the family to help him or her when he is in a crisis, or has no money. Even though the family members, most likely parents, will seek help for their child, the child will likely participate in therapy. In this instance the place to start is with the family members who are enabling by becoming strong enough to cut the person off until he is willing to change. Once the family member or others stop the enabling and resist the accusations, complaints, and threats from the addict they will notice that the person will eventually become humble enough to want help. Again, when enabling exists the need for change is diminished. It may take a while before the addict decides to change. Those who are helping the addict must exercise patience and allow the person to experience whatever is necessary to cause a desire to change.

A married man with 4 young children started using methamphetamines with friends in the neighborhood. After about 7 months he abandoned his family and stayed with these friends. His wife and children would see him wandering the streets on occasion and about every 4 to 6 months he would come home to get food, rest, and to regain his health. After about 5 days he would leave again, and his pattern was repeated for over 3 years. His wife eventually sought help after being counseled to by some close friends. She was helped to understand his actions and how she had been prolonging the problem by allowing him to come home at his pleasure and then leave again when he felt better. She said she felt it was her duty as a wife and a Christian to love him no matter what. She learned in therapy that enabling was not love but was contributing to his demise. She finally told him to never return home unless he had stopped the drugs. He eventually realized she meant what she said and he decided he did not want to lose his family so he sought help. In the beginning he wanted to be admitted to inpatient treatment but was denied because of the lack of money. He did find a program, but soon left because he was neglected for several days at a time and received no help except to have a bed and food. He immediately returned home and received therapy through a charitable organization. He sought help from the State Vocational Rehabilitation Agency and had his education funded. He became a Respiratory Therapy Assistant. He had a difficult time getting his license to enter the profession because of his honesty regarding his drug history, but because of persistence it was finally issued to him. According to his and his wife's report, he remains clean and sober and is happily married and loves his children and grandchildren. As with many other such cases he admitted that he felt he did not have to change until his wife cut him off, which put him in the position to seek help and keep his family.

Some depressed individuals will feel so hopeless that they refuse to seek help. In many of these instances, the spouse or parents will come for family therapy to learn how to help their family member. For most of these family members saying what they intuitively know they must is frightening because they fear making the person feel worse. In this case they are contributing to the problem. As they are helped to not act on their negative feelings they begin to insist that the person get help and they do not stop until the individual agrees to get help. When the family is through with therapy they feel empowered and are able to place the problem where it belongs, on the shoulders of the patient. Furthermore, they begin to see this as love.

The depressed husband mentioned in a previous chapter who stayed in bed for days at a time finally sought help when his wife became strong enough to tell him to either get help, or she would be his second divorce. She was not trying to scare or to manipulate him. She meant what she said and he knew it. After coming out of the depression he admitted that it frightened him so much that he decided to do all necessary to keep the marriage, including receiving therapy. It helps the family member of the depressed person understand how to help when comparing depression to hypothermia, or freezing to death. In this example, the person who is on the verge of freezing to death will become delirious and will feel warm, like everything is okay, and will want to go to sleep. If the person is allowed to go to sleep he will slip into a coma and die. Since this cannot be allowed the person taking care of the individual will do anything necessary to get the person moving, even if it includes making the person mad. Depression is, in comparison, freezing to death mentally and emotionally. As has been mentioned, it is not kindness to allow the person to continue in the depressed, withdrawn state because the behavior becomes reinforced. The wife of the depressed man stood her ground, and he decided to take charge of his life and get better. How kind would she have been if she had tolerated his depressive behavior? It would have destroyed him.

Another theme of negative thinking found in many patients is the need for approval from other people to increase one's self-esteem. Patients do not understand this, and many therapists do not understand that this thinking is unhealthy. The reason is that the other person's behavior toward the patient is often perceived as a reflection of the patient's worth as an individual. This goes back to egocentric thinking where the individual perceives that whatever happens around her is a reflection of that person, which is not the case. The other person's behavior is simply a reflection of what's going on with that individual. When this is understood by the patient, pressure is taken off of her to act the way she thinks she needs to get the other's approval. This also leads back to the double bind. The person may try to please the other individual to get approval, but that approval is short-lived and in many cases it will never come. As a result, he will misread the person's behavior as being a reflection of the other individual, not him. This type of thinking can lead to depression or anxiety. Depression will be the result of this thinking because the individual feels like she will never be able to measure up and will likely have a poor self-esteem. The anxious person will feel as though he is in trouble and will try and try to fix the problem but never feel successful. This type of thinking is one major component leading to the final problem to be addressed in this chapter.

A good number of adults have not learned to establish themselves as individuals and as result will feel depressed or anxious because they are always taken advantage of. Therapists in this case must help the patient identify the thoughts and feelings that interfere with her meaning what she says or expressing her desires. These thoughts and feelings are usually centered on the fear of one's approval as mentioned in the previous paragraph.

A couple had been married for about 20 years and had problems with her parents who felt that they needed to be involved in the couple's family affairs. The wife knew that she did not agree with what they were doing but was afraid to say anything for fear of them becoming angry with her like they did when she was a child. Her husband wanted to put a stop to it but was afraid to do so because of harming the relationship between his wife and her parents. Both knew what had to be done but acted on their fears and said nothing. The wife sought help for depression and as this problem was revealed in the second session, she tearfully said that her parents were running their lives and potentially ruining the marriage. As she was allowed to express and explore her feelings, she was able to see how she learned as a child to fear the disapproval of her parents which led to the current situation. She was also able to see her parents as anxious people who were insecure and as result had to control every situation they were in. When she understood that their behavior was not because she was a bad person, but that they had a problem, she talked with her husband and they decided together to establish rules with the parents. When initiated, the parents became upset and accused the couple of not caring about them and severed the relationship for several months. But because the couple did not budge the parents eventually came around and respected the couple's wishes. It was also found later that the parents had more respect for their daughter and her husband than they did for any of their other children because they could not manipulate the couple. By the end of therapy, she was able to understand how she learned her self-doubts and by changing her understanding of other's behavior she was not fearful of other's reactions to her and their behavior in general. She was able to establish herself as a person.

This same principle applies to dealing with peers. A couple was ostracized from their neighborhood for over one year because of a misunderstanding by the other couple. This couple was helped to understand that the actions by the other couple was a reflection of them, not this couple. They were able to keep to themselves and not try to defend themselves with the neighbors and over time one by one the neighbors began to warm up to the couple. Ultimately the people lost respect for the other couple and they were essentially left alone by the neighborhood. A young man in high school was taunted by some class mates and he was depressed and fearful of going to school. In therapy he was helped to understand the teasing and manipulation by the peers and to not take what they were doing as personal against him. He ignored their behavior which was different from before when he would try to fight back. Fighting back only encouraged the others to continue with the bullying. His parents were fearful of encouraging him to stop reacting, thinking that it would only cause the others to taunt more. The boy eventually learned that the father had been teased a lot in school and when he learned that his son was going through the same treatment he felt the same helpless feelings as he did as a child and thus felt that he could not help his son.

To summarize this chapter, it is necessary for the therapist to not only understand the presenting problem, but to also help the patient by understanding his or her thinking and perceptions of the problem and life in general. If the person was controlled, ridiculed, ignored, or mistreated, his perception of himself and his world will be revealed by his behavior and what he says. If the person has learned that by manipulating she will get her way, this will become apparent in the behavior and thinking patterns revealed in therapy. Then, as this is explored in therapy, the patient will hopefully be able to see the consequences of the behavior and then be willing to change. If the therapist becomes drawn into thinking that it is up to him to "fix" the patient, little will be accomplished, and the therapeutic experience will be an exercise in frustration. The role of the therapist is to help the patient become able, through insight and support, to help himself and not rely on the therapist to tell him how to live his life. Again the role is to help the person learn to help himself, to rely on his own wisdom and commonsense, and to become brave enough to acknowledge it and follow it.

Chapter 13 — Worksheet

1. When providing therapy for an adult, why is it important to understand the person's history?

2. If the patient does not want to change, what should the therapist do?

Chapter 14
Therapy with Couples

Olimpik / Shutterstock.com

The most challenging therapy is with couples. The reason being that the therapist is working with two people who present with their own difficulties and are hopefully trying to make the marriage work. The most important information to have clarified in the beginning of the therapeutic relationship with the couple is their desire to succeed in the marriage. This commitment needs to be from the individual and not motivated by pressure from the other to give a specific answer. In many instances, both will initially say they want the marriage to work. It does not take long to discover if both are committed, or who is and is not. This becomes apparent by what the person says and how the persons acts in the marriage and especially in the therapy sessions. In some cases the one who is not totally committed will resist attending therapy or will be detached in the session. This is illustrated by the husband who was not willing to be fully committed even though he said he was. He would miss about 75% of the sessions, when he did attend, he was quiet, and if he talked it was in sarcastic tones. The person who is committed will attend regularly and diligently try to figure out the problem and what he or she needs to do to fix it. One middle-aged couple came for couple's therapy and both openly admitted in the beginning that they were committed to the marriage. Even though the husband attended every session, he was quiet and would agree to change, but week after week stayed the same. The wife on the other hand was constantly trying to figure out what she had to do to be a better wife including losing weight, cooking better, and being less demanding of his time. In these instances, therapy can become quite tedious and frustrating because of the lack of progress. When both are fully committed to making the marriage work they will attend regularly, but also invest in the sessions and work diligently on what they learn in each meeting. In these situations therapy is rather brief and successful because of both people investing fully in the relationship.

Taking Sides

A common problem with couple's therapy is both wanting the therapist to take his or her side. The spouse wants the therapist to tell the other person that he or she is wrong and that person must change. It is tempting for the therapist to want to take sides if he feels that he can see clearly where the blame lies. If the therapist is drawn into this trap, the person who is sided against will become resistant after unsuccessful attempts in trying to be what the other person is saying the spouse needs to become. The individual with whom the therapist is taking sides will eventually become disgruntled because he is not seeing the change he wants. In either case, the therapist is blamed for the unsuccessful therapy. The wife in one instance spent every session complaining about the husband and telling the therapist to make the husband understand that he was at fault for the problems in the marriage. According to the husband, he was doing everything she wanted including doing all the outside work and most of the inside work, which left her with little to do. She also complained that he was not earning enough money for which he apologized, but after changing jobs he discovered that the increase in income was not enough, and he concluded that it would never be enough. After several months with no change, the wife finally decided not to continue because the therapist was not helping. The husband attempted to continue therapy, but eventually quit because he was unwilling to become strong enough to put his foot down and not give into her manipulation.

Commitment

Another reason for lack of success in therapy goes back to the lack of commitment because of the individual's attention being drawn somewhere else. A young husband was attending college and admitted to the therapist that he was dissatisfied with his wife. He was open about being attracted to blondes and that his wife was a redhead. He also said that she had a speech impediment that bothered him. In the initial session he was told that if he would begin to invest in his wife, she would appear more attractive to him. After several weeks, the wife attended therapy, and it was apparent that she was not a redhead but a light strawberry blonde and very attractive. Also, after listening to her for the entire session, no impediment was detected in her speech. He eventually admitted that he was spending most of his time with his girl cousin and her single friends who were also attending the University. When he admitted this, he was able to see that his attention was not in the right direction. He changed and invested his time and energy in his wife and two young children and eventually said he needed no further help. About a year later he saw the therapist and told him that they were able to work together as a couple. He said he thought that what the therapist said about his wife looking different to him was impossible, but after he directed his attention to her and their children he found that she was extremely attractive. In another case a public servant who was high in authority started finding fault with his wife. He began to give a lot of unnecessary attention to a woman at their church, and she was also within their social circle. He had the same complaints of the man just mentioned and decided his wife was not as attractive and intelligent as he wanted her to be. He convinced himself that the other woman had the qualities that his wife lacked. He eventually realized that he was heading down a thorny path and decided to change this and invested in his wife.

When a couple seeks help, and it becomes apparent that one is not willing to invest in the relationship and that the problems are serious, the focus needs to be placed on the person who will regularly attend therapy and try to make things better. As mentioned earlier, in most cases the one who is not invested will stop seeking therapy, which leaves this person to come alone. As the therapist help's the spouse who is attending to consider the other person's behavior and how it affects her, she will likely begin to see the manipulation and put a stop to it. The person who does not invest causes the other person to feel doubtful and helpless. This is due to assuming that the other person is detached from the marriage because she is not good enough, thus causing her to try harder to make things work. When this happens the other person will lose respect for her because he can manipulate her. Again, when she can see this she can then consider what it is she is getting out of the marriage. It does not take long for this spouse to conclude that the other person's behavior is because of him not her. When this is understood she will most likely decide that she does not need the marriage, which will put the other person in the position of having to decide whether he wants it or not.

A perfect example of this is the couple who presented with problems regarding communication. It was apparent that they had difficulties relating to each other. The husband said that to progress he had to be honest and admitted to having committed adultery frequently throughout their 15 years of marriage. He said that he confessed this to his wife about 6 months earlier and that he wanted to change. After the third session, he stopped coming, claiming he was too busy. The wife kept her appointments and during this time was encouraged to explore the return on her investing in the marriage. She realized that the investment on his side was almost nonexistent. She announced after about one month of therapy that she had filed for divorce. When asked why, she said that she was not going to live under such circumstances any longer. She said his behavior had a negative effect on her and her children, and she would not allow it to continue. She reassured the therapist that she was not doing this as a ploy to get him to change or to make some sort of a statement. Several days later the husband called the therapist in desperation and said he needed to see him immediately. When he was able to see him, his first statement was that he had gotten over his desire to commit adultery and would never go back to it again. He said it took about five minutes to make the decision because he realized that his choice was either his wife and children or the other women. He wanted his wife and children and was willing to do all that was necessary to prove to her that he wanted the marriage. After approximately 8 months of separation she slowly began to allow him back into her life with the understanding that if he faltered in any way she would dissolve the marriage. He was eventually allowed to move back into the home, and it did not take long for them to resolve the communication problems as well as other concerns. Four years later the husband told the therapist that he and his wife were still happily married and he was at peace with himself. There are instances though where the person is not willing to change. If that is the case, there is no hope for the marriage and the one who is not willing to change will most likely end up losing a potentially strong and fulfilling marriage. If the other spouse has traits that need to changed, and is willing to do so, that person can become a good candidate for a new marriage. The person not willing to change will probably take his behavior with him into the next relationship and will have a long string of failed relationships.

Acting on Emotions

When asked what is required to succeed in marriage, most people will have good insight and understanding of what is required. The reason they are unsuccessful is not because of the lack of knowledge. It is because of acting on impulses or emotions rather than being strong enough to follow their conscience and good wisdom. This inability, or unwillingness to follow one's common sense, but act on emotions or impulses is commonly learned in childhood. If an individual was allowed to pout as a child to get her way, she will do this as an adult, which can be very destructive in a marriage.

An elderly couple had no marriage per se although they stayed together. After years of trying to be a better wife she quit and withdrew into her own world. It was revealed that he would pout and act like a mortally wounded person when things did not go his way. This would put pressure on the family to conform to make him happy. Not only did he lose the relationship with his wife, but also that of his children because they each felt frustrated by trying unsuccessfully to make him happy.

In another instance, a mother had poor self-esteem and as a result she would try to get people's approval by flirting with men and tried to do anything she thought she could to get female acquaintances to like her. She did this at the expense of the marriage thinking her husband would love her no matter what she did. She was raised in a family where both parents loved her unconditionally, which meant they would tolerate her behavior, whether acceptable or not.

A husband who spent money as fast as he could earn it put the family in financial jeopardy. He eventually decided to take control of his impulsive behavior when his wife threatened to leave him and bill collectors were demanding that he pay his debts. He was about to lose everything. A man who was married and had two children sought help when he had put himself in a dangerous position financially. He became a victim of a scheme to defraud him of a large amount of money. He said he knew it was a fraudulent scheme. However, the promise of getting a large inheritance from an unknown relative in Europe had him thinking if he paid the fees required he would get the money. He eventually stopped sending money and confessed in therapy that this was not the first time he was taken in and that his wife said she would divorce him if he did it again. She did divorce him, but he decided to never become involved in such propositions again and reportedly never did.

Communication

Couples typically present with problems communicating. This is not due to difficulties with the language; each can understand clearly what the other says. The root of the difficulty lies in negative thinking and resulting emotions. This usually causes people to cut each other off and stop the communication. Many individuals have said that they only want to be listened to and not lectured to or given advice. If an individual has learned throughout his life by experience that talking on a feeling level only brings about embarrassment and ridicule, he will be unwilling to risk talking. When a sensitive subject is approached, the immature person will feel threatened and do all he can to avoid potential hurt. The mature person, on the other hand, may feel uncomfortable when a sensitive subject is brought up, but will communicate or listen and not avoid the subject. If one assumes she is always in trouble and acts on the resulting feelings, the communication will either stop or end up in an argument. As in all other cases the ability to communicate on a feeling level is learned in the family. If communication is limited or nonexistent in the family, the child will likely learn to keep thoughts to himself. On the other hand, if an individual learned that mother and father were nurturing and comfortable in talking with the child as well as with the rest of the family, he will likely have no problems communicating honestly and openly as an adult.

Communication is a two-part process. It is important that the person is an active listener. Active listening means wanting to understand what the other person is saying. Active listening accomplishes two important points. First, as a person is allowed to talk freely, she will likely begin to answer her own questions. Second, by listening to understand the spouse, is able to better see the person's concerns and thereby not get upset and take what the person says personally. The husband says to the wife he is disgruntled about life. Active listening on her part would mean wanting him to clarify more so she can understand what he was thinking. Many misunderstand active listening as agreeing with the other individual. This is not the case; it means practicing empathy by trying to comprehend the other person's thoughts and feelings. If the person feels threatened by what the other is saying, active listening will stop and the conversation will be cut off. If, after a couple has built their dream home, one evening the wife says she wishes they had never done it, the husband may feel frustrated, thinking that no matter what he did it was never right. If he acts on these feelings he will cut off the conversation by either ignoring her, verbalizing his frustrations, accusing her of something, making light of what she says, or changing the subject. If, on the other hand, he does not act on these feelings and tells her he wants to understand, she will hopefully be willing to start talking about her concerns. The likely outcome will be either the wife figuring out on her own what she is concerned about, or the husband will have a clear picture of her worries. In either case they will both feel better by not cutting the other off.

The other element of communication is being a good, open talker. For some people listening is a risky proposition, while others find verbally sharing feelings and thoughts is frightening. If one does not open up and share, the other person will be left to guess. In most cases, when a person guesses, it is usually in the negative. Unfortunately, when negative assumptions are made, the person will begin to act on them which will likely reinforce in the mind of the other person that talking is too costly.

A young man was sharing some childhood experiences during a therapy session. He said that when he was about 8 years old and was with his parents who were building a new home. He stepped on a board with a nail sticking out of it that punctured his shoe and went into his foot. He then said he stepped with his other foot on the board so he could pull his foot off and stepped on another nail in the board. When asked what he did he said he wiggled and wiggled until he got the nails out of his feet. He was asked if he went and told his parents to which he answered no, but climbed up in the tree and cried for a while. This young man had learned not to communicate with his parents because they would either ignore him or become upset. Another patient said she learned not to talk about problems because when she did her mother would start worrying and become upset. In a marriage, being unwilling to open up causes greater problems than not listening.

A group of married couples attended group couples therapy for 90 minutes weekly for 8 weeks. In the first session, communication was introduced. The couples were helped to understand the importance of listening and talking. They were helped to see the frustration when cut off and the problems resulting from not opening up to each other. The next week one couple said that listening and opening up worked. When asked to explain what happened they said that on their way home they decided to try what was introduced and started talking with each other. They became so taken in by revealing their thoughts and feelings to each other that when they arrived home they retired to the bedroom and kept talking until about 2 in the morning. The wife said that this continued throughout the week. She said one of the younger children approached her and asked if mom and dad were going to divorce. Mother said no and asked why this question came up. The girl said that the children were assuming that because they were so occupied and talking in the bedroom that maybe the parents were deciding on which child will live with whom after the divorce. Mother lovingly reassured her that this was not the case and the children relaxed. A side note here is that the husband no longer suffered from migraine headaches that were, at times, debilitating. He realized that his headaches were the result of stress mostly brought on by unsettled feelings in the marriage due to lack of communication.

Another couple was struggling with communication because the wife was afraid of listening to what the husband had to say so she would retreat to the bedroom and lock the door for fear of him talking himself into what he was saying. They learned about emotions and feelings interfering with communication and, after some tense moments, she began to relax. The first success was when he saw a car like the one he owned when they were engaged, and he reminisced about the fun times they had with the car. After talking openly, he mentioned that it would be fun to have that car again, and she panicked thinking that he was then wanting one like it. She took a deep breath and allowed him to continue and even make comments. After about 10 minutes he looked at her and said that it would be nonsense to buy such a car because it would never be driven but only take up space in the yard. She readily agreed and began to understand that by listening he was able to process his ideas and hopefully come up with a healthy answer. The real test came later when he arrived from work one evening very upset. Earlier that day he found out that the large order that he had sold was canceled which meant the loss of a large commission. He felt betrayed by the company because the loss of the sale was the fault of the front office making a mistake. He had the entire day to think about this, and by the time he got home was very upset. He opened the back door and said in a very loud voice "I hate my job. I'm going to quit." This frightened his wife and her immediate response was to retreat to the bedroom thinking that he was going to quit his job, which would leave the family in a financially difficult position. According to her they would likely have to sell their home and live with her parents. She remembered to listen and let him talk, which she did. During the next 30 minutes, he spoke vehemently about hating his work, wanting to quit, and would say this while yelling or crying. She had decided then to follow the instruction in therapy and be a good listener. As she listened she became frightened thinking that he was going to talk himself into quitting, but after about 30 minutes he settled down. He eventually looked at her and calmly said that he was not going to quit his job unless he found the one that was as good as, if not better than, the one he had. She asked if he really meant it, and he said yes. She then asked if he wanted to talk more and he said no he was fine. Four years later, he was still at the same job.

One particular couple, both of whom had been divorced previously, struggled because of communication difficulties. The wife was anxious and always sought reassurance from her husband. Her childhood was difficult because of inconsistency in the family.

She learned at an early age to not trust what her parents said because they rarely followed through with their promises. She said on many occasions she would worry about terrible things happening, and when this was explored she revealed that her father was anxious and unpredictable. One day he may be happy with his life and the next day be upset and even threaten to leave the family. This then caused her to feel anxious and fearful when she was not clear what the other person was thinking or going to do. Her husband, on the other hand, did not verbalize but kept almost everything to himself. He was the youngest of four boys, and the father was verbally and physically abusive. This man, along with his brothers, learned early in life to not let anyone into their worlds for fear of some serious negative outcome. This couple fed off of each other, which caused severe problems, not only for them but also they're 3-year-old daughter who was showing signs of anxiety. The wife would push the husband to find out what he was thinking or feeling, and he would withdraw and not say anything because of his thinking that she would become angry if he revealed his thoughts or activities to her. So she would push, he would withdraw, and as he withdrew she would become more anxious. After long periods of this type of struggle, they would both quit and go their separate ways for several days at a time. Unfortunately, these difficulties were never resolved and they divorced.

Successful Marriage

To conclude this chapter it is important to determine what leads to a successful marriage. The key to success in any endeavor, but especially marriage, is maturity and commitment. Immature people for whatever reason are unable to work in a cooperative way, which is required for a healthy marriage. Immature people don't communicate, or if they do, it is often confusing to the other person. Immature people have to have their way, which destroys many because of manipulation. Manipulative people will do whatever is required to get what they want. Getting their way can range from being left alone and never questioned about extramarital relationship, or affairs to being timid and withdrawn and not wanting to interact with others. Along with manipulation comes the ability to follow through with responsibilities. In such instances the immature individual is typically unwilling to take responsibility for the welfare of the marriage, and family and will blame others, more specifically the spouse, for a number of problems. On the other hand, some spouses will start projects, but consistently insist that someone, or everyone else, help to finish it because the task is too overwhelming in the person's mind. Immaturity for any reason will prove to be the demise of the relationship.

An example of a healthy marriage is a couple with three boys. On one occasion they were in the car leaving town to go on a weeklong vacation. At about 20 minutes on the road the wife leaned over the husband and said something to him, and he took the first exit and pulled off to the side of the road. He then explained to the boys that mother had made a mistake in the checkbook, and they both realized they did not have enough money for the vacation. In many marriages if this were to happen the couple would start fighting or blaming and would very likely act on angry feelings for the remainder of the vacation. Others might decide to go anyway and put the money on a credit card, which would create debt and possibly further problems later. This particular couple did neither. There was no blaming, no fighting but acknowledged the problem, and then the parents decided what to do to remedy it. The father told the boys that they would go home and spend the week together doing things locally. At the end of that "staycation," the boys readily admitted that they had more fun that way than they would have traveling. There is a misconception that healthy families don't have problems and unhealthy families do. This is not the case. Every family will face problems. The difference between healthy and unhealthy families is the healthy family, or couple, will reasonably and rationally work through difficulties, whereas unhealthy couples do not. They will blame, argue, fight, or avoid any difficulties, which leaves the problems to grow and ill feelings to increase.

In a healthy marriage, communication is open and genuine. It may be that one, or both, did not learn how to communicate during childhood and adolescence, but if the determination to succeed in the marriage is strong enough that person will learn how to communicate. Active listening comes naturally when one truly wants to understand the other person and what he or she is thinking. The mature person will not act on her defensive feelings or fears, which would lead to cutting the other person off, but will listen to a fully understand. On the other side of the coin the healthy couple will be open about concerns and share the concerns with the assurance that there will be no blaming, but understanding, and possibly even accountability. If one has a problem, he will share with his wife, and as she listens she will understand what he is talking about, or if she does not she can ask for clarification. He on the other hand will have the opportunity to verbalize his concerns and thereby sort the out situation. If advice or direction is needed it can be given because of a clear understanding of what the person is experiencing. In the same vein discussing finances and resolving problems related to money will not be a problem. Again, it is not that good families don't have financial problems and that unhealthy families do. All families will at some time face financial difficulties. The healthy couple will talk together and come up with strategies to resolve whatever their concern is regarding money. They will not jockey for position to have their way at the expense of the marriage but will work together to come up with the best way to resolve the problem.

Healthy couples will also work to be united regarding child rearing. They will not each try to undo what the other is trying to accomplish or sit back silently and say nothing when he or she disagrees with the other. Both will be willing to share their concerns and learn from each other. Discipline will be consistent because they will both agree on limit setting and accountability and how to discipline if necessary. They will not fight against each other in order to calm their own feelings, or those of the child, but will have the child's welfare in mind and support each other in parenting. It is a given that children will test the limits to get their way, and when they realize that mother and father stand together the testing soon stops. All couples with children will experience limit testing and this can be frustrating. If the couple has good communication with each other, they can discuss the problems with the child and come to a consensus how best to approach the child. It is not uncommon for the couple to disagree initially, but if they respect each other enough they will hopefully communicate and not act defensively or protective toward the child.

One young couple disagreed about the best methods to teach the child to behave in preschool. Because they were attending couple's therapy they had already learned the basics of communication and were able to practice working together to come up with a reasonable solution.

Finally, because of healthy communication and the desire to succeed in the marriage, couples will likely learn to counsel together. Unfortunately, most married people typically feel that if there is a problem that person's solution is the best, and if not agreed with by the other spouse will feel hurt or offended. It is as a result of the person's insecurities brought about by thinking that if the other person doesn't agree with him, he is not held in very high regard, and if that person acts on those negative feelings and thinking no solution will ever be achieved. An example is a young couple with small children trying to plan a vacation. It might be that the wife's family always went to the beach when she was a girl and not only to just any beach but one particular spot at a campground next to the ocean. The husband, on the other hand, might feel that they need to visit relatives and spend the entire time traveling from one family member to the next to see as many as possible within a week's period of time. Because each person's experiences of vacation while growing up will feel most comfortable, each will want their way. If the husband insists on visiting relatives the wife will be upset. On the other hand, if the wife insists on going to the beach, the husband will probably feel slighted. The wise couple will learn to counsel together to come up with the best solution.

Counseling together as a couple requires maturity and the willingness to consider options and not hang on desperately to his or her ideas. It might be that neither option is the best or that one is feasible at a given time and another at another time. An example might be buying a new car. Each may have a specific idea of what is the best to purchase. If the two can discuss the options, needs, cost, and so forth and not insist that there is one absolute right or wrong answer, they will eventually come to a consensus with which both can live. One may know something about the children's safety laws and the other one might know more about the mechanical workings of a car. An example is a couple counseling together while buying a new family car. They had five children, and the car they had was not sufficient for what they needed, and they both knew they had to buy a more practical vehicle. Both knew that there were practical vehicles to consider. Instead of getting upset because one couldn't have his or her way, they both began to look together at the options. They first considered station wagons and decided that was not enough mobility within the vehicle while traveling to take care of problems that may arise with the children. The minivan was discussed and considered, but they decided against it because of the smaller size. Finally, they decided on a full size van, and the wife relied on the husband for the mechanical features including the engine and transmission. He wanted an engine big enough to take care of the load and maneuver adequately, and both decided on an automatic transmission. She knew that automatic door locks and windows were important and requested that there be a locking system on the windows and doors for the children's safety that could be controlled by the driver. They consulted together on options for the interior and decided on a custom interior over the factory interior. She had a good eye for color and color coordination and was asked to decide on that. Finally, when the van was delivered and the interior was installed, the couple had everything they wanted with the exception of the outside rearview mirrors being too small.

Couples must remember that each has an understanding of anything they are facing and each will have a different perspective. When this perspective is appreciated and encouraged, options can be considered and worked on until the problem is resolved and both can feel comfortable. As mentioned earlier, mature people can give-and-take, which is required in the process of counseling together. If a person acts on his or her emotions, the counseling process will be ignored and the problem will not be resolved and will very likely continue.

Chapter 14—Worksheet

1. When a couple seeks couples counseling, what is the first thing the therapist needs to find out and why?

2. If one person wants to change and the other person does not want to change, what is the best course of action?

References

Bateson, G., Jackson, D.D., Haley, J, & Weakland, J. (1956). Toward a Theory of Schizophrenia. *Behavioral Science*, 1, 251–264.

Baumrind, D. (1971). Current Patterns of Parental Authority. *Developmental Psychology Monographs*, 4, 1, p. 2.

Berk, L.E. (2007). Development Through the Lifespan (4th ed.). Pearson, Allyn and Bacon

Bisson, J.I., Jenkins, P.L., Alexander, J., & Baumeister. (1997). Randomized Controlled Trial of Psychological Debriefing for Victims of Acute Burn Trauma. *British Journal of Psychiatry*, 171: 78–81.

Blotcky, A.D., Tittler, B.I., Friedman, S. (1982). The Double-bind Situation in Families of Disturbed Children. *Journal of Genetic Psychology*, 141, 129–142

Chance, P. (2008). Learning and Behavior: Active Learning Edition. Wadsworth Cengage Learning.

Cutajar, M.C., Mullen, P.E., Ogloff, J.R., Thomas, S.D., Wells, D.L., & Spalaro, S.D. (2010). Psychopathology in a Large Cohort of Sexually Abused Children Followed Up to 43 years. *Child Abuse and Neglect*, 34, (11) 813–822. Doi:1016fjchiabu.2010,04.004.

DeCasper, A.J., Spence, M.J. 1986). Prenatal Maternal Speech Influences, Newborn's Perception of Speech Wounds. *Infant Behavior and Development*, 9, 133–150.

DSM-5. (2013). American Psychiatric Association: Diagnostic and Statistical Manuel of Mental Disorders, Fifth Ed. Arlington, VA, American Psychiatric Association.

Ferreira, L.R.C., Miguel, M.A.L, DeMartino, M.M.F., & Menna-Barreto, L. (2013). Circadian Rhythm of Wrist Temperature and Night-Shift Work. *Biological Rhythm Research*, issue 5, 737–744

Flesner, M.K, (2004). Care of the Elderly as a Global Nursing Issue. *Nursing Administration Quarterly*, 28, 67–72.

Geen, R. G., & Quanty, M. (1997). The Catharsis of Aggression: An Evaluation of a Hypothesis. In L. Berkowitz (Ed.) *Advances in Experimental Social Psychology*, 10, 1–36.

Grundman, & Others. (2004). Mild Cognitive Impairment Can Be Distinguished from Alzheimer's Disease and Normal Aging for Clinical Trials. *Archives of Neurology*, 61, 59–66.

Haan, M.N., Wallace, R. (2004). Can Dementia Be Prevented? Brain Aging in a Population–based Context. *Annual Review of Public Health*, 25, 1–24.

Heider, F. (1958). The psychology of Interpersonal Relations, New York, N.Y., Wiley.

Kisilvesky, B .S., Haines, S.M., Jacquet, A. Y.Grainer-Deferee, C. & Lecanuet, J.P. (2004). Maturation of Fetal Responses to Music, *Developmental Science*, 7, 550–559.

Kivisto, K.L., Welch, D.P., Darling, N., & Culpepper, C.I. (20-5). Family Enmeshment, Adolescent Emotional Dysregulation, and the Moderating Role of Gender. *Journal of Family Psychology*, Vol. 29, Nov. 4, 604–613.

Lewin, K. (1935). A Dynamic Theory of Personality, New York, NY, McGraw–Hill.

Madon, S., Willard, J., Guyll, M., & Scherr, K.C. (2011). Self-Fulfilling Prophecies: Mechanisms, Power, and Links to Social Problems. *Social and Personality Psychology Compass*, 5 (8) 578–590. doi 10,111/j.1751-9004.2011.00375.

McNally, R.J. (2004, April 1). Psychological Debriefing Does Not Prevent Posttraumatic Stress Order, *Psychiatric Times*, p. 71.

Merriam–Webster Dictionary (2016). Merriam–Webster, Inc.

Putnam, F.W., Guroff, J.J., Silberman, E.K., Barbon, L., & Post, R.M. (1986). The Clinical Phenomenology of Multiple Personality Disorder: A Review of 100 Recent Cases, *Journal of Clinical Psychiatry*, 47, 255–293.

Santrock, J.W., (2008). Life–Span Development, 11th Edition, McGraw–Hill.

Seligman, M.E.P. (1975). Helplessness, San Francisco: Freeman.

Taylor, S.E., (2007) Social Support. In H. S. Friedman & R. C. Silver (Eds). Foundations of Health Psychology. New Your, NY: Oxford University Press.

Travers, R.M.W. (1982). Essentials of Learning: The New Cognitive Learning of Students of Education, Macmillan Publishing Co., Inc.

Uchino, B.N., Cacioppo, J.T., & Kiecolt-Glasser, J.K. (1996). The Relationship Between Social Support and Physiological Processes: A Review with Emphasis on Underlying Mechanisms and Implications for Health. *Psychological Bulletin,* 119, 488–531.

Von Bertalanbby, L. (1968). General Systems Theory, New York, NY, Braziller.

Weiten, W., Dunn, D.S., & Hammer, E.Y. (2015). Psychology Applied to Modern Life, Adjustment in the 21st Century, 11th Edition, Cengage Learning, Stamford, CT.

CPSIA information can be obtained
at www.ICGtesting.com
Printed in the USA
LVOW02s1318170716

496095LV00004B/17/P